THE PART

THE PARTING YEARS

A British Family and the
End of Empire

Sheila Bevan

The Radcliffe Press
London · New York

Published in 2001 by The Radcliffe Press
6 Salem Road, London W2 4BU
175 Fifth Avenue, New York NY 10010

In the United States and Canada
distributed by St Martin's Press
175 Fifth Avenue, New York NY 10010

ISBN 1–86064–734–0

A full CIP record for this book is available from the British Library
A full CIP record for this book is available from the Library of Congress

Library of Congress Catalog card: available

Typeset in Sabon by Oxford Publishing Services, Oxford
Printed and bound in Great Britain by MPG Books Ltd, Bodmin

'Parting is such sweet sorrow'
(William Shakespeare, *Romeo and Juliet*)

THIS BOOK IS FOR MERILYN, SIMON AND CHRISTOPHER

To Merilyn a special thank you for much of the typing and reminding me of certain happenings. To Simon and Christopher for filling in the details of their eventful flight to and from Sana'a. My late husband Trevor always encouraged me to take notes and keep cuttings, which has left me with a record of our varied, exciting and fulfilling life.

Contents

Illustrations

1. Granny Rice in her wedding veil, 22 July 1868.
2. Merilyn wearing Granny Rice's veil at her own wedding, 12 May 1979.
3. Author (in Granny Rice's veil) and Trevor at their wedding, 10 November 1951.
4. All loaded up for the game reserve.
5. Trevor, Sir Edmund Hillary, Lady Hillary and Hunt at Singapore airport.
6. Rab Butler and Trevor at Singapore airport.
7. Sir Robert Armitage and Trevor, Limbe tobacco auction floor.
8. Chris, Nanny and Simon, Limbe.
9. Sir Robert Armitage, Queen Mother and Major Imray, Blantyre, 1960.
10. Farewell dinner, Shire Highlands Hotel, Limbe. From left to right, Gwenda Long, Trevor, Cyril and author.
11. 4 July American Beach Barbecue invaded by the Brits. Trevor as Boadicea and landrover complete with cannon that fired blanks.
12. Author (top left) as lone woman at Manama Rifle meeting.
13. Pirate towers along Ras al-Khaima coast, later adopted as police badge.
14. Hammerhead sharks (with their hammers removed) laid out on fish quay, Ras al-Khaima.
15. House on the rock, Yemen.
16. Ras al-Khaima fort, which served as police headquarters, gaol, court and barracks between 1967 and 1972.

Acronyms and Abbreviations

AA	Automobile Association
ADC	aide-de-camp
ALC	African Lakes Company
B & B	bed and breakfast
BOAC	British Overseas Airways Corporation
BSAP	British South Africa Police
CAF	Central African Federation
CI	(Imperial Order of the) Crown of India
CID	Criminal Investigation Department
CMR	Cape Midlands Regiment
CPM	Colonial Police Medal
DC	district commissioner
DCVO	Dame Commander of the Royal Victorian Order
DIO	district intelligence officer
DSG	Diocesan School for Girls
ENT	ear, nose and throat
FCO	Foreign and Commonwealth Office
GBE	(Knight *or* Dame) Grand Cross of the Order of the British Empire
HE	His Excellency
HMG	Her Majesty's Government
ITN	Independent Television News
JCB	Joseph Cyril Bamford (excavating machine named after its manufacturer)
KAR	King's African Rifles
LTC	Limbe Trading Company

MC	Military Cross
MV	merchant vessel
o/c	officer commanding
PC	provincial commissioner
PE	Port Elizabeth
PNEU	Parents National Educational Union
POW	prisoner of war
PWD	Public Works Department
RAF	Royal Air Force
RAMC	Royal Army Medical Corps
RN	Royal Navy
RNR	Royal Navy Reserve
SAAF	South African Air Force
SABC	South African Broadcasting Corporation
SCF	Save the Children Fund
TB	tuberculosis
TOS	Trucial Oman Scouts
TT	TB-tested
TTF	Tarka Training Farm
UMCA	United Mission to Central Africa
UNIP	United National Independent Party
VLCC	very large crude carrier
WAS	Women's Agricultural Society
WRNS	Women's Royal Naval Service

Glossary

abbra	ferry
askari	soldier
barusti	shelter made of palm fronds and branches
bedu	Arab peasant, often nomadic
birja	face mask
boma	district offices
bwana	master
djambia	curved dagger (Yemen)
dona	madam
fadil	feast
Kamuzu	Messiah
katundu	luggage
khonde	veranda
kosa	sheep
kunja	curved dagger
lungi	skirt worn by males (Yemen)
nkuda	captain
panga	machete/long knife
shifta	raiding tribe
sjambok	short whip made from hide
skrik	shock/terror (Afrikaans)
souk	market
stoep	veranda
tripple	horse's gait between a trot and a canter
ulendo	safari
wadi	dry riverbed
yam sing	Chinese toast

Foreword

Not enough has been written about the colonial service and the fine body of men and women who served in far-flung outposts of the old empire. My late husband Trevor Bevan, who joined the British South African Police (BSAP) (Southern Rhodesia) at the age of 18, was such a man. In 1935 Mussolini had invaded Abyssinia (Ethiopia) and in 1941 a contingent of the BSAP was sent to Eritrea and Somaliland, on the horn of Africa, because the Italians had been defeated and it was necessary for civil administration to be restored and certain 'clearing up' to be done. This Red Sea coast — real bandit and tribal feud country where camels are the only form of land transport — is little known to the rest of the world. The hinterland, known as the Danakil depression, is below sea level and unbearably hot — the area being a dried up lake and now a saltpan. Because of the intense heat, the locals, who cut blocks of salt to be loaded onto camels and taken away for sale, could endure only a few hours at a time on the Danakil plain and no one could live there. A lot of smuggling took place along the coast with dhows from Yemen, Aden, Saudi Arabia and from the small fishing villages subsisting along the shore. There was also a certain amount of capturing and raiding of each other's wives, daughters, camels and water wells, which Trevor and others had to sort out. As John Doody, an ex-officer with the Palestine Police and a friend of Trevor's, writes in *The Burning Coast*.

This was Trevor's métier: he was happy to be alone, hundreds of miles from any other white man, for month after month. Working from his base, riding out with his cameleers to keep the Shifta (raiding tribe) at bay, he welded his little force into a well knit unit that was to earn the respect of lawless men of mountain and plain.

His bases were at Merssa Fatmah and Thio — east of Massawa, only accessible by sea and only marked on large-scale maps. Enough provisions would be taken to cover a patrol and a little boat would call from time to time to top up the stores. Having learnt to speak Arabic and Italian, after this solitary sojourn he was moved to other parts of Somaliland with the British military administration. On being released from duty in this part of the world in April 1948, he made his way to Southern Rhodesia to find that he was due for six months' leave. He promptly left for Cape Town from where he embarked to enjoy a well-earned holiday in England; and it was there that we met.

Despite occasional adverse comments in the press, the British colonial service had no reason to feel ashamed — other colonial powers ran things differently and in the journalistic world all colonial countries are apt to be lumped together and judged the same, which we felt was unfair and incorrect.

Trevor and I were stalwarts of Britain's colonial history; after all, we were there and saw the results. The British were not hated; we were admired and respected. My Indian cook in the Gulf, an ardent Roman Catholic from Goa, prayed twice a day that the British would go back to India. The rule of law and order under which trade prospered and the rights of all individuals were preserved prevails over every country with which the British colonial service was actively connected. It was a cardinal rule to ensure that British traders did not exploit overseas populations to their detriment. Roads, hospitals, houses, schools and universities were built for the benefit of the local populations. Our colonies achieved their independence with an administrative structure and framework for development and security already in place. A big difference between the way in which Britain and other countries governed their colonies was that we had relatively few administrators or police officers in comparison with the local population. We taught the inhabitants how to run their own infrastructures, administrations and police services; when independence came they were not left high and dry. If ambitious, indigenous people chose not to follow the pattern we had left, that was not the fault of the colonial service.

I am proud that we were able to have been part of the British Empire and Commonwealth, albeit at the end of the colonial era. There was a great tradition to uphold and, in my own family, several generations of dedicated men and women made significant contributions to education, engineering, the military, banking, missionary work, teak extraction in Burma, farming practices and, not least, Trevor in his own brand of policing.

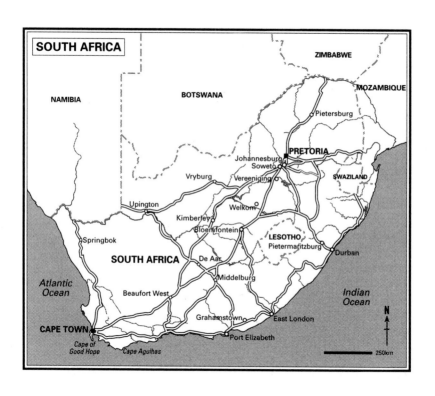

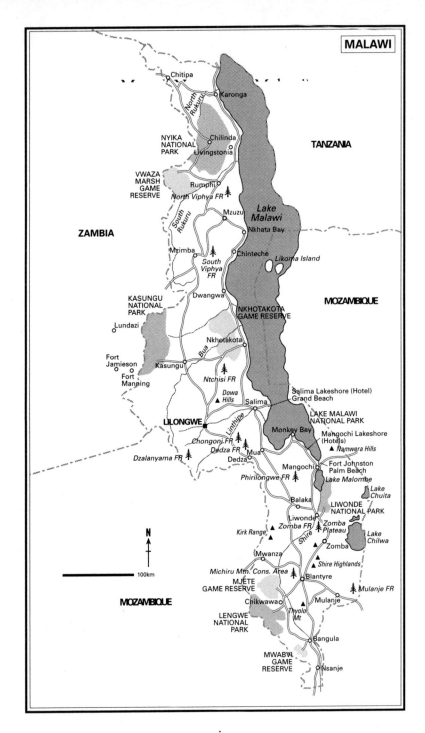

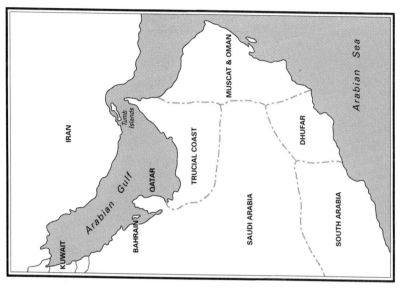

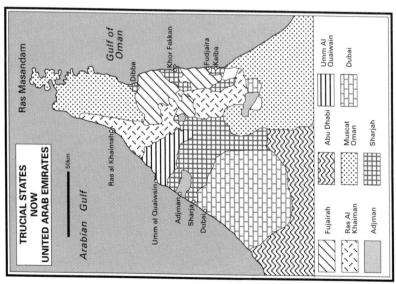

xvii

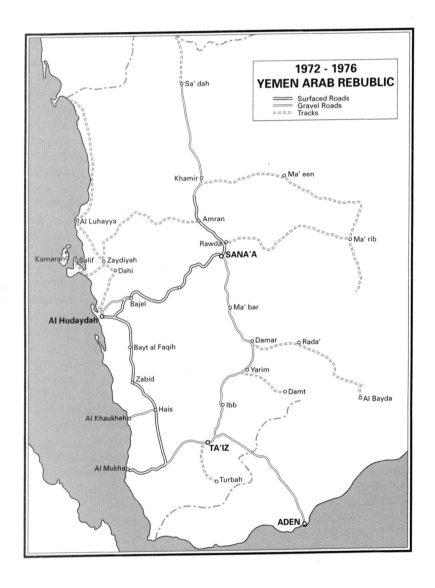

1972 - 1976
YEMEN ARAB REBUBLIC

Surfaced Roads
Gravel Roads
==== Tracks

Sa' dah

Khamir

Ma' een

Al Luhayya

Amran

Ma' rib

Rawda

SANA'A

Kamaran

Salif

Zaydiyah

Dahi

Bajel

Ma' bar

Al Hudaydah

Damar

Rada'

Bayt al Faqih

Yarim

Zabid

Damt

Al Bayda

Ibb

Hais

Al Khaukhah

TA'IZ

Al Mukha

Turbah

ADEN

1

Grandparents, Parents and Background

M y paternal grandparents had equally suitable heritages. My grandmother Mary Sophia's family had given many years' service to God, Queen and King. Her father John Garrett had gone to India as a missionary in the Wesleyan Mission in 1837 (the year Queen Victoria ascended the throne) and was posted to Bangalore in south India. The journey from Madras took ten days of daily marches on horseback and bullock cart. Pioneers of the first order, John Garrett married Sophia Austin, also from a missionary family, in 1842 in Mysore and they lived in Bangalore. In 1854, my grandmother Mary Sophia, aged nine years, was sent back to England because the Indian climate was considered bad for young children; the journey was by sailing vessel round the Cape of Good Hope. In 1856 her parents came on leave to England and returned to India the following year, also sailing around the Cape. They reached St Helena six weeks after leaving England and arrived in Madras in May, just in time for the Indian Mutiny.

In 1860 my grandmother's education was deemed to be complete and she set sail for India with a chaperone and a cousin. In those days you hired an empty cabin on the ship and furnished it with all that was necessary for the three of them for the voyage, which lasted three months.

With half the distance between Madras to Bangalore now by rail, the journey was shortened considerably in 1860, though half was still by bullock cart. There were travellers' bungalows on the route where one could stop for the night and a meal. My grand-

1

mother's luggage followed on another cart or two as she had brought her piano with her, a Collard & Collard specially made for the Indian climate. It was considered the best piano in Bangalore and was very much admired. Having got the piano, she practised for two to three hours every day and became an accomplished pianist.

The Rice and Garrett families had seen a lot of each other and my grandparents became engaged in 1867. Lewis Rice was then Inspector of Schools. Shortly after, Granny's parents returned with her to England on leave. The first-class fare was £100 per person and that included everything and anything one wanted. There was no extra charge for having champagne or port wine as often as one pleased. This time they went up the Red Sea to Suez and then by train to Alexandra, by paddleboat to Marseilles, by train through France, and finally by ship across the Channel to England. Granny was sad to leave her fiancé in India, but Grandpa took leave the following year and arrived in England in July 1868; they were married on 22 July at St Mary's Wimbledon. An extensive honeymoon was spent touring Europe and back in England. In March 1869 they went to hear Charles Dickens's farewell readings at St James's Hall (*David Copperfield* and 'The Trail' from *Pickwick Papers*) and in May they embarked, once again, to return to India via Suez in June 1869. Faster steamships had speeded up the voyage considerably.

The photograph of my grandmother on her wedding day is of some interest. I wore the veil she was wearing on my wedding day in 1951 and my daughter wore it on her wedding day in 1979. It was also used as a shawl to wrap my daughter Merilyn in at her christening in 1953 at the Garrison Church, Tanglin, Singapore.

In 1870 the first of grandmother's ten children was born; she had a baby nearly every two years for 20 years and never turned a hair. She lived to the age of 88 and all ten were healthy and strong and lived well into their eighties.

The story goes that my grandfather was away quite a lot, looking for his inscriptions, and used to say on returning home, 'and how many children have we got now, Mary?'

When I think of the hardships my grandmother had to endure I feel quite faint, yet she did not think she was a martyr. The saddest occasions must have been when she had to send two or three of her children aged six, eight or ten back to England with a chaperone to be placed in a boarding school. This was par for the course and all colonial families accepted it as the norm. My father went to prep school in England at the age of eight and did not see his parents again until he was 18. In fact, he did not get to know his parents until he was an adult. This constant parting with children gave me the idea for the title of this book. (I wonder if Granny had so many children to keep replacing the ones she sent back to England?) We also had to part with our children at an early stage, but thanks to contemporary communications we were less cut off than Granny had been from her brood; even so, I was forever having to choose between being with my husband or my children and I did sometimes feel torn apart.

Herbert, my grandparents' first child, was a studious type who read theology at Queens' College, Cambridge, and then went on to take holy orders. He married Iris and they had one daughter, Angela, who for a time was Lord Jowett's (Chancellor) secretary in the House of Lords. When Angela showed Trevor and me around the Palace of Westminster we took great delight in sitting on the woolsack.

Mabel arrived a year later. She married Harry Gratham in the RAMC in India and had one daughter, May, who married a tea planter in Assam. Sidney was next; he was a dear person who had a distinguished career in the Indian Army. Lily followed Sidney and she too married a doctor in the RAMC who rose to the rank of general. He was small of stature and was always referred to as the 'Little General'. He was a lovable man. Harold, who was next and very tall, was an excellent tennis player, still playing at Pinner Tennis Club in his eighties. He was an engineer who built important dams in Mysore Province and was much loved by the Indians. On his retirement, the local maharajah made him his agent, which entailed doing all his shopping for him in London and sending the goods out to India. Arthur, who appeared two years later, decided on banking for a career. He joined the Chartered Bank of India & China and served in several Far Eastern countries, including Burma. He had two children, Desmond and Tricia. Desmond joined the Queen's Bays and, after a successful army career, ended up as Major General Sir Desmond Rice. On retirement, he worked at St James's Palace as secretary of the Central Chancery of the

Orders of Knighthood. He dealt with all the investitures, kept all the records of the various orders of knighthood and organized all the big church services of the order in St Paul's, Westminster Abbey or St George's Chapel, Windsor. Tricia was in the WRNS during the war and in Ceylon she met a dashing young naval officer whom she married. Roy, my father, was the seventh child to be born to Granny and that was lucky according to the Indians. Charles, who was next, also went into banking, into the Hong Kong Shanghai Bank. He saw service in China, Japan and Ceylon and was in the 1927 Yokohama earthquake, but thankfully escaped injury.

At one stage both Charles and Arthur were agents (as they were then called) at the top of their professions in Colombo at the same time. There was naturally tremendous rivalry between them and it was agreed generally that the banks had not done their homework, for this was not an ideal situation. Charles was a sociable person who loved golf and the entertaining side of his job, whereas Arthur was the opposite. He loathed entertaining, but since he had to do it, he cunningly set several alarm clocks for the time he thought the guests should leave and hid them under cushions or in other strategic places. His ploy worked — at least that is the story.

Granny now had a gap of four years before Glad was born (more of Glad elsewhere), and last came Puss (Maud). Puss was a vivacious person, full of fun, with a difficult husband, also a medical doctor, who always seemed to miss the boat in his attempts to secure good appointments, so Puss did not have an easy life. They had one daughter, Eileen, who never married. There were 11 cousins in my generation and eventually I got to know them all. What a family! My mother always said it was a privilege and quite something to be a member of the Rice family.

When my grandfather Rice retired a slight problem arose over his beloved and faithful white pony, which he had ridden for many years over many miles looking for the 'inscriptions' on stones for which he became famous. This pony, it is said, never passed a stone of reasonable size in case it bore an inscription. This caused consternation with the new owner who could never get a decent long ride because the pony kept stopping and waiting for him to dismount to inspect the stone that had caught his eye.

The year 1906 saw grandfather's retirement realized and they sailed away from India on the P & O liner *Caledonia*, embarking at Madras and disembarking at Tilbury, having thus travelled full circle between England and India. This shortened voyage must have been a great relief. They settled in Harrow where Grandpa kept in touch with the Indian scene by setting and marking examination papers on his subject — Kannada literature — for London University. He would travel regularly up to London, but in his later years, when the journey was too much for him, the university came to him. All his scholarly works, including the *Edicts*, are housed in the Institute of Asian Studies at Cambridge.

While Pa was at Berkhamsted School with his two brothers Arthur and Charles, Grandpa Rice (being an educationist) presented a splendid Indian silver rose bowl for the best English Essay. The title of the essay, which was nominated annually, was usually relevant to the British Empire or Commonwealth.

Jonathan Driver, son of the Revd Joss and Phyllis Driver (Joss married Trevor and me and Phyllis's father baptized me) became headmaster of Berkhamsted School in 1985 and one day while rummaging in a cupboard he came across a rather battered silver rose bowl. The inscription revealed that a B. L. Rice had presented it in 1892 for the English Essay. Since this annual competition had been forgotten, Jonathan decided to reinstate it in view of his connections with the Rice family. When Jonathan and his brother were at St Andrew's Preparatory School in Grahamstown in the early 1950s, I sometimes helped them with their homework. Phyllis and Joss's house was a second home to me and my cousin Ken had a handsome wooden stand made for the silver bowl. Jonathan sensibly altered the title of the essay to the best essay on a subject of topical or international interest. Among many distinguished winners of the Rice Bowl is Robin Knox Johnston. I was thrilled that the bowl was found, restored and reinstated; I am sure Grandpa would have been delighted. While Jonathan was headmaster at Berkhamsted, he let me know each year who had won it.

Before Jonathan became headmaster at Berkhamsted, he was headhunted to run the International School in Hong Kong. Not surprisingly, he made a tremendous success of the job and, on returning to the UK, he was appointed master of Wellington. C. J. Driver, as he is known in the literary world, is an accomplished poet and novelist.

* * *

On leaving Berkhamsted, Pa was asked what he wanted to do. 'I want to be a farmer.' This took his parents by surprise because all their other sons had taken up professional careers. The post of paymaster in the Royal Navy was suggested, but he failed the shorthand exam; then he was put into Lloyds Bank and, in his words, 'had the softest job in London'. His boss was hardly ever there, so Pa spent most days on the top deck of various buses getting to know London and going to music halls. Meanwhile, Grandpa had made arrangements for him to attend the Colonial Agricultural College at Hollesley Bay in Suffolk. However, the Boer War broke out and Pa joined the Imperial Yeomanry — the Wiltshire division. When the war ended, he went back to England and was dismissed from his regiment, but decided to return to South Africa because the government there was handing out farmland to ex-servicemen; he applied and was sent to a farm at Theba Nchu in the Orange Free State. This venture was not a great success, so he moved to Southern Rhodesia to the Globe and Phoenix Gold Mine near Gweru. He did not make much money there either and had some frightening experiences, so he decided to return to South Africa to become a farm manager at Newcastle in Natal. However, wanting to be his own boss and hearing that Canada was also running a land-settlement scheme, Pa packed up in South Africa and took a voyage via England to Quebec and eventually on to Winnipeg. There he found it too cold and returned once again to England. The sun in South Africa won the day, so he took ship and went to work on the Premier Diamond Mine at Pretoria for three years from 1905 to 1908. He was working there when the great one-and-three-quarter-pound Cullinan diamond was found, 3206 carats. The Cullinan diamond, named after the owner of the mine Mr T. Cullinan, was presented to King Edward VII in 1907. It was then cut into two stones one, the 'Star of Africa', was set into the King's sceptre and the other into the imperial crown.

Mining lost its charm when Arthur, Pa's banking brother in Burma, sent him a letter suggesting he join a teak extraction firm and work with elephants in the jungle. So, once again thanks to Union Castle and its liner *Saxon*, he was back in the UK preparing to go to Burma. When the First World War broke out, Pa left the jungle life, which he loved, to join the Indian Cavalry. He was sent to France, where he spent three years in and out of the trenches and was awarded the MC, and then to Palestine where he was finally discharged in 1920. He then returned to South Africa and managed a farm belonging to an author named Leonard Fleming in the Orange Free State and another owned by a retired naval commodore. Then he received a letter from Grandpa Berry and the rest will be revealed.

* * *

Ma was born on 17 October 1898 and, the youngest of four children, two boys and two girls, was brought up in Sheffield with a very strict Scottish governess who had a great influence on her life. When she was older she went to a girls' school in Harrow, Middlesex. Grandpa Berry had been educated in Yorkshire and France and spoke fluent French; his grandfather had founded a brewery. Thirsty steelworkers needed good ale and, in due course, Grandpa became managing director. Being fond of golf and hunting, he hunted with the Grove on the same roam mare called Gipsy (of which we had a picture on our dinning room wall) for six seasons. His two previous hunters had carried him for like periods, so he had the extraordinary record of having hunted for nearly 20 years on no more than three horses.

An early member of Lindrick Golf Club, he served on the committee and played regularly. His son Douglas had been killed in the First World War and his other son Gordon was a disappointment to him. For this reason he instilled into my mother the rudiments of handling money and investments, which was unusual in the 1920s. As a Shakespeare fan, Grandpa read most of the plays to my mother and never missed a chance of seeing a production.

Much of Ma's social life as a young girl was connected with the church, Ranmoor in Sheffield, and like most congregations — as today — there was a drama group. Ma was a keen amateur dramatist.

Among the young drama group in Sheffield was one John Derbyshire. John took holy orders and ended up as Archbishop of Cape Town. He once spent a holiday at Greenhalgh and great fun he was too — totally relaxed in rather scruffy clothes. He never married and I do not think he ever grew up, for he played games with Dick and me endlessly. His elderly sister, who was his house-keeper, spent many of her holidays at Greenhalgh. Miss Derby-shire was a sedate spinster — the very opposite of her brother. Children, she felt, should be seen and not heard. I remember her putting about six grains of sugar in her tea — to strengthen her heart. 'Damn nonsense', Pa said.

When I think about it, Ma gave up a lot to marry Pa and leave the life she knew. She was brought up in a large, comfortable house and lived a full social life, spending holidays in Ireland, the Lake District and with her father in France. She spoke excellent French but sadly never taught us — not that she ever used it in South Africa. She was very musical and loved going to concerts and, of course, the theatre. She never went to a concert in South Africa because there were none nearer than 600 miles away at either Johannesburg or Cape Town. The only theatre available to her was what she produced herself, though I remember one very special and thrilling evening. The National Theatre (UK) was on tour and, wonder of wonders, staged a one-night performance in Cradock of *Quality Street* by J. M. Barrie starring Gwen Franken Davies and Peggy Ashcroft. I found it, the first professionally pro-duced play I had ever seen, spellbinding, with costumes exactly like those depicted on sweet tins. The only other play we saw that Ma had no part in producing was *French Without Tears*, which the RAF brought from Port Elizabeth and performed (with dif-ficulty) at the Mortimer hall. This was to show their gratitude and appreciation for the hospitality they had received on various farms between 1941 and 1945. Ours had not been the only farm with doors ever open to RAF and RN young men on leave. The people of Mortimer flocked to see the play, which was a great success.

When Ma knew she was going to marry Pa and live on a farm in South Africa she enrolled at an agricultural college. So far I have been unable to trace which college this was — there were very few such colleges in the 1920s and even fewer that took women. But we have her notebook (without its cover) and the course included dairy work, dairy farming, pigs, poultry and cheese making. Though written for England, from reading her notes it appears that the management of animals and various procedures are universal and she certainly put what she had learnt to good use. She kept two to three pigs and we made our own home-cured ham and bacon; she also kept poultry (Australorps) and sold eggs. At one point she kept a few dairy shorthorn cows and sold butter, which was a nice bright yellow without added colouring. Ma did not come from a farming background, but she loved the country and met the challenge of living on a farm in South Africa with great confidence. She had married the man she loved and, though 18 years older than her, she did not see this as a barrier.

Ever since my father's eldest sister and my maternal grand-mother became firm friends, my father's family and my mother's family (the Berrys) were well known to each other. Consequently, if my father and two of his brothers had nowhere else to go for their holidays from school in England, they would be invited to the Berrys at Sheffield, which was how my parents first met, when Ma was still a toddler. A close relationship grew up between Pa and the Berrys and in the early 1920s Grandpa Berry asked Pa to buy a suitable farm in South Africa for my Uncle Gordon and to teach him to farm. Pa duly found a suitable and attractive farm in the Conway district north of Cradock, near Middleburg, and the two bachelors launched enthusiastically into merino sheep farm-ing. It was then suggested that Gordon's sister come out to South Africa to keep house for the two men. Ma jumped at the plan because she would then be with the man she loved — though Pa was unaware of her devotion, or so he said. The good news was that the love affair flourished and they decided to spend the rest of their lives together; the bad news was that Pa was becoming dis-illusioned with Gordon's attitude to farming — Pa was always full of energy and very hard working, whereas Gordon was the oppo-site; having tired of the lopsided partnership, Pa pulled out. Ma returned to England to sort out a few things and get her trousseau ready (young brides today do not know what they are missing in the excitement and anticipation of collecting a trousseau) and sailed back to Cape Town to marry Pa in 1929.

2

The Early Years

On a hot afternoon in January 1931, an old model T Ford came to rest beside a peppercorn tree in an unmade street in Cradock, Cape Province, South Africa. My father had arrived to see my mother and me, the newborn infant. My mother was in a small private nursing home (one did not have babies in hospitals in those days) and Sister Lanham was the midwife under the instructions of Dr Scholtz. Sister Lanham delivered all the babies in the neighbourhood and was much loved. As was the custom in those days, Ma remained in the nursing home for about three weeks to ensure that all was well. The farm where my parents lived was 25 miles from Cradock and had no telephone.

Before driving back home in an open car along very dusty and bumpy roads, my parents took me to St Peter's Anglican church to be baptized by Canon Gould. As responsible Christian parents they felt this was prudent under the circumstances; I was then taken to my home, Greenhalgh.

Pa bought Greenhalgh in early 1929 and cabled Ma to join him. They married in Cape Town Cathedral and drove the 550 miles from Cape Town to their home by taxi. Their second honeymoon night was traumatic. They drew up at the Wilderness Hotel only to find a shell — it had been burnt down the night before. The taxi driver found them a room in a kind stranger's home, for there was no other hotel in striking distance and the headlights on those old cars were not very good for night driving.

Greenhalgh was small compared with most farms in South Africa, but virtually all arable with very little veld. Situated 3000 feet above sea level in the Great Fish River valley in the district of Mortimer, and surrounded by the ruggedly beautiful Winterberg and Coetzeeberg ranges to the east and west respectively, it has a healthy, unpolluted and invigorating climate. The mountain farms support merino sheep and Angora goats, the valley ones cattle and crops. The Great Fish River, from which the land gently sloped away into arable paddocks laid out for irrigation, formed the northeast boundary of our farm.

Mortimer housed a mixed community of English and Afrikaans people. In the 1920s there had been several large ostrich farms in the area, not for meat but for feathers, but these died out when the fashion waned towards the end of the 1920s. In fact, the farm my father had just bought had been an ostrich camp.

The house to which Pa brought his bride was built of soft (unburnt) bricks and had a corrugated zinc roof; it had four rooms. There were also two thatched rondavels, which, properly built with burnt bricks, were ideal for the climate — cool in summer and warm in winter. The one with a fireplace was used as a sitting room and the other was my parent's bedroom. There was of course a stoep (veranda) attached to the house, where one probably spent more time than in any of the rooms.

This part of the Eastern Cape Province was in the geographical area known as the Karoo — designated a semi desert. I always felt insulted when this point was made, but in fact it referred only to its low rainfall. As long as there was water for irrigation you could grow anything. Pa used to say that the topsoil was at least six feet deep. For drinking purposes, we had a borehole and windmill, which brought water up to a tank that fed the house and animal troughs.

The farms were irrigated with water from Lake Arthur, about 35 miles away. Except during a drought, we had a 'run' of water for three or four days a month. Pa converted a small dam that had been used to store drinking water for ostriches in front of the house into a duck pond. When that dried out he turned the sunken area into the main flower garden, consisting of a traditional lawn surrounded by herbaceous borders. A macrocarpa conifer hedge on one side created a sheltered area for roses, so there was always colour in Ma's garden.

When it was our turn for the monthly water run, the correct amount of water allowed for the acreage of the farm would be calibrated and our sluice gate set accordingly. A farm worker

11

would lead the water along furrows to whichever field Pa decided needed watering. This was fine during the day, but with no over-night storage dam on the farm, a reliable farm worker armed with a spade, storm lantern and pair of gumboots would be paid double wages for night work. Sometimes of course he fell asleep with disastrous results — precious water in the wrong places and Pa furious.

Merino sheep were bred on the mountain farms for their wool. As ours was not a mountain farm Pa first tried mutton sheep — the fat-tailed black-headed 'Persian' breed. When this proved less successful than he had hoped, he decided to switch to the love of his life, horses. Over the years he built up a rewarding thorough-bred stud and took in racehorses for rest periods. These were on the whole good horses that had been doped to win races by their greedy owners; in other words, they needed time for the 'poisons' of the dope to work their way out of the horses' systems so that they could regain their strength and stamina. Nothing special in the way of diet was needed, but they were given plenty of fresh grass, green lucerne (alfalfa) and unlimited water, along with oats, bran, a little salt and sometimes carrots or apples. They were out in the fields during the day, but stabled at night. Sometimes the owners of these 'doped' horses would turn up from Port Elizabeth or East London to see how their animals were faring and very often they did not recognize their own horses because they looked so fit with their shinning coats and bright eyes.

When I was about 18 months old Ma's father died and, as executor of his will, she found it necessary to go back to Sheffield. Her brother Gordon did not accompany her. We embarked on a Union Castle liner and in due course arrived in England. I was shown off to Pa's parents in Harrow and the remains of Ma's fam-ily in Yorkshire. My dear grandmother had no idea how to wind up Grandpa's estate. Grandpa had always shielded her from any financial and practical matters. Grandpa had come to terms with Gordon's limitations, which was why he made Ma his executor.

Once again we boarded a Union Castle liner and returned home to Greenhalgh. Why Greenhalgh? Pa's mother's family history can be traced back to the eleventh century to a place called Greenhalgh near Preston in Lancashire. When my grandparents retired to Harrow they named their house Greenhalgh; Pa called the farm

Greenhalgh and my poor brother got lumbered with the name. My husband and I called our last home together Greenhalgh and I hope the younger generation will continue to use the name.

While Ma and I were away, Pa altered the farm for horses and built an extension to the farmhouse. He also built more stables, fenced paddocks and planted trees to give shade for the thoroughbreds. Over the years he planted thousands, I mean thousands, of trees — our farm stood out in the valley because it was so well wooded. As a result he built up a microclimate without realizing it. We always got more rain than anybody else and the other farmers used to say that Pa topped up his rain gauge. He planted blue gums and other types of gum, poplars, willows and a few conifers. Around the house he planted an arboretum with many colourful and interesting trees of different shapes and sizes — deodars, Persian lilacs, pines, myrtles and olives — and all under planted with Kikuyu grass. Some horse paddocks were planted with lucerne, others with oats for use as feed and straw. Pa was a very traditional farmer, organic without consciously following a creed, just common sense. All the stable manure was put back on the land and I never remember him using chemical fertilizers.

The same practice was applied to the flower and vegetable gardens. There was also an enormous orchard with figs, mulberries, vines, apples, pears, plums, peaches, medlars and almonds and, protected from the frost, even a few citrus fruits like oranges, lemons and grapefruit. We could have up to 18 to 20 degrees of frost in the winter when the nights were very cold but it was always dry, sunny and invigorating by day. Apparently, Grandpa Berry sometimes used to stand on the stoep in winter and watch the temperature fall by 20 degrees between 3.30 and 6.00 p.m. and say, 'I can't believe it.'

* * *

It was explained to me that I was to go and stay with my 'other mummy' because I was going to have a new brother or sister. (I did not mind a bit because she was a great friend of Ma's, had three children of her own and I had often spent a day there or they had come to us.) Ma had decided to have this baby at home and did not want me to be in the way. Once again Dr Scholtz and

Sister Lanham did the honours and, in due course, brother Dick arrived. I remember being taken by my 'other mummy' to see Dick. There was Ma resting in the spare room with a cot beside her and this tiny human — very red faced — was introduced as my brother. I was not very impressed as he was so small. I was used to foals and calves that could get up and walk within minutes of being born and did not think much of this helpless infant.

Pa wanted to ensure that Dick and I grew up to be self-confident, able to think for ourselves and not easily frightened. However, his methods for ensuring the latter were somewhat novel, not to say eccentric. His attempts to render us 'shock' or '*skrik*' (an Afrikaans word meaning shock or terror) proof consisted of firing off a revolver near our prams. I do not recall this, but it is true to say that I did not grow up with a nervous disposition and loud bangs have never phased me.

Ma was the one who suffered most. I wonder what Freud would have had to say about it? Self-confidence and thinking for oneself, I believe, arose from the discipline of looking after our own horses. As soon as he could, Dick transferred his energies to disembowelling tractors and cars on the next-door farms.

When I was a baby Ma had engaged a young African maid Elsie to wash my nappies and generally help in the house. Elsie now had another set of nappies to wash and gradually became our much-loved nanny. Soon after Dick was born Elsie married Jimmy, one of the farm workers, and wore a long skirt, the prerogative of a Xhosa married woman. The maids who worked in the house were always provided with dresses and aprons.

They preferred cotton prints in navy blue with a white apron for making beds and waiting at table and blue aprons for general cleaning jobs, cooking and washing; they always looked clean and neat. The men working on the farm were given overalls and leather boots. Alfred, the old cowman, had very odd toes, which fell over the top of one another, so he always cut holes in the tops of his boots to allow his misshapen toes to stick out. They always fascinated us kids and in those days there was nowhere to get special footwear for farm hands. Alfred's wife Ida, a large, fat, full-bosomed, cheerful person with umpteen children, was the washerwoman. Very early each Monday morning she would appear and light a fire under a 40-gallon drum of water (African boiler). When the water was hot, she would pour it into a tin bath in which she would wash all the sheets, tablecloths and clothes. There was another tin bath for rinsing, another for blueing and another for starching. This was all done out in the open in the shade of the peppercorn tree. The washing usually dried in no time at all and then Tuesday was ironing day. There was no separate laundry room, so Ida did the ironing in a corner of the kitchen near the kitchen range, which had been stoked up to heat her set of flat irons. Meanwhile, Ma, the ever-practical one, took advantage of the stoked-up range to do her weekly baking. Cakes, biscuits, bread, pies and tarts were made. The bread dough would have been prepared the night before, wrapped in a blanket and put to rise on a shelf over the range. On Tuesday morning it would be kneaded and placed in the baking tins and left to rise again and then baked. I can see Ma now, with sweat pouring down her face, fiercely beating butter and sugar together for a sponge cake, enduring a very hot kitchen in summer to provide for her family. She always thought we would drop dead unless we had three good meals a day. She was an excellent cook and always used fresh ingredients. We had half a sheep a week, sharing a carcass with a neighbouring sheep farmer. This was mostly mutton and how good Karoo mutton is — people who have only eaten lamb do not know what they are missing.

Another treat, which tasted divine (if we were caught we got into terrible trouble), was within minutes of the freshly baked bread coming out of the oven, to cut off a really thick chunk of hot crust and add liberally about half an inch of butter. My mouth waters just to think about it. Of course it did not do the rest of the loaf much good and there was the tell tale sign we had 'stolen' a crust again, and again, and again.

In the early 1930s, a neighbouring farmer's wife sadly died leaving three little girls, Anne, Joan and Helen Lawford. The deceased's sister, a doctor practising in Stanmore in London, gave up her career to go to South Africa to look after her three nieces. Helen Foster ended up marrying Arthur and taking on a ready-made family. Helen became my mother's greatest friend and together they were an enormously beneficial influence on the community. Helen produced a fourth child, a daughter Margaret, and then finally a son, David. David was born at Greenhalgh, the second boy to be born on the farm. Again Dr Scholtz officiated, but this time two nurses from Holland, Toos and Pop, who had come to live in the district, assisted him. Sister Lanham had retired. I was sent to Littlefield House to stay with Anne, Joan, Helen and Margaret with Wy our governess to look after us girls. Toos was the resident nurse to look after mother and new baby. She had recently married a local farmer having gone to that farm to nurse her future husband's father during a terminal illness. Pop was our district nurse who happened to be a great friend of Toos.

✻ ✻ ✻

Ma and Helen were responsible for founding the Mortimer District Nursing Service. It was a wonderful idea and pioneering work, for so little was being done for African health at that time. As a doctor, Helen recognized the need and Ma, with her strong sense of duty to the community, set up the whole organization with the support of the farmers. They received a government grant and set up clinics in three areas of the valley. A doctor from Cradock would attend on certain days. Sister Pop had a car and a skilled man made a special dispensary/pharmacy, which fitted into her boot like a glove; it was even dustproof, for it had to withstand very dusty country roads. If someone on a farm was too ill to get to a clinic, Sister Pop would do a home visit and of course there were farm accidents with which she coped. Most of us by now had telephones, so we could phone Sister Pop. TB was rife among many farm labourers and their families and a routine inoculation programme was evolved, which included vaccination against smallpox at the same time. In time, the general health of the Africans did improve. In summer, eye infections were common as flies were in abundance and carried all sorts of diseases. The district nursing service grew from strength to strength and government support increased. A smart, properly built clinic was built with accommodation for the sisters at Mortimer village. Hitherto, converted rooms on farms had been adapted as clinics, but as the service expanded appropriate buildings sprang up at each end of the valley, Mortimer being in the middle.

The time had come for my parents to give serious consideration to my schooling. The little local state primary school was ruled out and the only alternative was to have a governess until I was old enough to go to boarding school. There was a good girls' school, Rocklands, in Cradock but that was 25 miles away and not a practical consideration. Anne, Joan and Helen were in the same predicament, so our parents got together and decided to share a governess. Anne was old enough to go to boarding school at the Collegiate in Port Elizabeth, so that left three of us.

Our parents then approached the PNEU (Parents' National Educational Union) based in Ambleside in the Lake District. This organization, which was tailor-made for children in the colonies, ran a worldwide correspondence course. Under the scheme, the college trained governesses before sending them abroad and the subjects taught and standards achieved were admirable. One theory behind it was that from the infant class onwards, the children would be taught and marked to a standard comparable to that of an English school so that they would be able to cope should they return to the UK to complete their education. For this reason, the syllabus had a definite English slant and some of the natural history we were taught hardly applied to the veld and the Karoo. Textbooks and exercise books were sent from Ambleside to suit our various ages. Even when very young we were examined, with the questions asked verbally and our answers written down verbatim by the governess and posted to the UK for marking. It is an excellent organization and I have met many families in various parts of the world who benefited from it. (When considering schools for our own children we selected PNEU ones.) Our first governess, Olive Dickinson, was selected by PNEU head office and interviewed by a close friend of Ma's and a close friend of Helen's. Olive duly set sail on a Union Castle liner to Port Elizabeth and from there was brought to Mortimer. Olive came from a small country parish in Wales where her father was the local rector. She had led a very sheltered and secluded life and the contrast with our way of life was a terrible shock to her. As there were more children at Littlefield farm the schoolroom was built there. (The name Littlefield was chosen because of Anne, Joan and Helen's mother's connections with Littlefield House at Marlborough School.) A rondavel was built and conifers planted all the way around to keep it cool in the summer. There were windows on two sides and a stable door so that when the top part was open the sun kept us warm in the winter and the breeze kept us cool in the summer. We had proper school desks, a piano, a blackboard, a bookcase and a governess table. I do not remember a single thing Olive was supposed to have taught me, but I remember my parents discussing how worried they were about her because she did not seem to know the facts of life and several young youths from the local training school were paying her constant attention. I can hear Ma telling Olive that it was not the done thing to spend almost the entire night on our koppie with a young man. We had a koppie (small hill) consisting of about 20 acres of Karoo bush just behind our house. Being responsible for Olive, Ma refused to tolerate such outrageous behaviour and sent her back to England.

Joan had kept in touch with Olive over the years and, to my utter astonishment, in the early 1980s Olive phoned me when I was living in Torquay because she was on holiday in Dawlish. Could she come and see me? 'Of course,' I answered. She duly arrived with her husband and friend in a Morris Minor (my children call these cars poached eggs). Her husband and friend decided not to stay and left Olive with me to catch up on 45 years. We had a pleasant salad lunch in the shade in the garden and, sadly, she died soon afterwards.

After Olive was sent back to England on the Union Castle liner, much to my mother's relief, the gap in our education was temporarily filled in two ways. First, Aunty Glad, my father's spinster sister and my godmother, was out from England on a prolonged stay and she took me in hand. She taught me the rudiments of reading and writing and all three verses of God Save the King, which I shall never forget. Aunty Glad was quite an accomplished artist, but I do not remember her teaching me any art. Second, Molly carried out the more formal teaching. She was a proper governess who had been brought out from England to teach David, Jocasa and Diana, whose father and uncle were partners on a nearby dairy farm. David, Jocasa and Diana were much older than we were and had moved on to higher education. Meanwhile, Molly had married George, a local chicken farmer on a farm called Burnham Thorpe. Burnham Thorpe is a small town in Norfolk where Nelson was born and George claimed that he was a relation. For some reason, though I cannot recall why, we met Molly for our lessons in the ladies' changing room at the

Mortimer Tennis Club. I remember it being very cold and not lasting for very long — so I returned to Aunty Glad's tuition.

Meanwhile, Ma and Helen had been furiously writing letters to PNEU to produce a more mature and responsible person; under no circumstances were they to send out any more 'Olives'.

Laura Wyatt arrived in due course and we were all told to call her 'Wy', which we did. I remember being taken down to Littlefield to be introduced and being impressed by her blonde hair. Wy became part of our family and energetically entered into all aspects of Mortimer life. She made wine from the super abundant grapes that grew at Littlefield and a beautiful evening cape from ostrich feathers, which intrigued us enormously. She was a competent horsewoman, soon had her own horse 'Helmet' and we had many happy rides together. She not only taught us the three Rs, but piano, singing and drama, and we learnt long recitations. Her lessons were memorable and effective and I am grateful for the good grounding I received from her. She encouraged us to put on little plays, for which we charged our parents or any other long-suffering adults three pence to watch and then solemnly gave the proceeds to the war effort. I was Piglet once when we enacted Christopher Robin, and recall Pooh Bear, Eeyore and Piglet having to fall on a balloon.

※ ※ ※

While Aunty Glad was staying with us she insisted on riding side-saddle. No one in the length and breath of the valley had even heard of side-saddle, let alone ridden on one. Somehow, Pa managed to find a horse from somewhere that was trained to take a side-saddle. Unless a horse is trained to accept this lopsided way of riding, with most of the weight on one side, there can be problems. Pa said it was damn silly to ride with one leg trapped under the pommel. It had to be a docile animal and, in due course, a big brown mare arrived, a weight carrier because Aunty Glad was no lightweight, and off they went for their first ride. All went well at first until they were cantering and her horse spooked, over-balanced and fell on top of Aunty Glad, who was hooked under the side-saddle pommel. Her glasses were broken and she was badly bruised, but no other harm was done. After this brief encounter, no more side-saddles were seen in Mortimer and Aunty Glad's riding career came to an end. She was not a novice, for she had ridden a lot in India.

One day, while Aunty Glad was still with us, we were visiting old friends north of Cradock and, on approaching Cradock, Pa did an unheard of thing. He asked Ma to drive because his eye was watering and he could not see properly. Ma drove into Cradock and, since it was not Dr Scholtz's surgery time, she stopped at the chemist. Pa assumed that he had had a fly in his eye and that some drops would soothe the irritation. After examining his eye and doing a few tests, the chemist concluded that there was only one thing to do; that was to take the night train to Port Elizabeth and go straight to the eye specialist, for he thought it was very serious. Aunty Glad and Pa stayed in Cradock until they caught the night train, while Ma drove us back to Greenhalgh. The specialist who saw Pa explained that he had a detached retina and that this was why he could not see. He recommended an immediate operation with no guarantee of success. He questioned Pa about any blows he may have received to his head at any time. The only thing Pa could remember was having been hit on the left temple by a polo ball, which had knocked him out and off his horse, about 40 years previously. As it was the left eye, the doctor thought that this was probably what had caused the retina to detach. Pa had the operation under a local anaesthetic and then had his head put in a cradle, so that he could not move it and in which he remained for three weeks. Meanwhile, Aunty Glad and Ma swapped places, with Aunty Glad looking after Dick and me and Ma being with Pa; I do not remember it being a particularly happy time. Pa lay in bed in his straightjacket and blindfold talking to Ma, or whoever else was around. Ma read to him constantly, for there were no radios or cassettes at hand in those days. He was in St Joseph's Hospital, which was run by nuns and they were marvellous. He used to pull their legs to such an extent that they did not know whether they were coming or going. To stop his fingers from fidgeting he had a piece of string that he would tie into a hundred knots and then undo the knots by feel. At the end of three very long weeks it was time to remove the bandages and move him to a sitting position. But snap, the retina parted once more. Pa said he was not going through all that again and would learn to live with one eye. He did this, but it took him some time to learn how to focus on things like pouring water into a tumbler, rather than just beyond it and spilling water all over the place. He did all the farm work, he drove and he rode. In fact, generally he did everything he had done before except play tennis. The eye specialist invented a special spectacle for one-eyed people. With one lens for reading and another for long distances, and with a swivel on the bridge and a reversible hinge on the earpiece, if Pa wanted to alter his lens he would take his glasses off, turn them round and replace them. There was no need to carry a second pair. For some obscure reason, as children we called this 'the changing of the guard'.

Aunty Glad came out to South Africa in 1938 on a prolonged visit with a view to living with us permanently. Pa was the last of the seven brothers to get married and, until then, Aunty Glad had seen her mission in life as looking after and keeping house for her brother Roy. Her plans were upset when Ma and Pa married. Ma told me that she had always tried to understand Aunty Glad's disappointment, but was not prepared to compromise her happy marriage. Aunty Glad must have been with us for about six months when Ma found her tidying the drawers of her dressing table in her bedroom. For Ma, that was the last straw and soon after Aunty Glad returned to England. But since Ma never bore malice to anyone, they remained friends and from then onwards Ma, Pa and Glad kept up a regular correspondence.

As the spinster sister of a large family, Aunty Glad now turned her attentions to keeping the Rice family tree up to date. On his retirement from the Indian Army, Uncle Sidney had undertaken all the research and had traced Granny Rice's family back to Doomsday, and Grandpa was not far behind. Uncle Sidney's army career had been curtailed by an accident; when out pig sticking, a panther had bitten him and when the wound turned gangrenous he had had to have an amputation. As children, we were intrigued to hear that he kept his socks up with drawing pins.

Members of the family returning from stints abroad in China, India or Africa were expected to 'report' to Aunty Glad and give her all their latest news. Long after I was married and had three children, we arrived in England on leave and, having caught my breath and settled in a hotel, I telephoned her. She greeted me very impatiently and added, 'don't you know I always listen to the

21

Archers at 6.45 p.m.?' and slammed the phone down. But, for all
her set ways, she was a great character and we all loved her. She in
turn just loved the younger generation and took a great interest in
what everyone was doing.

* * *

Dick and I had ridden down to Littlefield to school as usual one
day and were busy with our lessons when we were suddenly told
on no account to leave our rondavel schoolroom, break or no
break. The reason for this was that Arthur's bad-tempered old
Jersey bull had escaped from his pen and was rampaging round
the farm looking for cows and crashing through and over fences;
no sensible person would go near him, for he had gone berserk.
Since Pa was a good shot (one only uses one eye shooting), Arthur
had phoned him to come and shoot his mad bull. Pa came down
and, as luck would have it, the bull was roaring and churning up
the ground in a field not far from our schoolroom. We watched Pa
stalk into a perfect position for a clean shot. He then fired and we
saw the 'smoke' of the cartridge from the heavy rifle before we
heard the bang – a lesson in the speed of sound. Pa dropped the
bull with one shot, so his reputation stood. This was not the only
crazy animal Pa was asked to dispatch and those he was asked to
dispatch were not all crazy. Some had incurable diseases, a dog
with cancer I remember well. Some of the animals that were
brought to him were just too old and feeble for any quality of life
and killing them was the kindest act. He had a Winchester rifle, a
shotgun and several pistols. One, a Mauser, had been removed
from a dead German in the First World War. Whatever the
requirement, the appropriate weapon would be chosen for the job.
Pa's guns were kept in a state of readiness – cleaned regularly and
loaded in his office, which was locked at all times. He reckoned
that when you wanted a gun you usually wanted it quickly and it
was a waste of vital time to load the weapon. Everyone knew this,
respected Pa's views and there was never any problem. A few
farmers kept firearms, but they were used once a year, perhaps, on
a springbok shoot.

Once, when I was about eight years' old, I was walking round
the farm with Pa when we came upon two large cobras fighting in

a road quite far from the house. Their bodies were entwined round each other like a corkscrew and they were bashing hell out of each other's heads. Pa instructed me to stay and watch the snakes to see where they went while he ran back to the house for his shotgun. Having complete faith in him, I was smitten to the spot, mesmerized both with fear of the snakes and with fear of Pa's wrath should I lose track of where they went. When Pa returned, what seemed like hours later, the cobras were still fighting and probably had not even noticed me. He went up quite close before blowing their heads off. When untwined they were six feet long, big for one cobra let alone two. No wonder they were fighting. Could they have been king cobras?

* * *

Today we take telephones, electric lights, fridges and radios for granted, but I can remember the excitement when each of these innovations was installed at Greenhalgh in the 1930s.

The telephone was fixed to the wall and the mouthpiece could be moved up or down according to one's height. The earpiece was separate and to make a call one cranked a handle on the right-hand side of the apparatus. We were on a party line and we all had different rings. Our line was number nine and our number was 930, which meant if someone wanted to call us they would need to crank three short rings. Had it been 931, it would have been three short and one long ring. I remember the early excitement of hearing the three short rings and Ma or Pa answering. The phone was fixed too high for me to reach, so I had to stand on a chair if I needed to use it. Being on a party line meant that one just picked up the earpiece and if you heard voices you put it back on its cradle and tried again later. If there were no answer to your 'line clear?' question you cranked the required number. Decent people respected each other's privacy, but one woman in the valley spent day and night listening in to other people's conversations, so one soon learnt what *not* to say over the phone. Pa used to negotiate horse deals over the phone and would say, 'I cannot give you my final price because there is a woman listening in on this line.' 'No there isn't,' would come a voice down the line. Pa claimed that she even had her meals brought to her on the phone.

If you needed a number on a different line you had to crank one long and the operator would connect you. Long distance calls were a nightmare, especially in stormy weather. The surrounding ironstone mountains attracted frequent electric storms, with the result that all one could hear was crackling static.

The generation of electricity by means of a wind charger was a great step forward. Only those who have had to cope every evening with smelly paraffin lamps, burnt mantles, cracked glass funnels and overgrown wicks can properly appreciate electric lights; and our kind neighbours Ernest Gadd and Arthur Lawford undertook the installation for us. There was barely enough electricity generated for lights (let alone any other power), we thought that the 40-watt bulbs were rather impressive. The electricity was generated in two alternate ways. If there was sufficient wind, the wind charger blades rotated at high speeds and the electricity generated was fed into a row of batteries. If there was no wind, a small diesel engine was cranked into life to generate the electricity.

These batteries had to be kept tested and regularly topped up with distilled water. Cornwall, Denmark and other such places now have thousands of windmills generating free electricity for the national grid, but wind power is not new to those of us who were brought up on South African farms miles from any municipal supply of power. However feeble the electric light, it was better than a smelly hot paraffin lamp. Aladdin gave the best light, but was temperamental and could not be used in a draught, and the Miller lamp was fairly reliable. If one needed a light other than a torch outside at night, we used the old hurricane lamp and its superb design has not changed to this day. The wind charger was fixed to a very high pole, which was bolted to two sturdy supports sunk into the ground, and there were three anchor wires going out at 60° to help keep the wind-charger pole at 90°. The pole could thus be gently lowered once a year for servicing — with the tension on the anchors lessened, a car attached to the pole acted as a counterweight to lower it. Arthur used to do the servicing, as Pa had no clue — another example of how the farmers helped one another. Pa's skills were with animals, especially horses and dogs; Arthur's were electrical and mechanical.

A cooler preceded the fridge. To keep dairy products cool and water at an acceptable temperature for drinking, we had a huge round cooler on the shady part of the stoep where there was likely to be a breeze. This cooler had two parts. The lower two-thirds consisted of a double 'skin' of wire netting filled with clinkers and a door giving access to several slatted shelves of foods such as milk and butter. The top third consisted of a water tank that had to be kept filled. Small holes in the base drip-fed the clinkers below keeping them wet and cool. It was primitive, but it worked provided you did not expect too much of it. The fridge, which was paraffin powered, looked similar to modern fridges. Ours stood on legs and the paraffin tank had to be kept topped up to prevent the flame going out and the temperature in the fridge rising. Africans were puzzled by how a flame could cool things down enough to make ice cubes and ice cream. The flame was temperamental, it needed ventilation but not a draught and if the wind blew in the wrong direction it would go out; also, the wick had to be trimmed regularly to prevent the glass going black. But one took these normal routine household chores in one's stride for one was only too pleased to have a working fridge. We also had a large cool larder with stone (marble) slab shelves in which a lot of food was kept, including many shelves of bottled fruit — apples, pears, peaches and numerous varieties of jams and marmalades.

The next excitement was the wireless. Once again Ernest came to help Pa install our first set. A high pole on which to attach the aerial was put up near the house and a huge piece of furniture was trundled into the sitting room and placed by a window so that the aerial wire could be connected easily. Curious cylindrical 'things' called valves were inserted and a battery connected; the wireless was attached, switched on and, hey presto, out came the most awful squawks and wailing you have ever heard. Eventually, Ernest tuned into the nearest transmitter, which was broadcasting from Grahamstown, 100 miles away. The noises through the static eventually became voices we could understand. It was an earth shattering experience. A battery (accumulator) provided the electricity for the wireless. One had to be careful where one placed the battery because it produced an evil acid on the terminals that could burn great holes in the carpet.

Our wireless was not considered advanced enough for the coronation of 1937, so we went to Littlefield where Arthur knew all about wirelesses and had a more up-to-date and powerful set.

We listened to the whole ceremony in awed silence, consuming sandwiches. I was in my Brownie uniform because that morning we had been to a Brownie parade at the Mortimer village hall in honour of the coronation of King George VI and Queen Elizabeth.

Being on the main Port Elizabeth–Johannesburg line, with two passenger trains a day in each direction and frequent goods trains, Mortimer was well placed for communications. Trains were used to transport everything in those days and, with only a single line, there was nearly always a goods train in Mortimer station waiting for another to pass. Not only were goods sent by train, but also livestock for markets or shows and horses to and from Greenhalgh. If a truck (or cattle or horse pen) at the goods shed were meant for Pa, it would be marked in chalk on the side with his initials and the rail code for Mortimer (RAR/MMT). Pa was usually notified when a horse was railed to him so that he could meet the train and take the horse out of the truck immediately. Though railway personnel were supposed to water the animals, they were not very regular about it and the horses always seemed to arrive thirsty; I have seen a horse drink 20 gallons in one go.

At 3000 feet above sea level the nights were cold in the winter months and, without looking at the thermometer, we always knew if there had been a heavy frost because the heavily-laden goods trains going north would slip on the frozen lines. One could hear the train slipping back and its steam engine having another go at the incline — a distinctive chug, chug we got to know very well.

The invigorating Karoo climate is one of extreme temperatures and when Granny was staying with us, after a cold and frosty winter night, Ma would get the car out of the garage, park it in the sun and put Granny in it. (In 1936 we had a new Ford V8 closed saloon with wind-up windows.) There she would remain crocheting or reading until the temperature rose sufficiently for her to feel warm. The car in the sun was in effect a hothouse on wheels, for everyone knows how hot the inside of a car can become when left in the sun. By about 10.00 a.m. on winter mornings the sun would have warmed up to about 65° or 70°, but by 4.00 p.m. one would need to pile on the jumpers again and by 6.00 p.m. it would be dark and cold. The saving grace was the certain knowledge of a sunny day in winter. When the rains came it was summer.

According to Pa, there were drawbacks to being near a railway station. In his opinion, the worst day of the year was when the coal truck arrived with, I suppose, about three tons of coal, which had to be got from the railway station to Greenhalgh. There were no lorries to hire in those days, so all the farm hands (who hated it just as much as we did) were piled on the wagon with sacks and shovels; the mules were inspanned and off they went to Mortimer. The truck would be manoeuvred into a convenient spot so that the wagon could draw up alongside it and the coal was then shovelled into bags and put on the wagon. When the wagon was full the first load would be taken back to Greenhalgh. Everyone (whether black or white) would be covered in pitch-black coal dust, including the mules. With luck, and by working from dawn to dusk, the job could just about be done in one day, with the heavily laden wagon making several journeys to and from Mortimer station. The next chore was to get clean.

Ma insisted on having coal. It eked out the wood for the kitchen range, it produced a higher temperature for certain cooking and in the winter a coal fire in the sitting room was a great comfort. If we were ill in winter, the height of luxury was to have a fire in our bedroom. Two bedrooms had fireplaces and if we were ill and needed warmth we would move into a room that had one. Being high up on the Karoo plateau we could get frosts as cold as $-18°$ and there was often snow on the mountain peaks.

Mortimer village grew up round the railway station. There was a stationmaster's house, several gangers' cottages, a post office, a telephone exchange and a general store, which included a butcher. One could buy anything at this store, which Tom Underhill ran. It was said that farmers who could not meet their accounts during the 1930s' Depression owed him thousands of pounds. Tom was well liked, as was Mrs Underhill, affectionately known as Mrs TU. She ran a boarding house where Miss Minnie the postmistress lived, as did extra railway staff, the local state elementary school teacher (who had a crooked neck so her head was always to one side), a shop assistant and the telephone exchange operator, all very well fed at Mrs TU's table. The cobbler-cum-harness mender, designated 'poor white', a category peculiar to South Africa, lived on the edge of the village. This man would spend at least a week each winter pruning our fruit trees. Pa and Ma were good about finding jobs to help poorer people earn a little extra money. Poor whites often had large families and, with no welfare state, any extra income was gratefully received.

The little elementary school was fairly basic and taught mostly Afrikaans children aged between 6 and 12 years. If any of these children went on to secondary school they had to go to Cradock, 25 miles away. Cradock Boys' High had a good reputation, but unfortunately children from this social group seldom seemed to better themselves.

We had a much used village hall and the same building housed various offices, including the Lucerne Co-op run by Mr Shoesmith whose brother, known as 'Old Shoe', ran the last ostrich farm in the district. Old Shoe sold a few ostrich eggs (each equal to 24 chicken eggs) and a few feather dusters. No one knew how he made ends meet; he had no car and went everywhere on horseback. He was a bachelor and lived in a shack near the railway line, but slept on an ostrich-feather bed. He and his brother were erudite well-educated Englishmen. Old Shoe was a dropout, though we did not know that term then. He wrote furious letters to *The Times* on various subjects that fairly frequently excited him.

One man in the village who was indispensable to the farming community was the blacksmith-cum-farrier. Once or twice a year he would be fetched to spend the day paring horses' hooves at Greenhalgh. When racehorses arrived at Mortimer for Pa, the first job would be to have their racing plates removed so that the horses could feel natural. Farrier day on the farm was red-letter day for the old English white bull terriers Pa bred and of which there were always at least two in his shadow. Dogs love to chew the clippings of horses' hooves. One piece the shape of a horseshoe would last a dog for hours. They were very good for the dogs, for they both cleaned their teeth and exercised their jaws.

At Mortimer village there was a dry cricket pitch next to some stock pens (where an occasional stock market was held). With not enough cricket enthusiasts to keep it going, I was sometimes roped in to keep score and, as I was to find out, this requires great concentration. The tennis club, which was near the village, was well used and very popular. We had five courts in constant play and a sixth if needed. They were all hard, as most are in South Africa, being made of antheap soil, and very fast if properly maintained through constant watering and rolling. The African groundsman did a good job with the help of a borehole and windmill to pump the water up into a concrete reservoir, as on every farm in South Africa. We had a full day's tennis every other Saturday and half a day's on alternate Saturdays. The standard was generally high, which it usually is in South Africa because one plays the whole year round. The usual rota of hostesses produced marvellous meals and teas, with everyone bringing a plate of something that would be enjoyed by all. The groundsman's wife kept the Dover stove wood fire burning to boil kettles for tea or heat up food, and she did all the washing-up. Together they kept the club grounds and clubhouse neat, clean and tidy.

* * *

Looking back, Mortimer valley housed a generous share of slightly eccentric people, or perhaps there were more individualistic people around generally. The English-speaking community consisted for the most part of settlers, pioneers out from the UK, but there were also numerous old English-speaking South African families dating back to 1820. The British government had been keen to increase the white population in the Cape Province, particularly in the Eastern Cape where Bantu tribes were marauding and raiding isolated farmers and settlements along the Great Fish River, the flash point of black versus white. During George III's reign, the UK government promised volunteers a free passage, a grant of agricultural land, remission of rent for the first ten years, implements, seeds, a tent, wagon, two oxen and enough rations to keep them going until the first harvest. Some 24 ships laden with excited families set sail for Algoa Bay (Port Elizabeth) from Portsmouth, Bristol, London, Liverpool, Leith and Cork. The trying voyage took four months. The *Chapman* was the first ship to arrive on 9 April 1820, followed shortly by the *Nautilus* on 14 April, with the others anchoring at irregular intervals. Surnames like Bowker, Osler, Pringle, Murray, White, Southey, Cawood, Collett, Baines, Lanham, Pigot, Greathead and Cullen are all names with which I grew up and it is lovely to see those same surnames still on the register of my old school. Grahamstown was a frontier town and most of the people who disembarked at Algoa

Bay made their way northeastwards to Assegai Bush (their final dispersal point) just outside Grahamstown.

Each family was allocated 100 acres, which was insufficient for that sour veld area, and there was much hardship. They built fortified houses and effectively set up a human buffer between the European community and the warlike Bantu on the eastern border. They were tough, dedicated people and, though they suffered many setbacks, they and their offspring shaped the indomitable people of the Eastern Cape. Their spirit lives on in their descendants.

Between 1820 and 1853, these British settlers lost 62 of their people, a high proportion, and it of course devastated the families concerned, for it was very often the head of the family.

The Cape Governor Lord Charles Somerset had been advocating such a scheme to settle the border country since 1817 and at last in 1820 the settlers arrived. Little did they know just how many battles and skirmishes they would have to endure.

I remember a member of the White family, settlers in the Grahamstown district, saying how much they had suffered during a raid by marauding Bantu.

The Whites, of whom there were numerous members, were having a family celebration. The table was ready with all their best silver and glass laid out on a starched white damask cloth when a lookout gave the alarm that a group of armed Xhosas was approaching in wardress. With one accord the tablecloth was picked off the table with all the silver on it, placed in a hole and covered with branches. The family barricaded itself into the house and the men loaded their rifles and managed to scare the enemy away. The strange thing was that the silver was never found. It was a mystery.

An imposing monument to the 1820 settlers has been built on a hill with a commanding view overlooking Grahamstown. Opened in July 1974, the building serves as a venue for numerous events, including the renowned annual arts festival, Rhodes University graduation ceremonies, school prize givings (most schools have outgrown their own halls and Grahamstown is full of schools), examinations, exhibitions, conferences, concerts, reunions, wedding receptions and formal dinners. The monument has been integrated into the community and into the life of the country. It has exceeded all expectations. It is said that the best form of commemoration is active — this one certainly is. I do not know who said, 'while mindful of the past, to do things in the present that shape the future', but it is apt.

These early settlers formed the 1820 Association, which is still in operation and of which the Tarka Training Farm (TTF) was one fine illustration of its work in the Mortimer valley. The name is taken from the river Tarka, which joined the Great Fish River at the farm next to Greenhalgh. The TTF was like a modern agricultural college with proper student accommodation, a pedigree herd of Friesian cattle, Clydesdale horses for farm work (and later tractors), and the usual pigs, poultry and sheep. The students were allowed to keep their own horses, often their only means of transport because there were no buses and few had cars. Alec Carswell-Smith, the manager, had two daughters, Dorothy and Alison, both excellent horsewomen who competed successfully at the Cradock Show each year. Dorothy married one of the students and they went farming in Swaziland. Alison I met again years later in Nyasaland with her first husband Joe who ran the Central African Transport Company. She still kept horses and was to be seen riding regularly with her two children.

Back at TTF there was a large swimming pool, tennis courts and a big hall that was used for a variety of functions ranging from church services to Greek dancing. There were about 24 students at a time and, since most had their own horses, gymkhanas and paper chases were held, usually organized by Pa.

These gymkhanas were great fun and mostly patronized by the English-speaking community; a few Afrikaners took part and a few spectators came to watch the mad English.

My mare, Judy, was always in great demand at these events and I lent her to numerous age group heats. Judy had an uncanny musical gift. She knew before anyone else when the music would stop and in musical chairs she would come to a dead halt from a fast canter, usually unseating the rider and not always onto a vacant chair or cushion.

Judy was a firm favourite of mine and very intelligent; she was quarter Suffolk punch; quarter countrybred, half thoroughbred and a good ride. She also gave me a foal every year, which always sold well. I had been allowed to buy her on my seventh birthday with my own money taken from a post office savings' account. Pa had a saddle made to fit me, which I used until I was about 11. Dozens of children learnt to ride on that saddle.

The students at TTF added considerably to the social life of the valley. Some turned out to become excellent farmers; some were totally inadequate and sent back to England and some drifted into occupations that had nothing to do with agriculture. Most of these young men developed a love of Africa and chose to make it their home.

It all came to an end in 1939 with the outbreak of war. No more students came out from the UK, those on courses left and went into the forces, and a few who were not fit finished their TTF training and then left. The farm was managed as an ordinary mixed farm for a while and then, after the war, the 1820 Association sold it as a private farm with a village of redundant buildings.

Many of these students found their way to Greenhalgh. Our door was ever open to anyone and everyone and some of these young men needed a friendly family home in which to discuss their problems or successes with Ma and Pa. The advice, if asked for, and help my parents gave them was always rewarded by genuine gratitude. The students were all single — there was no accommodation for wives and families — but somehow Mary and her baby slipped through the net and pitched up at the TTF having come from England. What to do? Ma, being the kind of person she was, ended up housing mother and child and this of course meant frequent visits from the student husband. This went on for several months until he had completed his course and moved on, taking his wife and baby with him, much to Dick's and my relief, for we were detailed to push the pram and play with the baby.

Most of the students were sensible people, but one very hot day Pa was in Mortimer village and a horse staggered in gasping for breath, pouring with sweat and near to collapse with the TTF student riding it in a sweat too. Pa immediately went over to him, told him to dismount and asked him what he thought he was doing. Apparently, he had galloped for about ten miles on hard, rutted, uneven, dusty gravel roads to see how quickly he could get from TTF to Mortimer station. Pa gave him a severe dressing down, made him find water for the wretched horse and, when suitably rested, walk the horse back to TTF. Many years later I met that man in Zimbabwe and he said how stupid he had been and how he had deserved every word Pa had thrown at him. It was a lesson learnt the hard way. He bore Pa no hard feelings.

To repay Ma and Pa in a small way we were invited to use the TTF swimming pool. However, as a family we did not take up the kind offer very often because the water smelt of sulphur and this brought on Dick's asthma.

Some of the students became friends and several wrote to tell us of their new beginnings, where they had settled or got married. Some even wrote asking horse-related questions. One in particular, Anthony de la Hey, who was farming successfully in the Howick district of Natal had a beautiful place and invited us to stay. He had several good horses and, while we were visiting, Pa and I had some lovely rides. It was good to see him well established with a wife, child and well-run farm. He had made it and that was what the TTF was all about.

* * *

The valley was populated with a mixture of people. The valley farmers were mostly settlers of British stock whereas Afrikaners mostly ran the sheep and goat farms on the mountains. The merino sheep were reared for their wool and the angora goats for luxury mohair wool. The angora is a handsome beast with a long silky coat prior to shearing. The mixed farming in the valley was mostly of dairy, pigs and chickens on the one hand and of cash crops of wheat, oats, barley, lucerne and fruit on the other.

There were some odd people among the settlers. Our neighbour on one side was a retired British army colonel whose wife ran their pig farm and would not allow him to do anything, not even negotiate the sale or purchase of stock. Afrikaners are conservative by nature and would be thrown by encountering a woman when they came to buy a special sow or boar with which to improve their own stock. They were far too shy to discuss details of progeny and breeding methods with a woman, let alone an eccentric English one, and often left with the wrong pig or took the first one they came across and fled rather than deal with her. This did not enhance their reputation as pig breeders with good imported strains and they left not long afterwards. This same woman never wore conventional clothes. She rode about the farm or over to see us wearing an ex-military jacket of nondescript shape, riding breeches and, instead of boots, stockings or leggings, she wore silk stockings knotted at the knee and carried an open parasol when it was sunny, which it usually was. Needless to say, hers must have been an old moke, for no self-respecting horse would stand for that. They were not our neighbours for long and, from the way they conducted their affairs, I think they must have gone bust. If I compare the photograph of a British lady jumping a hurdle in India in 1905 riding side-saddle and holding up a parasol in Joanna Trollope's *Britain's Daughters*, I realize that Africa was not the only colony to attract eccentric women.

The next occupants of that farm were another unusual couple. She was at least 20 years older than he was and most people mistook her for his mother, which caused great embarrassment. He was an RNR engineer who built what for those days was a magnificent cow-milking parlour with water laid on and drains for the slurry, which was unheard of in the district. They filled it with Jersey cows and a stockade, like an elephant stall, was built alongside for their predictably fierce Jersey bull. (Surely all bulls are fierce if they are permanently isolated from the rest of the herd accept for a minute or two now and again when a cow comes in season and needs to conceive next year's calf.) This oddly matched couple had some magnificent furniture in their home; though I was unaware of antiques at the time, I could still appreciate beautiful furniture and always enjoyed being invited inside. I think they were reasonably successful dairy farmers. In those days all the milk was separated; the cream would be sold and the skimmed milk would go to the farm labourers and their families and to the pigs in the district. The cream was taken in large metal churns to Mortimer railway station and dispatched to the creamery in Port Elizabeth. This young RNR engineer had an exceptionally good tenor voice and as his wife did not play the piano he brought all his new songs to Ma to play for him. Ma was a superb sight-reader and anyone in the district who had a new song or aria to learn would come over and get Ma to play it for them. In this way I was introduced to many popular songs of the day, arias from operas and of course Gilbert and Sullivan. When war was declared

34

in 1939 the RNR farmer was called up immediately and we never heard of him again. The neighbours on the other side were given the farm to run as their own during the war and after the war it was sold.

The neighbours who took over the RNR officer's farm were not particularly wealthy, but they were one of the nicest and most hard working families in the area. The father had lost most of one leg in an accident on a threshing machine and his wooden leg gave him a limp, but this did not seem to deter him from doing any farming chore. I remember his wife telling Ma that he seldom went to bed without the stump bleeding. Theirs was a mixed farm — a few sheep, a few cattle and a few horses. Their one son, Tom, was very keen on horses and I know Pa helped Tom a lot with his great knowledge. Sadly, Tom had to leave the farm to make a living and went into mining in Johannesburg. Next came twins, Danie and Madelaine. Danie was equally mad about horses and Pa bought a country-bred one from him as my hack — it was a nice dapple-grey. After elementary school, Madelaine left the area and worked in Johannesburg; when she came home, she was so 'dolled up' that her old father failed to recognize her. Their mother became one of my mother's close Afrikaner friends — she spoke good English, which was just as well as Ma did not speak a word of Afrikaans.

Across the Great Fish River from us, our boundary met in the middle of the river, lived an ex-Indian Army couple. He, a peppery old colonel, was not much liked by anyone but she was popular, charming and always beautifully dressed. She played bridge (a major social pastime) and he did not. They had a fruit farm and he spent the first few years digging out mature fruit trees and replanting them in mathematically precise straight lines, like guardsmen on parade. The Africans were totally mystified by these instructions. As far as they were concerned the trees were doing well and looked good. (Africans rarely have a word for straight, which is perhaps why they still build round houses, one house for each purpose rather than different rooms for different purposes.) I do not recall impressive fruit crops. He was a jealous man and because of his wife's popularity and involvement in the bridge circuit, he sold the car so that she could not go out. Nothing daunted her, so she gave instructions for a deck chair to be lashed to the bed of the farm wagon and the mules to be inspanned. She climbed up onto her deck chair, complete with parasol, and the African groom drove her to her destination. My mother, among others, was good about driving round to collect Elsie Gillespie to spare her the humiliation of the deck chair and four white mules. Yes, the colonel had no less than four matched white mules. In 1939 he expected to be called up immediately, but was not — eventually he got a job guarding Italian POWs and the farm was sold. On leaving, he gave Pa the famous four white mules, Selous, Witbok, Nelly and Blesbok. Mules are sterile, so they all lived together on the koppie with the other mules, Bosbok and Ringhals, some donkeys and Thrussie.

As our farm was under irrigation, the water bailiff paid us a visit from time to time to ensure that we only used our quota of water from Lake Arthur. Mr Todd, an elderly bachelor, was always immaculately dressed in panama hat, polished shoes, Palm Beach suit and stiff collar and tie. Whatever the temperature, he wore the same clothes and carried a silver-handled ebony walking stick to check the canals. He also rather liked brandy and Cape brandy is good stuff. He invariably pitched up at our house just in time for lunch, for he knew Ma would never allow him to go away unfed and he could have his brandy first. Pa and Ma never drank alcohol before lunch unless they were out socially or on holiday. I remember Mr Todd once coming to do one of his inspections when my grandmother was staying with us. She was a very beautiful woman and could get away with saying anything to anyone. Mr Todd was into his second brandy when Granny scolded him for drinking spirits at all, let alone a pre-lunch drink. Didn't he know how bad strong spirits were in a hot climate? Mr Todd looked contrite, smiled and finished his drink; and we all went in to lunch as if nothing had been said.

In fact whenever anyone stepped out of line or caused a misdemeanour, and I mean anyone, Granny would say 'they need telling' and this became a family saying. She was never seen out of the house without a hat, cotton gloves and, however hot it was, a silk scarf round her neck to avoid burning a V that would look unbecoming in evening dress. She spent half the year in South Africa, mostly with us but with a short spell with Uncle Gordon, and half the year in England, usually in Worthing where she had cousins. Grandpa had left her reasonably well off. One day while back in Sheffield, the manager of the National Provincial Bank, where she kept her account, asked her to pay him a call, which she did. He explained that perhaps she should cut down her trips to South Africa because she was going through her money rather fast. She smiled at him and said, 'Oh, that's all right, I'll just write you another cheque.' The concerned bank manager then realized that Granny had no idea of how to manage money, so alerted Ma and she coped with her finances. Sadly, this did not last long. Shortly afterwards, while staying with us on the farm she announced that she would like to spend a week at the Victoria Hotel in Cradock to have her snow-white hair permed and to do some unhurried shopping. She had her perm and for some reason caught a chill, which turned to pneumonia and she died. There was no penicillin then and she did not realize how ill she was. We all missed her very much. The Africans loved her and she often recruited African children to collect *roll-bossies*, a weed that becomes detached from its roots when mature. The idea was to pick up as many as possible so that they would not be blown around the farm in the wind. Once a suitable pile had been amassed, usually in a corner of a fence, she would set fire to them, often forgetting that the fence was made of wood. Pa would get furious, but she never heeded his outcry and rewarded the children with sweets.

With horses, we would sometimes help Old Shoe, the eccentric ostrich farmer who believed that the boom in feathers was just around the corner, round up his ostriches for plucking. These ridiculous and vicious birds can outrun most horses and some horses will not go near them, for they know how dangerous they can be. The aim was first to herd all of them into a small paddock, then a selected few into a smaller pen and eventually one bird at a time into a crush pen where, with a stocking quickly pulled over its head, the bird became so docile that one could pluck the soft clean feathers from under its wings and breast. The stocking was then removed, the crush pen gate opened and, whoosh, it was away and just as fierce as before. You had to be extremely careful to avoid a kick. These birds are very strong and can break a horse's leg with one kick. Their claws are deadly and can make a horrendous flesh wound. One should never stand in front of an ostrich, always to the side, to avoid being clawed. Their eggs, however, are delicious. If we were given one, Ma would have a marathon baking session and make the best sponge cakes I have ever tasted. The eggs also make superb omelettes. You seem to be able to beat them more and, though the colour is a very dark rich gold, they do not have a strong taste. The shell, of course, is very tough and has to be cut open with a hacksaw or a hole drilled if you want to keep the shell in tact.

Old Shoe's sister came out from England to visit him, but not long after she arrived the war broke out and she could not return. She could not live in his shack but luckily the neighbours had to move because George Briscoe had important war work elsewhere. So May moved into his nice little house at Burnham Thorpe. However, poor May was totally isolated, for she neither had a car nor knew how to drive and Old Shoe went everywhere on horseback; May was unlikely to learn to ride at the age of 70. Old Shoe used to leave his shack and ride over every evening to keep her company and to sleep in the house. May, a typical Victorian lady, was very tall and thin and, when out walking, always wore long-sleeved dresses, a black velvet ribbon round her neck and a long string or two of pearls, gloves and buttoned kid leather boots. She decided she needed a dog for company, so she acquired a half-grown mongrel she called Doggy Doggy. Doggy Doggy had never been trained for anything, let alone to go on a lead, and May had no idea of how to train a dog. We would sometimes meet this ill-assorted pair on the edge of a dusty road and when we approached, usually on horseback and accompanied by two or three bull terriers, her dog would panic and wind his lead round and round May's legs. We would wait holding our breath to see if May and Doggy Doggy would collapse in a heap. By some miracle this never happened and they used to unwind themselves successfully and continue their walk, and we would ride on. May did not play bridge so she seldom went anywhere unless she was fetched and returned. She was a rather sad and lonely old lady.

* * *

When Dick and I were growing up Ma began to concentrate on the dairy side of the farm. The two or three shorthorn cows that kept us in milk were now added to and a serious study of line breeding and lactation records began. A magnificent bull was bought and one or two more cows. These dairy shorthorns were prize animals, so not only horses went to the Cradock Show. Basil was the name given to the bull and he was so docile that, as children we regularly fed him sugar lumps, carrots and apples, just like the horses. His great rasp tongue would take the offerings with enthusiasm but to get him into the show ring was another matter, for, with his vast tonnage, he was incapable of more than the slowest amble. We had to use devious lures, bribes, shoves and pushes to get into his thick woolly head that he must just try and walk a little faster.

Being children with unorthodox ideas, my brother and I tried every means to charm Basil into increasing his limited speed. One pulling his head collar at the front and one switching at the rear with a stick or sjambok worked quite well, except we did not think anyone would appreciate us entering the ring as a kind of mock circus act. However, after weeks of perseverance Basil did increase his speed and on the great day of the show fooled us all by practically trotting round the ring. The explanation was simple. We had done all our arduous training without a heifer or cow in sight.

Basil did us proud and was awarded Best of Breed; our cow got a second and the heifer a first. Ma was tickled pink at her first effort. The heifer was a beautiful roan colour and there was great excitement when Ma was offered £100 for her, which she decided to accept as a good advertisement for her new pedigree dairy shorthorn herd. With the increased volume of milk from more cows, Ma started to make butter, which she then sold. I can remember having to stand on an upturned bucket to reach the handle of the hand-turned churn. Lovely yellow butter was patted into one-pound blocks and wrapped in greaseproof paper that had been soaked in cold water with Ma's name and address printed on it. There were regular orders for Ma's butter and I must say I have never tasted butter to equal it. No one used it sparingly and it was in great demand. Most of the neighbouring dairy farms sold cream or milk, but no one else made butter.

The surplus whole milk was sold to Cadbury's, which had built a cooling plant at Mortimer railway station. Its lorry would go round twice a day to collect milk cans from the farm gates to take to the cooling plant where it was chilled before being bulked into a milk tanker for overnight railroad transport to the Cadbury's chocolate factory in Port Elizabeth. It provided a nice steady income and encouraged dairy farming.

Judy was my favourite horse but Ma was against me riding her when I was very young because, as a quarter Suffolk punch with a very broad back, she feared I would develop bowed legs. She persuaded Pa to let me ride a donkey until my bones were harder. We usually took long rides every Saturday with a gathering of people and I disliked being on a donkey; I could seldom get it to break out of a walk and was always left miles behind everyone else. I rode on a felt saddle and as donkeys have no withers (nothing in front of the saddle) and slope behind, it was necessary to have a crupper. I remember feeling inferior. In fact, I was so miserable that Ma eventually gave in and I was given Pickles. My brother was also subjected to a donkey in his extreme youth and he hated it as much as I did. Pickles only had one eye and I do not think I ever rode him off a leading rein, but at least I could keep up with Pa and the other riders. Ma then thought a Shetland pony was the answer, for Pickles could not be trusted. Ladybird arrived and, though she was supposed to be a reliable children's pony, I was unimpressed; she was so small and narrow that the felt saddle had to be brought out again. I mounted Ladybird and rode her, with Pa at her head, quietly round the stable yard a few times and she seemed docile enough. Pa let go, I kicked her in the ribs and off we went at full gallop to the horizon. I remained on, just. She had a long flowing mane and I remember clutching handfuls of it all tangled up with the reins. I could not stop her, but eventually she tired and slowed down on the open road miles from home. By this time Ma was in hot pursuit in the car and when I met her I was riding a very tired Shetland pony. I have no idea how long all this took, but, though unharmed, I disliked Ladybird. She had an evil eye and with their short little legs taking short little steps Shetlands are uncomfortable to ride. As my new mount had not come up to scratch and as she was about ten years old, not much training could be done. She had a mouth like cast iron and of course I was not advanced enough to school her and no adult could ride her to teach her, so she was given to Danie Pollard, a neighbour's son. He loved his wild little mare and could be seen riding her at breakneck speed with his feet barely clearing the ground as he herded sheep. It was the first horse he had ever owned.

The Early Years

When I was seven years' old Ma reluctantly let me ride Judy. She was a lovely ride and taught me a lot. She was a great show-off and I rode her for four consecutive years at the Cradock Show and got first prize each time in our age group. She knew how to catch the judge's eye, arch her neck and pointed beautifully at the trot. I was proud of her.

Pa's stud of thoroughbreds was becoming quite well known and in 1938 he decided to take a string of yearlings to the Rand Easter Show in Johannesburg and to the yearlings' sales, the South African equivalent of the Newmarket sales. Everyone was very excited, especially old Alfred, the cowman, and his two very reliable sons Gerry and Makwasa, who would accompany Pa and who were put in charge of six yearlings and of the under grooms. They were turned out in new white overalls and special leading bridles were made. One rein, the off rein, pulled through the near snaffle and could be pulled tight as a curb, but usually it was left relaxed. Four railway trucks were ordered, three with two yearlings in each and one for fodder, tack and the grooms. Pa travelled by passenger train and, so that Ma would not be on her own with us, Wy was invited to stay.

Some time after the Rand Easter Show Makwasa sadly had an accident with a badly behaved horse and his leg was very seriously broken. After a long hospital stay it eventually mended, but there was a shortening of some four to five inches and he had to wear a special built-up boot. Pa saw to it that he was only given jobs that did not bring him in contact with horses, for he had lost his nerve and, with a shortened leg, was less nimble. Ma and Pa had paid for his and Gerry's secondary education at Lovedale. Gerry later went to Fort Hare University (which was where Nelson Mandela had read law) and qualified as a teacher, but when Ma and Pa left Greenhalgh we lost touch with them.

While Pa was at the Rand Easter Show, I took it upon myself to oversee that the right feed was put in the right stable for the convalescing racehorses and stallion, Caribbee. The small amounts of freshly-cut lucerne that formed part of the evening stable feed were cut by scythe and I asked the scythe wielders to let me have a go. I do not remember whether or not I got an answer, but I picked up the scythe, which was well sharpened and much bigger than I was, and swung it around to cut the lucerne. I got such a swing going on it that it swung right round and nearly cut my leg off. The two farm hands were shattered. I do not know how I got back to the house, but I remember standing outside the sitting room window where Ma and Wy were talking and sewing and saying that I had hurt my leg in a very frightened voice. Ma came out immediately and was horrified because my calf was cut to the bone and was bleeding profusely, though without any pain. Within a very short space of time I was in the car with my leg bandaged and strapped up to try and stop the blood flow. Ma gave a few hurried instructions to the horse boys and, with Wy at the wheel, we shot off to Cradock hospital at 50 m.p.h. Wy was unfamiliar with the road so we had some near misses; parts of the road went along dry riverbeds and the drifts were poorly marked. We flew over one of theses ridges and it was a wonder that no springs were broken on landing, but Wy had only one thing on her mind and that was to get to Cradock as quickly as possible. I was carried into the theatre where Dr Scholtz was waiting for me. He gave me a local anaesthetic and I remember the needle going in and out and the tugged feeling of him drawing the two sides of my calf together. Ma remained with me in the theatre. My leg was then strapped up tightly, I was carried back to the car and we all went home in a slower and more sedately manner than before. For about the next three weeks I was not allowed to put any weight on my leg and spent all day on a bed on the stoep. Very boring but with Ma, Wy and eventually Pa, when he returned from his successful showing and selling, I was not given much chance to move off the bed.

The Cradock Show was due in a few weeks and Pa had entered me in my class age group. A terrific argument arose as to whether I would be allowed to compete. With me not having ridden for weeks and Judy having eaten her head off and being as fat as a tick, we would not stand a chance. In the end, commonsense lost and I just managed to get my jodhpurs over my still swollen and bandaged leg. Judy somehow sensed the situation and could not have given me a kinder or better ride. She excelled herself and we were lucky to take first prize once again — good old Judy. When I got home I had to be cut out of my jodhpurs; with the exertion of riding, the stitches had burst and I was back at square one. It was decided just to strap it and let it heal from the base up, which it did, leaving a huge ugly crescent-shaped scar on my calf, which I carry to this day.

Between the ages of 8 and 11, I would ride the three miles to school each day, I on Judy and Dick on Blackie or Mike, all faithful and reliable mounts. Blackie had a foal every year and an udder like a Jersey cow. She had a generous nature and frequently one could see her suckling two foals and not always hers. She was a godsend if a thoroughbred mare had very little milk or died in foaling. As long as Blackie was in milk she would save the day. Pa's reputation for successful breeding was spreading and a mare called Mustanquet was sent to Caribbee to stud. She had never conceived at other studs and her owner was particularly anxious for a foal, for she had had a good racing career and carried good genes. She got on with Caribbee and was in foal, but was watched carefully for any signs of abnormalities. All went well until she actually tried to give birth. Something was very wrong and she died of a heart attack before the foal was delivered. I was with Pa when he unhesitatingly slit her abdomen and delivered a beautiful live foal. Pa handed it to me and I was speechless with awe and admiration; I shall never forget that precious moment. Blackie had not had her foal yet so there was no milk from her, but that night another mare gave birth to a stillborn foal and Pa quickly skinned the dead foal, wrapped the hide around Mustanquet's foal and gave it to the foalless mare. They were put in a stable together and unobtrusively watched (just in case the mare did not take to the foal). After much sniffing, the mare began to lick the orphan foal, which found the milk supply and they never looked back. This is often done with lambs, but is not always successful with horses.

As our mounts were horses and not ponies we were still quite small to remount because we had to go through two gates to get to school. Judy was good about opening and shutting gates from the saddle, but Blackie was not. Pa put a mounting block at each gate just in case we had to dismount for whatever reason. We would get up in the morning and go with Pa to collect our horses, who had been grazing out all night, bring them to the stable yard, feed them with lucerne, give them a quick brush, remove any ticks, and return to the house for our breakfast and saddlebags. Once saddled up, off we would go. When we got to Littlefield there was a special shady place to tie up the horses. We removed the bridles and saddles, put the halter on and tethered the horses to the tree. We had been taught a special knot that would undo in a flash should it be necessary. At break time we would take the horses to the water trough for a drink, then tie them up again and return to our lessons. At lunchtime, when school ended, we would saddle up, ride home, unsaddle and lead the horses out to pasture before going into the house for lunch. We were tired by then, but I have always been grateful to Ma and Pa for instilling in us a sense of discipline and of looking after our animals before feeding ourselves. After lunch we were allowed two sweets while we had a rest on our beds. Sometimes Ma read to us, sometimes we read and sometimes we just slept. After a swim, tea and our homework if we had any, I usually helped with the evening stable routine, though Dick was far more interested in his dinky toys, bike and Meccano.

One day a week we had Afrikaans lessons. Dick did not join us for some reason, so he would ride home on his own with Blackie or Mike. I would remain at Littlefield for lunch and then we would all, including Wy on Helmet, ride over to Mrs Withers for an hour's lesson, once again tying the horses up under a shady tree. We did not have lessons with Mrs Withers for long, for Mrs Johnnie Sieberhagen who lived further down the Bedford main road soon took over. Mrs Johnnie was an excellent teacher and I have never forgotten the rudiments of Afrikaans she instilled into me. Although Afrikaans was not in our PNEU syllabus, we had to learn it because it was compulsory in senior school. Hearing and using it daily, one grew up absorbing the language naturally, but it was important to learn the finer points of grammar properly. Afrikaans is a very descriptive language and later I really began to appreciate its poetry and novels, though except on one occasion I never used it outside South Africa.

In summer, Pa would often ring up a farm between seven and ten miles away to ask if we could have breakfast with them during our Saturday morning ride. Riding in the early morning to avoid the heat of the day was to become a regular routine and a very enjoyable one because the bull terriers came too. The numbers varied according to the availability of horses, whether or not guests were staying with us, and who wished to join us along the way. On these rides there were places where we only walked or trotted, others where we cantered and, on a very few private roads, where we galloped. The horses knew our routine and this often took strangers by surprise. Of course we children all knew what to expect and delighted in the other people's predicaments. We had a dogcart on pneumatic tyres that could be inspanned to an old dual-purpose horse called Kroon. Every year our regular riding horses had to be injected against horse sickness and then have three weeks off work. Usually this happened in the school holidays, but there must have been an overlap because Dick and I were told not to ride to school but to take Kroon and the cart. I always did the harnessing and outspanning, but on that particular day I had a music lesson for which I had not practised and, having arrived early, I told Dick, who was about eight years' old, to out-span Kroon and tie him to the tree, and I walked off to the school-room to practise. A few minutes later there was pandemonium. Dick was screaming and a bolting horse was dragging a half-attached dogcart through the garden into the veld. People appeared from everywhere trying to catch the runaway Kroon and calm him down, which was eventually done without too much trouble. It had never entered my head that Dick did not know the order of outspanning a horse from a cart. He had half removed one trace and the blinkered bridle when Kroon panicked and bolted. Poor Dick was devastated and I was castigated and shamed. Pa was telephoned and he came down with an African to lead Kroon home with his few cuts and bruises and very unnerved. I do not think the dogcart was ever repaired, at least I do not remember it being used again.

Kroon came into his own some time later when Ma decided that Dick, being the only boy at Littlefield School, would be better off with other boys at the state-run one-roomed school at Tarka. This involved quite a long ride on the main road, but poor Dick had no option but to do what he was told. He had to start off before I did and I used to see him in the distance trotting along on Kroon while I finished my breakfast. Looking back on this period I think it was a mistake (and Ma did not make many) to subject Dick to this hardship. He was only eight; he hardly knew any of the other children at Tarka; and the syllabus was quite different from the PNEU one. With a governess we all loved, who had been brought out from the UK at some expense, why did Ma subject Dick to this humiliating experience? I still do not understand her reasoning and neither does Dick, for we have discussed it as adults. He hated it and still feels sore about it. But Kroon was the reliable old nag who carried him safely there and back on his own each day. Another of our more notable riding horses was Hypo — a handsome 17-hand broken-down chestnut racehorse descended from the great sire Hyperion. Hypo was Pa's special ride, a horse with beautiful manners, very gentle and very comfortable to ride. Pa seldom let anyone else ride him, but occasionally I was allowed to as a special treat and it was a treat. My usual mount at this time was Nobby, a smart 15-hand bay I adored. He was naughty and spirited, but always gave me a good ride, though he sometimes nearly pulled my arms out of their sockets when he was in the mood. Pa produced all sorts of devices to stop him pulling, or at least to ease the rider's arms. They would work for a while, but then he would find a way round by holding his head differently or just choosing not to pull one day and when you thought you had won starting again. However, he was also the gentlest pony and would take a lump of sugar from my lips. At that time I had a spaniel called Mickie who would come for rides with us and when he got tired Nobby would allow him to sit behind the saddle, though only at a walk.

Two stallions stand out in my memory — Caribbee and Clustine. Caribbee came to Pa with an impressive pedigree but as a man killer from a stud where everyone was terrified of him. Pa was known in the horse world for his 'gift' for getting on with just about any horse, so Caribbee's owner asked if he would have him at stud. Always happy to meet a challenge, Pa agreed and Caribbee duly arrived by train and his truck was shunted up to the crush pen enclosure. Ma did not want me near this dangerous animal, but I pleaded and promised to wait in the car while Pa met the horse. We went down to the station with head collars, ropes, lunging reins, three bridles (in case he broke one) and three terrified Africans who were not quite sure what was expected of them. Though horse boys, they were very apprehensive. The car was parked and I kept my promise. Pa took a bridle with a lunging rein and opened the top half of the truck door to confront Caribbee's tail, his head down in a corner ignoring everything. Pa, with carrots, apples and lump sugar handy, spoke to him. There was no reaction. Pa continued to talk to him and, in a little while, Caribbee's ear pricked up and he turned his head to see where the voice was coming from (he was not used to being spoken to in that vein). Pa went on talking to him and, before long, Caribbee turned right round and came up to Pa — no teeth bared, no ears back, no dash — he stood back from Pa and looked out of the half open truck door. When he took a step nearer, Pa slipped the bridle on over his halter, fastened the throat lash and adjusted the curb chain, talking to him all the time and giving him a carrot. He quietly asked the three Africans to open the truck doors so he could lead him out. They opened the doors and stood well back as Pa led Caribbee out through the crush pen into the enclosure. Calling the stallion boy over and introducing him to Caribbee, he told him to keep talking to him and handed over carrots, apples and sugar as he clipped another rein onto the offside and they walked Caribbee out into the open. He looked around, shook himself, and Pa said, 'right, take him home, there is nothing wrong with him.' With some disbelief the other two stable boys, one on each rein and one at the rear walked Caribbee the three miles to Greenhalgh and we never had a moment's trouble with his alleged savagery. We discovered later that at the other stud he had been used as a teaser and had never been allowed to serve a mare. This had gone on for far too long and one day Caribbee had attacked his groom, who later died. Caribbee, an import from the UK, had had a successful racing career, but in his last race had fallen and broken his fetlock. This had been left to heal by itself and it must have been very painful, which would not have improved his temper. Any other horse would have been put down in those days, but his then owner wished to breed from him. So Caribbee was given to Pa and six excellent brood mares became the nucleus of his own stud. I soon became devoted to Caribbee and was allowed to bring him to his loosebox in the evenings. He was such a 'gentleman', for he used to lower his head so that I could reach to put his bridle on, and then in the loosebox to take it off. He produced some excellent progeny that were sold as yearlings. If there was a particular good filly Pa would lease her for racing and have her back to breed when her racing career was over.

Beauty, a stunning half-Arab palomino mare and a great trippler (she would tripple for miles) produced some lovely foals.

Another memorable horse at Greenhalgh, and there were at times 100 or more, was Bonaparte, a magnificent dark bay 17½-hand riding horse. He had won every prize for which he could be entered in the Cape Province and was a five-gaiter — walk, trot, tripple, canter, gallop. To make him trot rather than tripple one just touched his withers. The Afrikaans taught all their horses to tripple and some did it naturally after generations of tripplers in their blood. Bonaparte's previous owners moved away and wanted him to go to a good home where he would not be overworked in his old age. He was a stallion, much in demand for breeding riding horses, and behaved exactly as a stallion should. It was a thrill to ride, and own, such a well-known, popular and beautiful horse. When I told my friend Bits Wattrus, who lived about ten miles away, that we had Bonaparte and that I rode him every day, he did not believe me, so I said, 'Right, I will show you. Will you be at home tomorrow?' When I rode him over Bits could not believe what he was seeing, for he really thought I was winding him up, which I frequently did. He was thrilled to meet such a famous horse face to face. The joy and thrill of the compatibility of a good ride is a special experience. You and the horse know instinctively what is required of the other and there is a total trust in each other — evident at Badminton and other trials and three-day events, and essential to great horsemanship.

Earlier on I mentioned Helen, the doctor with a practice in Stanmore in London who came out to look after her three motherless nieces. On her trip to South Africa on a Union Castle liner, Helen noticed a grey horse in a horsebox on the deck, which she visited daily. She became quite fond of this animal in the course of the 18-day voyage to Port Elizabeth. The horse was Clustine and destined for Greenhalgh, which Helen did not know until she saw the horse with which she had shared a voyage while visiting Ma and Pa.

The champion jockey Gordon Richards had ridden Clustine successfully and we had a photograph of them together hanging in the dining room. Clustine, a handsome dapple-grey, sired some useful progeny including my own horse Popples, also a dapple-grey. Popples remained my hack until I married. One day in about 1946 I was about to go for a ride with a friend and had in the meanwhile tied up the two horses to a tree near the stoep by our house.

Just then, the lorry arrived with our annual order of coal. While the lorry was unloading, Danie Pollard the driver, rushed round, untied Popples, climbed onto the saddle and cantered down the drive with a look of pure joy on his face. Danie's mare and Clustine were Popple's parents and Danie loved horses. He had sold me Popples because he needed the money, but he never lost his love for the horse. As it happened, an uncle and aunt were staying with us at the time. Uncle Arthur, who had been ill after the war, had come to South Africa from the UK for the good food and sunshine. Aunty Con witnessed Danie helping himself to and cantering off with Popples and was outraged at the young man's cheek. Not knowing the background, she was especially amazed that I was not the least put out by Danie's behaviour. She thought a mere lorry driver helping himself to my horse was beyond the pale and went on muttering about it for ages. South Africa is less class ridden than the UK and she could not understand my attitude.

I must have been thrown and fallen off horses umpteen times without turning a hair; the important thing is to get back in the saddle as quickly as possible. Pa claimed that he had never fallen off a horse (he was not boasting, merely stating a fact) unless the horse had fallen, which of course happened in the cavalry during the Boer War and First World War, the latter being the last war in which British troops rode on horseback. I think Pa may have participated in the last cavalry charge without knowing at the time that it would be the last.

Pa and I were out riding one day and cantering fairly briskly on a soft bit of road we knew well when all of a sudden Pa and his horse almost disappeared into the dry grass on the side of the road, which was between 24 and 30 inches high. I pulled up in horror, not quite knowing what to do. I caught Pa's horse, which was very shaken and tied a knot in the offside broken rein. Pa's glasses had fallen off but we found them, luckily unscathed. Neither Pa nor the horse seemed to have any bones broken, so he remounted and we continued at a slow walk. When Pa kept repeating, 'Why have I got a knot in my rein? I would never have come out with a knot in my rein,' I realized he was unwell, but I had not heard of concussion and thought the best thing was to continue on our ride to a neighbour for tea. What had happened was that Pa's horse had fallen into an antbear hole. These animals, about the size of a pig, dig enormous holes to get to ants' nests and the long grass hid this particular one. When we got to the neighbour's house for afternoon tea, Pa was still going on about the knot in his rein. When I told them he had fallen, they realized at once that he was concussed. They phoned Ma and she came in the car with an African to ride back with me on Pa's horse. Pa was put to bed, complaining loudly that there was nothing wrong with him. It is funny what one remembers. It had been my first experience of concussion.

* * *

Pa believed in not interfering with nature and, since we lived in a good climate, all the mares had their foals in a foaling paddock with plenty of shelter and abundant grazing. One knew when foaling was imminent (11 months' gestation) because the udder would become enlarged and wax would appear on the teats. At this point the mare would be isolated and old Bartman, the stonemason, would keep watch by night. He did not disturb or interfere with the mare, but if he suspected a problem he would call Pa. Usually by the time Pa got there, a healthy foal was already suckling.

Part of Bartman's job was to ensure that all the afterbirth had come away, and then to bury it to discourage jackals or wild cats from coming too close to the paddock.

On walking to the maternity paddock early one morning, Pa and I met Bartman on his way home. Pa asked if all was well and whether the foal was a filly. Bartman said that all was well with the foal but that he did not know its sex. Pa looked at him in a strange way and we continued on our way to see this lovely foal all licked and clean except for one thing — his penis was pointing outwards between his hind legs — this was Caribbee's son and clearly a throwback from somewhere.

Thrussie, as we named him, was reared in the normal way and as a yearling Pa offered to give him to the veterinary research station, Ondersterpoort, but they declined. Thrussie had grown into a strong horse with a good temperament, so Pa trained him to harness and he lived with the mules and donkeys as a draft animal and thrived. He came into his own during the breeding season as he had all the instincts of a stallion (there had been no need to geld him because he was incapable of serving a mare) and would be put in with the mares due to come into season to get them excited enough to accept Caribbee or Bancroft. Thrussie used to get just as excited sexually as a normal stallion, and have erections and ejaculations without penetrating the mares. When Pa decided to retire and sell the farm he himself put Thrussie down because he did not want him to be ridiculed or fall into wrong and perhaps unkind hands.

By this time Pa's reputation as a successful breeder and experienced horseman was spreading far and wide and we had frequent visits from people with a connection or interest in horses. On one occasion I recall a car arriving unannounced with two jockeys and two trainers while Ma and Pa were busy entertaining the Bishop of Grahamstown on his annual visit with the local vicar and entourage. Our dining room was too small to accommodate everybody, so the jockeys and trainers were put in the sitting room and fed on beer and sandwiches, while the Bishop and his attendants sat down to a proper lunch as arranged. Ma apologized to His Grace for the influx and the bishop said, 'Oh, I would like to meet them to get some good tips.' With this ecclesiastical visit an annual event, Ma thought it was time our lavatory, a pit latrine about 100 yards down the garden, was improved. This was a very deep pit over which a tin shelter was built with a wooden seat with an appropriately placed hole. As it was built for full-sized adults, I was terrified of falling in as a small child and we children were provided with two steps to get to the 'throne'. It was all very primitive, but if properly used there were no flies and no smell; when you finished you replaced a tight-fitting lid. There was a door, but I never remember it being shut; if you were approaching the latrine you could see if anyone was there and whoever was there could shout a warning to the approaching person. The *Farmers Weekly* was the main reading material and sometimes a church magazine. Ma thought this old pit latrine must be coming to the end of its life and that a new one should be dug and built; it seemed a good idea to have it ready for the Bishop's next visit and this was done. However, Pa decided that he did not particularly like the new latrine, which was not as secluded as the old one, so it was decided that the old one would be for men and the new one, which was nearer the house, for the females. Dick took the matter seriously and decided to make it quite clear by painting 'LADIES ONLEY' in huge white sloping letters. His spelling was never corrected and caused a few laughs. In the ladies loo our reading matter was the *National Geographical* and *Country Life*. It was pleasant to sit there and watch two large Cape eagle owls (Bubo capensis) on their daylight perch in the branches of a large conifer a few yards away. They grew so used to us being there that they never moved, just blinked down at us when they should have been asleep during the daytime. There was an interesting assortment of pelts under their tree containing the remains of mice, rats, little birds and other small mammals. If you unwrapped the neatly rolled little parcels you could identify very clearly what the owls lived on by the head of each skeleton.

Ma had masses of birds of all kinds at Greenhalgh. When my parents first moved there they inherited large brick-built chicken houses from the previous owners, so they kept white leghorn hens for their eggs, which they sold, but the hens soon became infested with tampan — a flat blood-sucking tick that crept into the soft brick crevices and cracks and were impossible to eradicate. So that enterprise came to an end and the chicken houses were cleared and burnt to kill off the ticks. Next Ma invested in big black Australorp fowls, a good-looking docile breed of good layers. They had a posh run built under the mulberry and quince trees; the hen house and egg boxes were made of zinc to stop ticks infesting everything. The chickens had to be secure at night to stop jackals and iguanas marauding. Australorps make good mothers and broody hens, so had their own maternity run in which they sat on and hatched their eggs before being moved to grass in an enclosed movable cage until the chicks were big enough to join the flock.

At a certain time of the year the hens would moult and look very scruffy as they lost their feathers and ceased to lay. When there was a surplus of eggs Ma used to preserve dozens in isinglass (gelatine from a sturgeon's bladder). The liquid stank and was kept hidden and covered until one needed to use the eggs. They were fine for cooking, but not as a boiled egg for breakfast.

There were geese and white Aylesbury ducks on the pond and, at one stage, a fierce gander of which Dick and I were terrified; we had to take a wide detour to get to the stables to avoid him, for he would fly at anything and anyone — Pa, dogs, horses and us. We then decided to stick to ducks until a more docile gander could be found. Ducks make hopeless mothers; they lay anywhere and, if they manage to hatch their eggs, they invariably squash most of their ducklings. Ma once found a duck's nest containing 40 eggs, so heaven knows how many ducks used that nest. Ma then began to collect the duck eggs and put them under broody hens to hatch. Ducks will only produce fertile eggs if they have access to water and, as the old hens proved, the eggs were fertile. Ma built up quite a trade in ducks for Christmas and it was a case of all hands and the cook to pluck and dress them for sale all over the country, not just locally but by overnight train to Port Elizabeth, East London and Cradock. Another reason to place the duck eggs in the brooding hens' safe maternity ward was to protect them from the iguana — a large lizard about four to five feet long that can move very fast, that is attracted to ponds and that likes eating eggs.

We had all shapes, sizes and colours of pigeons, not for eating but to look pretty in the farmyard. They had a cote but also nested under the eaves in the wagon shed or in stable windows. Pa even got some peacocks, which used to display on the lawn and look terrific, but they did not last long because they took to screeching outside Ma's bedroom window every morning at about 4.00 a.m. or at the first suggestion of dawn. Ma got fed up and said that either she or the peacocks had to go, so they went into the pot and made very good eating.

Dick and I were given a pair of budgerigars for which Pa built a beautiful aviary round a living conifer just outside the sitting room window, through which we could hear them chattering. Comfortable nesting boxes were provided and in no time at all we had many dozens of budgies. We gave lots away and every house in the valley must have had a pair. Sometime after Dick and I had gone to boarding school they were all sold as a flock.

Ma also had turkeys and the cocks were hilarious when displaying to the hens — tail up in full fan, red rattles dangling from their cheeks making much gobbling noise. The hens are the most stupid of all birds and quite hopeless mothers. So once again the Australorp broody hens were called upon to hatch the turkey chicks. The turkeys were a bit too big for the iguana to tackle so they had a free run to roost wherever they pleased. As there were hundreds of trees this was not a problem, but turkey brains being what they are they mostly chose to roost on low willow branches overhanging the pond. Invariably, one or two would either get pushed off or fall asleep, over-balance and splash into the pond. However, turkeys can swim, at least these did, so with much flapping of wings and squawks the bedraggled bird would scramble out onto the grass and find its way back to the willow branch overhanging the water.

The wild indigenous birds were too numerous to count, but the herons with their heronry in the large gum trees that shaded the walk to the ladies' loo were the most noticeable ones near the house. Swallows, swifts and house martins would arrive to nest under the eaves, as is their wont, when the European winter began. Yellow finches, or weaverbirds, would spin bottle-shaped nests on willow twigs overhanging the pond and sometimes on trees nearer the house. My bedroom, which was at one end of the house, had two outside walls with sliding windows with bamboo-like reeds planted outside to screen the room. These were just right for the weaverbirds, which would tear off 12- to 14-inch strips to weave into nests; some even made their nests on the reeds, which was unusual because they prefer to be over water for safety, but perhaps they felt safe next to the house.

Hoopoes nested near the river, as did dikkops with the huge piles of sticks and mud they used year after year. One hoopoe decided to make its nest and rear its young in a stable window, but the smell was unbearable; even the horses did not like using that stable. It took several years and much rolled-up wire netting and other barricades to persuade the hoopoe not to build there. This was very unusual behaviour for a hoopoe.

Turtledoves and ringdoves are now commonplace in England. The sound of their cooing here seems out of place, especially on a cold day, for I associate the sound of a cooing doves high up in a shady tree with a temperature of about 80°F.

* * *

Ours was not the only thoroughbred stud farm in the valley. A few miles away Monsieur Jean, a magnificent, temperamental French-bred sire was at stud. He and a goat that always accompanied him were inseparable. The farm was called Daybreak and its owner, a

Miss Reynolds, had built a row of very fine looseboxes, stallion paddocks, tack and food rooms, a sick bay, a crush pen and exercise yards. Because she lived in Durban, she had a manager on the farm and used to fly down to see her horses two to three times a year. Flying in the 1930s was not very common, but to fly in one's own aeroplane was a cause for great excitement. Quite large crowds used to gather at the Daybreak landing strip to see this phenomenon. Her pilot was her trainer Labuster, and sometimes a jockey would accompany them. For some reason they always arrived at about 8.00 or 9.00 a.m. and came to us for breakfast. The conversation of course was all horse talk. Miss Reynolds had some very successful racehorses running in Durban. Another stallion at Daybreak, a huge Percheron imported from France, became well known for siring crossbred draft horses. The plane, which was a four-seater Dragon Moth, was refuelled by hand and the visits usually ended in time for Miss Reynolds to fly back to Durban in daylight.

* * *

While 3 September 1939 is unforgettable for millions the world over, for me it was a remarkable date for a different reason. Judy gave birth to a beautiful chestnut colt, which was immediately named War Sunday, but known as Sunday for short. At the appropriate age he was gelded, broken in to the saddle and became a good ride. As we had so many horses, I was not allowed to keep him and he was sold to Old Shoe — poor Sunday with only Old Shoe and ostriches for company. We used to see Sunday regularly because Old Shoe came to supper and bridge every Saturday evening until I put my foot down a month before my marriage. One evening he quizzed Pa about polo (Pa had played a lot at one time) and asked to borrow a mallet and ball to get some practice in. I have no idea where or with whom he thought he would play, for the nearest polo then was in Natal about 400 miles away. Some weeks later Pa asked him how he was getting on and Old Shoe said he found it difficult to hit the ball, Pa said 'Oh' and quizzed him a bit, only to find that this highly educated eccentric was trying to hit the ball with the point rather than the flat of the polo mallet. I will not repeat Pa's exclamation.

In 1939 I was eight, Helen nine and Dick five. Joan and Anne had gone to board at the Collegiate in Port Elizabeth and Wy, who could have done with more pupils, was stranded in South Africa because of the war. A cousin of Helen's came to live at Littlefield and so Jean Cowden swelled the numbers, swiftly followed by an evacuee girl from Egypt. Her mother had come to live in South Africa for the duration of the war and Henrietta was too young for boarding school. Evacuees also arrived from Malaya, including the Lee twins whose father was taken prisoner by the Japanese, followed by some others. In 1942 Helen joined Joan as a boarder, but at Diocesan School for Girls (DSG) in Grahamstown rather than the Collegiate in Port Elizabeth. I joined them in 1943 because by the age of 12 I had outgrown Wy. From 1943 to 1947 I was a boarder at DSG and riding was limited to the holidays. This seemed a terrible wrench at first, but my companions were now girls of my own age and not horses.

Christmas on the farm in the middle of summer was very different from Christmas in the UK. On Christmas Day animals still had to be fed, milked, watered and turned out as on any farm in the world. We were not allowed to receive our presents until lunchtime at the earliest. Ma never had a Christmas tree; she said it did not seem right with the temperature in the eighties. After breakfast all the Africans arrived in front of the house with their entire families and each and every one was given a present. As we never knew how many children would turn up, a huge basket of sweets and fruit was produced and it was my job to scoop up a handful into each child's cupped hands. Some of the known and older African children were given clothes. Then everybody wished everyone a happy Christmas and they sang for us. Africans are very musical and break into song on all sorts of occasions. This is where I first heard and learnt 'Nkosi Sikeleli Afrika', which is now the South African national anthem. Africans naturally sing in harmony and some had lovely voices; their singing was a special part of Christmas. When they went home we had our Christmas midday meal complete with traditional Christmas pudding. We usually had duck or turkey, whichever was available on the farm.

Once the evening chores were done, Pa would give the adult workers a generous tot of brandy, at least those still sober enough to do their duties. They loved brandy and appreciated Pa's gesture.

I first came across Christmas wrapping paper in England in 1947 because for some reason we never had it at Greenhalgh. Ma tended to emphasize the spiritual rather than commercial side of Christmas and perhaps the war had something to do with it. However, I was thrilled by all the pretty paper and horrified to see people tearing it off their presents. To this day I remove mine as carefully as possible and use it again having ironed it if necessary. It makes good and cheerful draw linings. My son-in-law still pulls my leg over this idiosyncratic habit of mine.

During the Christmas holidays everyone at Littlefield went carol singing, including Toos and whoever else wished to join us. With the war still on and strict petrol rationing in force, we squeezed as many people as possible into each car to go round the farms singing carols. We took it very seriously with all the hymns and carols typed out for each person and glued onto cardboard so that it did not flap in the wind. We always decided beforehand which carol we would sing where. On one occasion we slipped up by singing 'God bless the master of this house, likewise the mistress too and all the little children that gather round the table' when two rather grumpy bachelors came to the door in their pyjamas. We never finished the verse because we all had a fit of giggles. One farmer came after us with a shotgun until he recognized a few faces and was then very embarrassed. A few ignored us, mainly Afrikaners who supported Germany (and there were a lot of them in South Africa), but most were delighted and came out and joined in the singing. Helen played the violin, another carried her music and stand, and a third held the hurricane lamp over the music. We were supposed to carry torches in case we forgot the words. If the petrol ran out or we were economizing for something else, we would inspan the four white mules and go by wagon — quite mad but great fun and it did create a Christmas spirit even if the temperature was in the seventies or eighties.

* * *

Although she was three years older than I was, Joan and I shared a birthday and we always celebrated the event together, either with a party at Littlefield or Greenhalgh, or by going on a picnic. For one birthday present Pa had assembled a large seesaw on the lawn at Greenhalgh. We all took turns on it and, probably because I was fooling around, I fell off and bit right through my tongue. Helen, the doctor, must have administered well to my needs because, apart from a swollen tongue, there were no ill effects, but the party did end ahead of schedule.

Another birthday treat consisted of a picnic miles away on the mountainside near Trelawny Farm on the way to Gannahook. Most of us rode there but Ma and a few others went by wagon with the food. The Africans could never understand the point of picnics. With a perfectly good house, kitchen, stove and dining room why should we choose to travel miles to collect firewood to build a fire between two large stones to cook sausages, bacon and eggs in the smoke and then wait ages for the kettle to boil for a cup of tea? Nevertheless, we all had a wonderful time, for eating out of doors is always pleasurable wherever you are in the world. Having eaten our fill and dampened down the fire to ensure it was properly out, we saddled up and rode home.

One day we were taken to see Bushmen paintings in some caves on the bank of the Great Fish River, which Joan's father, who had been brought up in the area, knew about. It was a long walk from the road, but exciting to find the paintings and to examine each drawing. The animals were all recognizable — kudu, springbok, elephant, jackal, hyena, zebra, lion and other cat-like creatures, along with a few hunters with spears. These Bushmen must have lived in the Mortimer Valley thousands of years earlier, for there is absolutely no wild life there now other than baboons, guinea fowl, jackals, hares and springbok. There were supposed to be some zebras in the mountains near Quagga Hook (*quagga* means zebra), but we never saw any. The mountain farmers did all they could to encourage springbok and if you were lucky you might be given a haunch of venison after a cull; if you were in contact with the right people you might even be asked to join a shoot for a day and bring home a whole springbok. Its meat is wonderful and its biltong, South Africa's famous dried meat, quite delicious. I wonder if anyone living in the Mortimer valley now knows of these Bushmen caves and paintings?

✳ ✳ ✳

No week ever went by without a few family rounds of our quiz game, which we called 'the general knowledge game'. Throughout my life I have had a good geographical knowledge and a fairly sound general knowledge, which I know I acquired from playing this game. For a quick version, ten subjects are selected (for example country, flower, mountain, river, capital city, sea, lake, make of car, colour and fabric) and then some random method is adopted to choose a letter in the alphabet. We had five minutes to think of an answer to each of the selected subjects beginning with the chosen letter. The scoring was simple. If you had an answer no one else had you scored ten, if this was shared you scored five. If you decided to make a longer game you chose 20 subjects and took ten minutes to find the answers. Pa always did the timing. It was good fun and if we had visitors staying with us, which we usually did, they joined in too. Later when I was married I spent many an evening playing this game with my own children.

Saturday night was Ma and Pa's bridge night. Old Shoe always played, along with anyone else who was available to make up the four. Ma and Pa were good players; Pa had a special penchant for cards and several excruciating card tricks, which he taught me about a week before he died aged 87. He played bridge right up to his death — with the old boys in the afternoons (as he said they could not keep awake in the evenings) and with the younger ones in the evenings.

Helen's grandfather was a brilliant bridge player — he used to set the bridge column in *The Times* — so Ma thought that she would be the best person to teach Dick and me bridge. At 15, I was not very interested, but in those days one had to obey one's parents, so we had to learn it. Helen had a very clear brain and I have never forgotten how well she explained the intricacies of bridge and the fundamentals, procedure and special bridge protocol. I only 'took up' bridge when I was 36 and went to evening classes to relearn the Acol system, after which I joined a bridge group and played regularly. On beginning again after another 20-year gap, I was amazed by how quickly it all came back. I had retained the feel of the game and the interest, but perhaps not the execution. It is a bit like riding a bicycle; if you are properly taught you do not forget the fundamentals.

Occasionally, there would be a dance in the Mortimer village hall. There would be no band, just someone on the piano, possibly accompanied by Johnnie Cawood on his accordion. They were painful evenings looking back, but exciting if a chap invited you to his car for a drink with him and his friends. There was no bar at the hall but all the young swains brought Castle beer or Lion lager, sometimes even brandy and orange juice. I do not remember anyone getting drunk except one young Afrikaner farmer who was never sober anyway, whatever the time of day or night.

The parents would sit round the sides of the room chatting while we got on with the dancing. Pa refused to come so Ma had to be the chaperone. Later, when I was old enough, a young man who had to return me by a stated hour and with no nonsense would collect me.

The imaginative games we played as children seemed so real to us. At Littlefield Arthur had an enormous old-fashioned steam-driven tractor, the sort you could steam up and attach to a plough; the tractor would remain stationary and the plough would go up and down the field on a pulley. I never understood how it worked, but once its working days were over we used to climb all over and under it. Having read Arthur Ransome's *Swallows and Amazons*, the old steam engine became our ship and we had a wonderful time sailing the oceans. Sometimes there would be six of us clambering all over for hours on end. The back wheels, the crow's-nest, were at least six feet high, but I never remember any of us coming to any harm or falling off.

✳ ✳ ✳

Among its personalities, the Mortimer district can lay claim to the author Olive Schreiner, who made her name with *The Story of an African Farm* and who had been the Cawood children's governess. She lived on the other side of the mountain from the Cawood family, who ran a large sheep and angora goat farm at Gannahook. Olive married Samuel Cronwright, an advocate and one of Cecil Rhodes's right-hand men, and they retired to Mortimer after the Boer War. Olive's brother W. P. Schreiner was prime minister of the Cape in 1908. Pa used to say that Olive, who had a reputation for being ahead of her time, followed Cecil Rhodes round South Africa in a Cape cart when he was prime minister of the Cape. The point of saying this is that she was entombed at her request on the top of the mountain on their farm, Buffels Kop, and her dog and canary are buried with her.

In her zeal for organizing entertainment, Ma once arranged a climb and picnic beside Olive Schreiner's tomb to celebrate Pa's birthday. About 12 panting climbers reached the top. For some reason, I did not join them that day, but they signalled us with mirrors when they got to the top.

On 1 October 1940 Cradock became the centre of civilization when the world and its wife came to see the total eclipse of the sun. Cradock was slap bang in the middle of its densest part. There was tremendous excitement as Prime Minister Jan Smuts flew in, along with the Astronomer Royal and other top-ranking astronomers, including South Africa's leading astronomer who soon afterwards came to Mortimer to retire. With government warnings that people could go blind unless they looked at the eclipse through smoked glass, Pa and the other farmers made sure that the farm hands and their families were well equipped. African women rounded up their children and locked them in darkened houses for fear of them going blind. At the appointed hour, which was in the afternoon at about 2.30 p.m., we saw the moon begin to cover the sun. We all went up to the koppie behind the house with our smoked glass, Pa with his camera and a large white sheet. This was to make it easier to see the earth's shadow racing across the country. It was very exciting and the birds began to make such a noise. We had a large heronry near the house in a row of eucalyptus trees and the birds were all scolding each other for being caught out. The ducks, geese, turkeys, chickens and guinea fowl together created a terrific din. Then came total darkness. It was eerie to watch this great ball of sunlight being extinguished; the aura was bewitching. The birds had hardly had time to settle down and be quiet when it began to get light again, with more squawking, trilling and gobbling. We saw the shadow racing across the earth and then it was all over and we went back to the house for a cup of tea. Pa took a lot of photos and there was a competition in the local newspaper, the *Midland News*, popularly

known as the Muddling News. He entered, but with hundreds of entries all equally as good as each other, he did not win, though someone must have. We were lucky to be in the middle of the belt; it was thrilling and a sight I shall never forget; it is unlikely to happen again in my lifetime and, having witnessed the total eclipse in the UK on 11 August 1999, I am even more glad that I saw a perfect total eclipse in 1940.

H. E. Wood, the astronomer who came to live in the house where the colonel had had all the fruit trees put into straight lines, and his wife Woodie did not farm the land though they kept a little piece round the house, were great craftspeople. A sheep's fleece would be brought in one door and a jumper would walk out another. They washed, spun, weaved, dyed and knitted. It was fun to watch them and we were sometimes allowed to help. Woodie was a fairly accomplished artist and her watercolours of local scenes were popular. She also worked in copper and brass. I have a copper platter of hers on my hall table, which is where we kept the car keys throughout our marriage, and a brass tray with an 'S' beaten out in the middle on my dressing table for holding hairclips and slides. They kept bees and we used to buy our honey from them by the gallon. Pa adored honey and ended every supper of his life with a slice of wholemeal bread, butter and honey, eaten with a knife and fork so that he did not get his fingers sticky. He said that eating honey was why he never had a twinge of rheumatism. He also ate a raw onion at lunchtime every day, a habit he formed many years before (pre-1914) in the jungles of Burma to keep him free of malaria. Ma said it did not only keep mosquitoes away. In any case, being 3000 feet above sea level, we did not have a malaria problem in Mortimer.

* * *

There was no nearby cinema, or bioscope as we called it, or for that matter any other form of entertainment; what there was, was homespun and Ma excelled at it. She would invite several children for the day and by the late afternoon we would be producing a play. On one such occasion Joan, Helen, their cousins John and Barbara Foster who were visiting from Johannesburg, and some others came for the day and Ma had us all learning and rehearsing

A. A. Milne's 'The King would like a little bit of butter with his bread' with John playing the king. I don't remember who played the queen, the dairymaid or the cow, but when the grown ups came to collect their children that evening we performed the play for them and it was a great success. Ma was involved in the Women's Agricultural Society (WAS), which met monthly in the Mortimer village hall, and there too she soon had people who had never acted before performing on stage in a full-blown play for the good people of the valley. Dick and I were usually roped in in some small way. She wrote and produced one nativity play that started with Dick and me on a table in front of the curtain arranging presents for Christmas Day the following morning; we grew tired and eventually went to sleep and our dream was the story of the nativity acted by Ma's cast.

She based another play on an A. A. Milne story of Christopher Robin losing his mouse. Helen played the aunt and Dick Christopher Robin: 'I opened his box for half a minute and he jumped outside. I tried to catch him; I tried. Has anyone seen my mouse?' Another was about Christopher Robin and his beetle named Alexander. Helen and I recited alternate verses of the whole of John Gilpin, most of which I still remember, and on another occasion we recited the 'Walrus and the Carpenter' by Lewis Carroll.

On one epic evening, 20 June 1942, we had a party at Greenhalgh, mostly for mothers and children for the young men had joined up and were in the desert in North Africa. We kept a huge map on the stoep wall on which each day, after the news, Pa made us mark the positions of Rommel's army and our Eighth Army. Though busy playing charades and guessing games, as one did at parties in those days, *everything* stopped for the BBC World Service news from London at 9.00 p.m. We filed into the sitting room, mostly to sit on the floor, in utter silence. In a sombre voice the newscaster announced that Tobruk had fallen and that most of the South African troops had been taken prisoner. Pandemonium and despair broke out, for there was not one person in the room without a brother, father, cousin, uncle or son who had been taken prisoner that day. Our local Cape Midlands Regiment (CMR) was included in the list of units taken prisoner. The party broke up in disarray and sadness; I shall never forget it.

Another memorable moment in the war was the announcement

of the fall of France. It was my day for Afrikaans and I was having lunch at Littlefield when I heard the news. I remember the meal very clearly because I was on my second helping of rice with a lovely thick gravy — at home we only had rice with curry or as a pudding, never as a vegetable. Whenever I have rice with gravy now I always think of that day.

The war was not going well for Britain and soon the Empire Training Scheme was launched and 42 Squadron RAF came to Port Elizabeth to train pilots and aircrew. These air training schools were all over South Africa, Canada and New Zealand.

Though Pa was too old for war service, he had served with distinction in the Boer War and the First World War, he and Ma still contributed to the war effort. The young, fit and able farmers joined up, returned to their units if they were on the reserve, or joined the local regiment or SAAF. Many families were split. I remember Michael Geldenhuis, with piercing blue eyes, joining the SAAF as a pilot and his father, who was on the other side, almost disowning him but his mother, who was English, being proud of him. Farms left without a boss managed marvellously, with wives becoming experts in Jersey cattle, angora goats or whatever; some farms were left to an African headman to run. When the Mortimer Vigilante was formed, Ma, Helen, Pa and two other men went round these farms to give advice, often pay the workers and help sort out problems to ensure that everything ran as normally as possible. If they did not know something they would find someone who did. Consequently, when the men came back from the war they found their farms intact and running reasonably well.

My parents and their friends also put up RAF and RN men on vacation or sick leave. They came by train from Port Elizabeth and the stationmaster sometimes rang to say 'Please come and collect two RAF men.' Most visits were prearranged and well organized, but those who had enjoyed previous stays sometimes jumped on a train to spend a couple of days or a weekend with us. Officially, they came for at least a week, usually two.

Those who came on sick leave were not always war casualties or postoperative cases. Sadly, they were often lads the Ossewa Brandwag had beaten up; it was not unusual for ten large Afrikaners to round on two to three RAF or RN men, for these thugs who supported Germany indulged in bullying tactics. One chap, Neil, who was in the navy and from Cambell town in Scotland, never saw the war at all. Thugs had deliberately driven a car into him during a blackout, which had broken both his legs. One leg was a simple fracture and healed quite quickly, but the other needed several operations and took months to heal, by which time the war was over. Joe, another frequent visitor, was determined to learn to ride and Kroon gave him the confidence he needed to learn. Ted Heath (the bandleader, not the MP) often visited Greenhalgh and would spend all day on the piano. There were never fewer than two young men staying at any one time and when Dick and I were at boarding school there would be even more. Ma wrote to the mother or wife of each one who stayed with us to give them a first-hand report on their health and well-being. Many friendships and much correspondence emanated from this period and some continued for many years after the war.

We kept an old 1926 Buick on the farm so that we could claim petrol coupons for two cars; the other car was a 1936 Ford V8. Joe and his pals decided to transform this old car, which had a wooden steering wheel and wooden spokes in the wheels, into something better. Dick and I learnt to drive in it and we reckoned that if you could drive it you could drive anything. In any case, Joe and his pals cut off the hood, wired the four doors shut (trying to keep them shut was a dodgy business anyway), smuggled some paint from the RAF camp and daubed the old car in camouflage colours with RAF roundels on the front doors. We had such fun with that old banger. It was not fully licensed, so was not supposed to go off the farm, but it was often at Mortimer village to collect the post or undertake some other farm errand. In 1951, Helen junior's husband Keith Collett adapted its engine to pump water.

In January 1943 I was sent to boarding school at DSG in Grahamstown. It had three terms a year, whereas the state schools and a few of the independent ones had four terms a year. Woodridge, the prep school selected for Dick, had four terms. One reached Woodridge, which is beyond Port Elizabeth, by mainline train to PE and then a miniature-gauge train to the actual school. With me having three terms and Dick four, Christmas was the only holiday that coincided and Ma thought we were in danger of losing touch. I do not know why she thought this, for I was three years older than he was and we were never close at that stage.

However, during one of my Easter holidays Ma took me with her to visit Dick at Woodridge on the famous train. Dick had always been prone to asthma. On countless occasions I remember seeing him as a little boy sitting up in bed fighting for breath under a tent of pinned-together sheets suspended from the ceiling with a kettle on a primus stove belching out fumes of Friars Balsam. Doctors advised Ma that a school near the coast would suit Dick better because Greenhalgh was over 3000 feet above sea level and the air was too dry. At the time of our visit Dick had spent the whole term in the sickbay suffering from asthma. Ma was naturally concerned and I remember 'A GOOD PATIENT' being written right across the page of his school report for that term. As Dick grew physically, he became stronger and eventually stayed the course at Woodridge before going on to St Andrew's in Grahamstown. Dick now says that he was only cured of his asthma when he began to smoke at the age of 17.

The year before we were sent to boarding school it was considered a good idea to spend the month of February, the hottest month of the year, at the seaside. So, both families from Littlefield and Greenhalgh, complete with Wy, schoolbooks and dogs, moved to the Bonza Bay Hotel outside East London. We were no strangers to Bonza Bay as we had been there for short holidays most years. It was a well-known medical fact that people who lived at high altitudes needed to go to the coast every now and then to keep their blood pressure down. (It has always been said that if Johannesburg had not been 6000 feet above sea level there would have been no Jameson Raid and no Boer War.) School lessons were held each morning and taken very seriously at first. We were let off our homework and it gradually became more and more difficult to concentrate during the morning. After about two weeks the lessons were abandoned and we spent the whole glorious day on the beach. There is a blind river, which is wonderfully safe for swimming, and a huge beach that went on for miles, with rock pools and sand dunes. We just loved it.

We had tried other places but always came back to Bonza Bay. We had been to Bushman's River and stayed in a primitive hotel where our host had served at meals in bare feet; this was more than Ma could take.

One year the two families went to Port Alfred and were having a lovely holiday — I was well on the way to winning a competition Helen organized over who could produce the best collection of shells — when, about a week before Christmas, I went down with measles. The hotel told us to leave and, since I was really quite ill, Helen, who was after all a doctor, said that I should not travel. Eventually, a good Christian family heard of our predicament through the church and offered their home to Ma and me until I was well enough to travel again. I spent Christmas in a darkened room with these kind people, who could not do enough for us, looking after us extremely well.

Most civilians who lived during the war will recall the minute silence each day at noon. We did not keep to it on the farm, but when the clock struck 12 in big cities like East London everything stopped — traffic, shop assistants in the middle of transactions, or waitresses pouring coffee. The total stillness of that minute was impressive.

Ma and Pa were good Christians and all our meals were preceded by grace, which I regret not having continued with my own children. There were no churches in Mortimer — the nearest was Cradock where I was baptized as an infant — so the rector used to come once a month to Mortimer village hall and we would have matins followed by Holy Communion. Ma usually played the piano for the hymns and psalms. Molly Cawood also sometimes played, but Pa disliked Molly's playing because she thumped too much. Ma kept the suitcase containing the altar cloth, the two wooden candlesticks, cross, collection plate and hymn books. Pa usually took the collection plate round, though he preferred someone else to do it as he enjoyed singing hymns. He had been in the choir at Berkhamsted School and had a good bass voice. Dick and I were usually the only children attending this service and until our confirmations we were allowed outside after matins and before the sermon to wander round Mortimer village or sit in the car until the adults came out. On the Sundays when there was no visiting priest (the priest alternated his services between Mortimer and Tarka), we held our own little service for the family or whoever else was staying. Ma chose the prayers and the reading, which Pa read and we knelt down as in a church; he also read from the Bible. We would then cluster around the piano and sing as many hymns as Ma wanted to play. It was not until I was about ten that

I discovered that not all families held a service at home on a Sunday; I was quite shocked.

* * *

Ma and Pa had an outstandingly good reputation for treating their farm labourers well. Though the system was a bit feudal, it worked admirably and their kindness was amply rewarded with loyalty. For a start, each family was given a properly built stone house, similar to a crofter cottage in Scotland. Several quarries on the koppie provided the stone with which Bartman, our stonemason, built the workers' houses, as well as all the stables, barn and wagon shed.

With Xhosa (Bantu) and coloured (mixed-race) people working on the farm and with relations between the two groups invariably strained, they preferred to live separately. There was a bit of land round each croft on which the family grew vegetables, mostly maize. They gathered their firewood from the indigenous trees on scrubland down by the river. Many farmers paid their workers lousy wages, which they compensated with food rations. Pa preferred to give them good wages and let them buy their own food, though they all got free milk. On the farm he kept stocks of sugar, flour, matches, tea, tobacco (they loved to chew tobacco) and mealie meal. He kept account of their purchases and deducted the cost from their wages, and they seemed happy with the arrangement. Some kept chickens for meat and eggs. Working clothes were supplied, but those who lived on the farm but only did casual work did not get their clothes issued. I have particularly fond memories of Alfred, with the crooked toes, and Ida and their swarm of children, as well as of Jimmy and Elsie. When Alfred was pensioned off Jimmy took over the cows and the vegetable garden and mowed the lawn. Kate worked in the house with Elsie, and Harry looked after the horses. Fred was very dopey and frequently got sacked for smoking dagga (marijuana) and being useless with horses when high. He was always repentant and said he would never do it again. His father was Bartman the stonemason who was indispensable and called me Little Princess. Poor Bartman eventually went blind and senile and had to be placed in an institution. Aaron was a hard worker but was eventually sacked for absenteeism and too much womanizing. He then got a job as a ganger on the railways and we used to see him travelling along the railway lines on those strange trolleys that are conveyed by pumping a handle up and down. Those were the mainstays, but casual labour was called in at harvest and other crisis times.

Harvesting was done in the old-fashioned way. A mule-drawn reaper cut the corn, mostly oats and some wheat, while a binder gathered it into bundles, which were stood up in stooks and left to dry thoroughly. Then all were collected by wagon and a stack was built in the threshing yard. Later in the year Mr Meyer would arrive with his thrashing machine and an old tractor with huge leather belts going this way and that with no protection for anyone. All hands and the cook were involved on thrashing days and endless cups of tea and other drinks were brought down from the kitchen. It was hot and dusty work. I was allowed to place the sacks on the hooks. The sacks were filled with grain and to direct the grain into another sack one shut off the fall of oats or wheat by pulling a lever. Though I could not lift the full sacks, I was a dab hand at fixing empty sacks onto the hooks to be fed. The oat sacks were loosely tied, heaved onto a wagon, taken to the stables and poured into silos for horse feed for the year. The little wheat we grew was taken to the appropriate mill after being thrashed, bagged and sewn up. The ground wheat was then used on the farm for cooking, particularly for making our own bread.

* * *

As children we spent a lot of time at Littlefield both socially and at school. Joan and Helen's grandparents lived across the Fish River from them on the other side of a terrifying suspension bridge. The bridge consisted of a cradle of wire netting suspended by strong wires attached to poles anchored on each bank. Planks about six inches wide and laid together in three or four parallel rows provided a surface on which to walk at the base of the wire cradle. There was a wire to run your hands along for support, provided one could reach it, and there were gaps in the planks here and there. When the wind blew it swayed and there was a drop of at least 40 feet to the water below. Joan and Helen used to run across it to have tea with their grandmother without batting an eyelid, but to me it was sheer hell. I did it, though, as children do; I never let on how frightened I really was and had nightmares about this bridge well into my adult life.

I had another, but different, terrifying bridge experience, this time during torrential rains when all the rivers were in full flood and the drifts were totally impassable by car. A river drift on the outskirts of Mortimer village, the Gannahook River, which flowed into the Fish River but was dry for 11 months of the year, was in spate on this day and Pa had to go to the village on business (telephones were down when the weather was this bad). Pa decided to walk across the railway bridge and I followed. The bridge consisted of a viaduct with solid stone pillars with a steel girder either side on which railway sleepers were positioned at regular intervals, and the railway line lay on the sleepers. Pa set off and easily strode the distance between each sleeper, but my legs were too short and for some reason I did not tell him of my difficulty. Anyway, I got across very slowly, jumping from one sleeper to the next, but was terrified that I might slip and fall into the raging torrent below. Having made the crossing I wondered how on earth I was going to get back, but on the return journey Pa must have seen how frightened I was and he carried me back. I had nightmares about this crossing well into my adult life.

I had another frightening experience while helping to rake lucerne. The rake was a fairly large implement pulled by two mules, on this occasion Ringhals and Bosbok. I asked Pa to let me have a go. I was always out on the farm unless I was actually riding or doing something with the horses. I must have been 10 or 11 and my reach was limited, for the rakes were built for men. One had to push down on a pedal and lift a hand lever in the same movement to raise and lower the rake teeth. The lucerne or hay was then collected into neat 'sausages' ready to be picked up and baled. I went up and down quite successfully for a few rows and then, turning at the headland, one rein broke. I felt mild panic, but the mules knew they had to turn and they did. The next row down was towards the gate, which thankfully was shut. I could not guide the mules into a straight line and when we got to the bottom near the gate they stopped and I got down as quickly as I could. I had contemplated jumping off if the mules had not stopped, but that was a risk I mercifully did not have to take. Fortunately, some farm labourers appeared and I departed hastily, never again wanting to help with the raking.

* * *

Cradock, where I was born, was a fairly large strategically well-placed town on the Great Fish River with an important railway station that fed a vast agricultural area. The smaller towns within a radius of 100 to 150 miles were not on the railway and between 1910 and the 1950s everything was transported by rail. There was great excitement one year when General Smuts was invited to open Cradock's annual agricultural show. By then the streets were mostly paved and Cradock had grown beyond the frontier town stage. It supported a beautiful Dutch Reform church that had been built to resemble St Martin-in-the-Fields in Trafalgar Square, as well as a town square, well-kept municipal gardens, a town hall, library and three hotels — the Victoria in the main square, commonly known as the 'Vic' and thought to be the best in town, the Grand, which we were never allowed near because it was considered third rate and full of undesirables, and the Masonic. There were also two banks, the Standard and the National (formerly Barclays). Ma banked at the Standard. In those days a bank manager would remain at his post for many years, getting to know his clients and becoming their friend and adviser. Ours used to come to the farm from time to time and bring his family.

I recall three admissions to the local hospital other than having my leg stitched up. The first was when Dick and I had our tonsils and adenoids removed. For this Ma booked a private ward and engaged a friend, who was a trained sister but did not work at the hospital, to look after us. On waking up after the operation our little ward was packed with nurses trying to subdue Dick who was screaming blue murder. It was not doing his throat any good and there was an atmosphere of unease. I went back to sleep and the next time I woke up all was quiet. We were there for a few days before Ma and Pa came to collect us and take us home; on that day we were allowed to get dressed and play outside until they arrived. Dr Scholtz, the surgeon, was there to hand us over to Ma, Pa and Sister Hockley, who came back to the farm with us for a few days.

The second occasion was when Ma was admitted with excruciatingly painful eyes caused by ulcers on her pupils; we were sent off to our other 'mummy' Margaret Gadd so she could keep absolutely still and quiet. No doctor could throw any light on the cause and they tried all sorts of things. Dr Scholtz then suggested she have her tonsils removed and, once this was done, she never had any more trouble with her eyes.

Then, several years later, she was admitted to a private ward for a hysterectomy, which in the 1940s was less routinely performed than it is today. However, with careful convalescing she made a good recovery and was all the better for the operation.

Cradock really was a bustling market town and supported its own weekly newspaper, the *Midlands News*, which an English couple ran; their son Guy Butler, who achieved literary fame with *Karoo Morning: 1918–1935*, *Bursting World*, and *A Local Habitation*, has recently retired from Rhodes University where he was professor of English.

When our gentle English dentist who was very patient with children retired, a large and quite different Afrikaner, whom we called the 'Beard', replaced him. When I was about 17, I developed abscesses and, to my mother's horror, this dentist removed two of my front teeth and later fitted me with a plate. He did his own mechanical work and one Saturday afternoon he embarrassed me by turning up at the tennis club, where I happened to be playing, with a colour chart because he had forgotten to match the colour of my teeth. He was a flamboyant man and when he decided to acquire a white bull terrier, instead of getting a puppy and training it, at great expense he bought the reigning bull terrier champion of South Africa. The Beard had no experience of handling such a dog, which was not a family pet, and could not cope. He had small children and, with his wife frightened of the dog, he asked Pa to take him over and train him. Pa explained the problems of trying to train an eight-year-old dog that had spent its entire life at shows and at stud, but agreed to take the dog and see what he could do. He was a magnificent specimen, but could not be trusted, did not get along with other dogs and had never been let off the lead. Pa did his best and there was some improvement, but when he attacked and nearly killed my dog, a spaniel that was not a stranger, with the Beard's consent, the dog was put down.

The main street in Cradock housed the usual range of shops, including outfitters, newsagents — Mr Boughton of White & Boughton (the bookshop stationer) was a particular friend of Pa's — and, most important, the Maatskappy Algemene Handelaar (general dealer), which sold all and any farming equipment, tool or machine. In the 1930s a number of Estonian and Lithuanian Jews came to Cradock; they were all hard working and eventually became successful businessmen. Mr and Mrs Bergavitch ran a very good clothes shop for men and women from which I often bought garments and from which Pa got all his clothes. Besides Badgers, which Garlicks later bought out, there were Mr Hyam's furniture store (I still have a five-drawer chest made of imbuna wood Ma bought from him), a Greek café, a jeweller and a fish shop. After a visit to Cradock we always had cooked fresh fish for supper.

On reaching the age to take my driving test, Pa, Dick and I merely turned up at the town clerk's office in the town hall to ask to take a test. The examiner came out and we all got into our Ford V8, Pa and Dick giggling in the back and Mr Vester in the passenger seat. I remember him saying something like, 'we know you can drive and have been driving round the farm for ages, so this is just a formality. Drive round the block.' This I did, but it was the first time I had driven in town. Having completed the block, we returned to his office and he gave me my driving licence. It was all quite painless, except for Dick's giggling in the back.

Around this time about ten miles of the main road north of Cradock had been tarmacked, which was a great improvement. Along with some of his friends, the son of Mr Moy, who ran the garage and serviced our car, decided to test the newly laid tarmac. They drove so fast that when they ran out of tar and hit the rough corrugations, the car turned over and the son was killed. This was the first road death I recall in the valley and it certainly sobered up the driving community. Because the roads were so bad most of us could not travel fast. Dust was a hazard. When one passed a car the cloud of dust often left you driving blind for some yards and, since anything could be in the road, one drove slowly.

A natural spring on the north side of Cradock discharged warm sulphur water in which it was a pleasant and therapeutic treat to bathe, with a smell quite different from that of the pool on the Tarka training farm. The hotel attached to the waters has now been developed into a tourist complex with chalets, caravans, and camping sites with picnic facilities, children's playground and good fishing in the Great Fish River. We did not go very often because the farm was about 25 miles away from Cradock and our average monthly trip there tended to be taken up with shopping, the dentist and the bank.

Visits to Cradock were generally all-day affairs and it was a great thrill to have a picnic lunch at the zoo, which was well run with lovely gardens and trees. We would have our picnic on a bench near the monkeys, for we found them amusing. Once while I was handing a banana to a baby monkey through the wire netting, the mother monkey grabbed my hat. Pa and the monkey then proceeded to have a tug-of-war with my hat through the wire netting, which ended with Pa holding the crown and the monkey the brim, which she promptly put over her head to give herself a straw necklace. Ma was furious, for this was my best hat; we always wore hats in that climate.

I remember great excitement over a powerboat regatta on Lake Arthur. Aunty Glad was staying with us at the time and we all set off to watch the regatta in our Studebaker. The windows of this car consisted of flexible see-through sheets of Bakelite, which one buttoned on. This was fine in hot weather, for at 30 to 40 miles an hour one got a nice breeze to keep one cool, not to mention covered in dust. Many adults wore dustcoats to protect their clothes when driving, which they removed on arriving at their destination. In winter we had to wear lots of warm clothing and if caught in the rain without the windows, we would be soaking wet by the time we had stopped to button them on. Anyway, we arrived at the regatta and everyone had a great day until it was time to return home, for not long after setting off the car came to a grinding halt. Pa knew nothing about engines, but fortunately spotted a friend who did. He came over, looked under the car and saw that the flange on the rear axle had gone, which was a disaster, for a qualified mechanic was needed to fix it. Pa's friend said that he was going into Cradock anyway, so would get the mechanic to come and fix us up. Eventually the mechanic arrived, the repair was made and we were able to drive home at a snail's pace. With the bad state of the roads, potholes, poor headlights, dust and being cold, we were glad to get home. Breakdowns were frequent in the 1930s and all cars carried a full set of tools, which was never much good to Pa because he could never diagnose the problem in the first place.

It used to be considered important to have one's photographs taken by a professional and I recall several visits to Mr Leadbetter, the local photographer in Cradock. He seemed very old to us then — keeping us for hours, making us turn this way and that, look here and there, and always telling us to *keep still*. On one occasion, when I was about seven, Ma produced a new dress for me to change into at Mr Leadbetters, for these were to be special photographs. I can still feel that green lawn dress with a starched muslin collar that scratched my neck and finding it almost impossible to sit still long enough for Mr Leadbetter to disappear under his black blanket to make the necessary adjustments to his camera while Ma kept dashing out to comb my hair a certain way.

When we were very small, Elsie would come with us on these monthly shopping expeditions to Cradock and we would be left at the rectory. The Canon and Mrs Gould were kind enough to allow Ma to leave us in their garden to play while she did her shopping and other business in peace. Phyllis and Ashly Gould were already away at school then, but I met up with Phyllis later and we became good friends; we still correspond and occasionally I stay with her.

Cradock had two good secondary schools — Rocklands for girls (which was independent) and Cradock Boys' High (state). The boys used to wear very brief shorts, and the more senior they became the briefer the shorts. These schools took boarders to cater for the widely dispersed farming communities.

Cradock had two cinemas and a change of programme about once a week. Living out of town made going to the cinema a major expedition. When we did go, it was always to the matinée because of the hazards of driving at night. Ma and Pa very seldom went; in fact Pa never went. Ma thought the acting in films was third rate and preferred the live theatre, which was not on offer. When I was old enough to join other teenagers (we were not called teenagers then) we would persuade a reluctant parent to drive us to the cinema. Ma never approved of this and still less did she approve of me going to the cinema at 16 or 17 with only one escort. This was not the thing to do, but she said she trusted me.

Two nights were set aside for dancing during the Cradock Show.

The first was a ball, a very grand affair with black tie but strangely no bar — only water and glasses were supplied. For the second night, which was an informal dance, there was still no bar but everyone brought their own drinks, which they kept in their cars. In between dances, everyone went back to their cars for a drink and, if lucky, a cuddle. When I was old enough Ma let me go to the ball provided she approved of my escort. I remember Ma being absolutely furious with me on one occasion because I had accepted an invitation to join another party for the dance. She thought the dance was only for the riff-raff. I eventually won and had great fun dancing the night away, but I was not forgiven for going against Ma's wishes.

✻ ✻ ✻

When I was sent to boarding school in Grahamstown in January 1943, DSG was considered to be the best school in the Eastern Cape. Girls from Northern Rhodesia (now Zambia), Southern Rhodesia (now Zimbabwe), the Copperbelt, Chingola and Ndola, spent about five days on the train getting to school. In fact girls came there from all over southern Africa.

If the two families between them had saved enough petrol coupons, we would be taken to Grahamstown by car — a three-hour journey on dusty corrugated roads — but we often went by train. This was great fun because the train would be full of boys from Rhodesia, Johannesburg and Bloemfontein, plus some girls from DSG. We caught the 10.20 a.m. at Mortimer and changed to the Grahamstown branch line at Alice, which for some reason occasioned a three-hour wait. There was absolutely nothing to do at Alice, which consisted of only a few houses built round a railway junction, so we naturally got up to a few pranks, though we were constrained by having to travel in school uniform and thus being at risk of letting down our school name. When we eventually got to Grahamstown, Mr Tooley would be waiting with a fleet of taxis to take us to our respective schools — DSG, St Andrew's or Kingswood College. There was also a Roman Catholic boys' school in Grahamstown, St Aiden's, but I do not remember any of its pupils ever being on the train. With Rhodes University, a teacher training college and various other excellent schools, including the state-run Graem for boys and Victoria Girls' High, Grahamstown was quite a seat of learning. St Andrew's College had its own feeder prep school, always referred to as 'Prep', with Grif Mullins as the head in my day. His family gave a lot to both DSG and St Andrew's.

I was put into the pink dormitory in Merriman House and was horrified at having to share a bedroom with 25 other girls. This huge dorm had a partition down the middle, but not up to the ceiling, and after lights out the more obstreperous girls would scramble up and along this narrow partition and then jump down on a bed. As our beds had traditional black iron frames with wire springs and very thin mattresses, one can imagine the noise of beds giving way and springs flying in all directions. The bathrooms were next to the dorm but the lavatories were far away at the other end of the corridor past the housemistress's bedroom door and the headmistress's flat. You were supposed to go to the 'fort', as the outside loos were called, before you went to bed. If you were taken short, there were potties but I never remember anyone ever using them. One could pull a curtain round one's bed, as in a hospital, but that was the only 'privacy' one had. I hated the dorm, but enjoyed school in the day. The next year I moved to the green dorm, which was half the size, but less cramped and nearer the 'forts'. At 15 we moved to the senior boarding house, Crewe. The junior boarding house was named after N. J. Merriman, the Archdeacon of Grahamstown in the mid-nineteenth century. Crewe was named after Lord Crewe, the Colonial Secretary at the time the London Parliament passed the South Africa Act, which brought the Union of South Africa into existence in 1910.

I had cubicles in various parts of Crewe House, but in my final year I had the best and most envied one of all. At each end of the long building, there was a wing at right angles to the corridor containing a set of five cubicles and mine was the middle one with a double window overlooking our brother college. Girls would queue up to look out of my window in the hope of catching a glimpse of their boyfriend; some of these waving sessions were prearranged and successful. If too many wanted to look I would charge them a penny each. We did not have much pocket money and were not supposed to keep any money on our person.

One night the girl in the end cubicle gave us a terrible fright. We had an ineffectual housemistress at the time and I had had a quarrel with this girl the previous evening, which ended up with me pouring cold water all over her. The following evening, I called to her over the cubicle wall and, on only hearing a muffled reply, went into her cubicle to find her clinging to the window ledge on the outside of her second-floor window with very white fingers. I called to one of the other girls and we managed to get her back in safely before she let go and fell. We calmed her down and put her to bed. This girl was different from the rest of us; she was more scholarly and did not have any friends. I decided not to report the incident to either our housemistress or the prefects, but instead went to the headmistress, Miss Miller. I was not punished, for which I was grateful, but a close watch was kept on the girl. From then on, the headmistress frequently 'popped in' to our end of the house at bedtime.

Crewe House, which was said to be fireproof, was a three-storeyed building overlooking St Andrew's playing field on one side and two boarding houses on the other. Though very cold with concrete stairs, long draughty corridors, cubicles divided with partitions and with curtains rather than doors, I remember it as a happier place than Merriman. All Saint Chapel was at the heart of the school. School began there three mornings a week and the boarders attended every evening, with a Communion service on Sundays. As seniors we went to evensong at the cathedral, which was exciting because the St Andrew's boys also attended, but it was difficult to catch more than a glimpse of them because they sat in a gallery overhanging the seats on which we sat. It is unusual to have gallery seating in a cathedral. This one had been installed during the Boer War to shelter the women and children, but when I visited again in 1997, the gallery had been removed.

The SABC regularly used to broadcast a service from the cathedral and sometimes the DSG choir was invited to augment the cathedral choir. I was lucky to be in the school choir and found this a great thrill. The organist, Professor Ronald Kirby, was also our school choirmaster and we had choir practice every Friday morning between breakfast and chapel.

I remember All Saint Chapel with great affection, for I was lucky enough to be a sacristan in my final year. There were three of us and we were responsible for quite a lot really. We had to change the alter hangings to match the religious periods (Lent was mauve, Trinity green and Easter white), put out the robe and vestments for the priest in the right order, choose the hymns, ring the chapel bell, take collection to the headmistress and generally see that everything was in order and tidy, make sure there was enough wine and wafers, and perform our duty at the altar during communion as a server.

On a recent visit I was delighted to find that the chapel is still at the heart of the school, though enlarged since our day to cope with the growing number of pupils. I was impressed and felt privileged to take part in what was for me a very emotional service of Holy Communion with the present school. I had so much to be thankful for in the 50 years since leaving school. DSG had given us all something very special with which to cope with life and all its vicissitudes. For that I shall always be grateful.

In November 1997, All Saints Day, the matric class of 1947 was invited back to DSG and 11 of our class of 20 turned up for the reunion and what turned out to be a wonderful weekend. Jenny Hirst and I came from England and as we both had relatives in South Africa we decided to make a long holiday of it. Jenny had spent most of her working life in England and was now retired and my husband and I had retired to England. Our classmates, who came from Cape Town, Johannesburg, Bulawayo and Port Elizabeth, were all surprised by the progress and development of the school. There was little time or funds for expansion during our school days because of the war. We had no school tours, but now the girls were travelling all over southern Africa for various matches, projects and visits. The school motto is 'Forward', and they had certainly lived up to it over the past 50 years. It was always a live and pulsating school, now it is in overdrive and positively exhilarating. I was thrilled to be able to go back.

One incident I was reminded of at our fiftieth reunion was when we were responsible for putting on a concert in the Lower VI. In addition to the various songs, piano recitals, duets and so forth, a group of us decided to perform a cancan. We had practised hard, got our kicks quite high and were feeling very pleased with ourselves when we were suddenly summoned to the headmistress's study and given an almighty dressing down. We were threatened with expulsion if we presented this low, disgraceful, distasteful, rowdy and common act. Did we realize that cancan girls were prostitutes? What were we thinking of? We would bring the school into disrepute. We left her study very subdued, for Miss Miller meant what she said. Our problem was what to perform instead in such a short time. We must have chosen something pretty tame, for I have no recollection of what it was.

We had some memorable teachers. Miss Tilley came out of retirement to be headmistress during the war when there was a shortage of teachers and, though I was there for two years under her headship, I had little to do with her. Miss Miller, who took over from her, was quite different and a very good classroom teacher. Some years after I left she started to behave strangely and had to be asked to resign. Among the more notable staff were Miss Charlton for English who dressed very well and Miss White for history who dressed appallingly badly. Mrs Jennet, the maths teacher, frightened the life out of me but I have never forgotten the mental arithmetic she taught us. Miss Frost was the gym mistress; this subject was very low key by today's standards. Miss Miller taught geography and maths and was excellent. Our Afrikaans teacher was hopeless, in fact so useless that we had to borrow the Afrikaans teacher from St Andrew's to ensure that we knew enough to sit our matric exam. Scripture was taught by a succession of well-meaning ineffectual women of dubious ability. Subjects like biology, physiology and anatomy were taught well enough to pass, but I do not recall very good or very bad teachers. The outstanding staff member was Miss Gwenllian Mullins. The entire Mullins family was involved in education in Grahamstown and was well respected. Miss Mullins taught art and coached hockey and tennis. I was useless at art, so was allowed to work with leather and pewter instead, which I thoroughly enjoyed. Miss Mullins was an excellent coach and I was overjoyed to be picked once or twice for the first hockey XI. We all loved her accessibility. She invited friendship and guidance without being patronizing or losing her authority. We all respected her and still do. She married Rex Woods, a master at St Andrew's and, with her brother the headmaster of St Andrew's Preparatory School, she had strong ties with all three schools. Before Jenny and I went to our fiftieth reunion, we went to Plymouth, Devon to see her as she and her husband had retired to England.

The Early Years

In my final year at school, Ma decided that we should have a memorable family holiday together before I left school and went to England. She bought a brand new Ford V8 saloon 1947 model and we went to the Victoria Falls. This was quite an adventure, involving a drive of more than 1000 miles. We went north up through the Cape Province and on through the Orange Free State. I remember stopping at Parys on the Vaal River and going on a powerboat at an alarming speed, sending up huge clouds of spray. Then, on the Great North Road, we drove through the Transvaal, circumnavigating Johannesburg's traffic, to the lovely Soutpansberg mountains in the northern Transvaal, where we stayed overnight at the Mountain Inn. It was a charming place with individual rondavels for each couple scattered round a lovely garden with magnificent views of the mountains. We then carried on to the customs post, over Beit Bridge and into Rhodesia — across what Kipling described as 'the dirty green greasy Limpopo' — and on to Bulawayo where our cousin Meredith Rice, his wife Ena and our three girl cousins lived. Meredith was chief engineer of Southern Rhodesia Railways and lived in a lovely big spreading bungalow with several smartly dressed African male servants. This was new to us as in South Africa we had female house servants. One, called Pacey, was Meredith's special valet and went everywhere with him. As chief engineer, Meredith had his own railway carriage, which he hooked onto whatever train he needed to do his work. The plan was for us to go by train from Bulawayo to Victoria Falls with Meredith and family in his special carriage. We were thrilled with this exclusive mode of travelling and revelled in it. We left Bulawayo in the evening and had a superb meal from hampers supplied by our host, slept well and woke up at the Victoria Falls Hotel where we detrained. The railways owned the hotel, which was possibly the best in Africa. We were then shown to our sumptuous accommodation.

A few weeks before King George VI, Queen Elizabeth and Princesses Elizabeth and Margaret had stayed in the same rooms. We touched everything with great reverence; it was so exciting. The hotel is crescent shape with all the front rooms having a view of the falls. Ma and Pa occupied the suite the Queen had used. The five children were given the rooms reserved for the ladies-in-waiting and equerries — it was luxury beyond our wildest dreams.

Meredith guided us down to see the falls and we stood in awe and wonder at the majesty of it all. It was high water season and this was surely one of the most magnificent natural sights in the world. We got soaked to the skin walking through the rainforest from the spray opposite the main falls. The actual falls are over a mile long and are gazed on by the stony statue of their discoverer, David Livingstone. In those days one viewed the falls in style on trolleys. These were like back-to-back garden benches on a flat base and with a canopy to keep off the sun that some smartly dressed Africans pushed along a railway line in superb colonial style — a splendid conveyance that alas no longer exists. After a wonderful few days we returned to Bulawayo by train and retraced our drive back to Greenhalgh. It was a memorable and happy family holiday and I shall always thank Ma for thinking of it and organizing it. It was our last holiday together as a family.

On leaving school I wanted to be a vet but Pa sensibly talked me out of it. He said that farmers were not ready for women vets and that I would be left with overfed dogs and cats I would not enjoy. I decided to go into nursing instead, which was a sort of compromise. I was all set to go to Groote Schuur Hospital in Cape Town when I was 18 in 1949.

To fill in the year Ma thought it would be a good idea for me to do a one-year domestic science diploma course at Cheltenham Ladies' College, so in April 1948 she and I set sail for England on the *Durban Castle*. Before the ship had even left Cape Town I noticed a striking young man with a huge handlebar moustache standing next to me on the rails watching Table Mountain disappear over the horizon. Indeed, he stayed there for the next two to three hours to watch Africa disappear from view. We were inseparable for the duration of the voyage; and, thanks to an understanding mother, I had a wonderful time. On arrival at Southampton, as we were both London bound we arranged to meet the next day. This meeting led to many more, to theatre visits, to Regents Park and much else besides.

Trevor was on leave from the British South Africa Police in Southern Rhodesia having just been released from the British military administration in Somaliland. He found he had about six months' leave due to him, of which he promptly took advantage.

Ma had arranged an itinerary for us between landing at Southampton and depositing me at Cheltenham, but this did not prevent Trevor and me keeping in close contact by telephone and numerous letters.

Ma and I travelled all over England seeing old friends and relations, including some cousins on Ma's side of the family in Worthing. To fill in my mornings I registered at a reputable riding school to be coached in jumping, which I knew to be my weak spot. I took the bus each morning to the village of Findon just north of Worthing. A strict coach frightened several in the class; I found him daunting, especially when he said, 'anyone can see you have been taught to ride by a cavalryman. That's no good for jumping. Before you leave here you will have adopted, under my instruction, "the forward seat".' And I did. I was keen to make the most of this opportunity and thoroughly enjoyed my short time there. I wished I had been able to spend longer at the riding school; it was hard work but well worth it.

During the latter part of the summer Ma booked us into a little guesthouse in Folkestone to be near some close friends of hers. Trevor asked if he could join us for that week, which turned out to be one of the happiest of my life. A friend knew of a reputable riding stable, so we went for lots of rides, froze on the pebbly beach and walked for miles. We took the bus to Canterbury and saw the beautiful cathedral at the centre of the Church of England. On a walk down a disused railway line one day we came across an isolated and unlocked country church, so we went in, opened a musty old Bible on the lectern and began to read familiar passages to one another. It was a touching experience and a memory I shall always treasure.

One evening Trevor took Ma and me to an up-market restaurant in Folkestone. He chose the wine and when asked to taste it, pulled a face and told the waiter it was corked. Ma's face was a picture, for one could see her thinking 'bumptious young man showing off'. The wine waiter disappeared with the bottle and the headwaiter came to apologize and to ask Trevor to choose another wine with the compliments of the house. Ma was impressed; it was the only time we were ever served corked wine.

Ma had fallen in love with Pa in her teens and had never looked at another man, so she understood what was happening to me. I was head over heels in love with Trevor, but everyone was saying that shipboard romances never lasted. Trevor was born to Welsh parents living in Chingford, London. His mother had been a nurse during the First World War and had died quite recently. His father was an ordinary 'tommy' working in the rag trade. Trevor had been to Sir George Monnoux Grammar School and later I found glowing reports of his time there and a glowing reference for his first job. After collecting his school certificate in 1934 his father set him up with Sun Life Insurance in Threadneedle Street in the City of London. Trevor and his father did not get on very well and Trevor hated the job, and so loathed commuting every day to the City that he was determined to get right away and make something of his life as soon as he possibly could. While in Threadneedle Street he joined the Territorial Army's Artists' Rifles. This kept him sane, for he enjoyed the camaraderie among the men and going on training exercises. The friends he made in the Artists' Rifles lasted a lifetime as they kept meeting each other later on in different parts of the world. The only thing Trevor and his father had in common was rugby, for Grandpa Bevan had been capped for Wales in 1908/9 and was very involved with the London Welsh Rugby Club. Trevor played rugby at school, with the Artists' Rifles and with the London Welsh Rugby Club. Eventually, Trevor had interviews to join the British South Africa Police (BSAP), Southern Rhodesia, and the Fleet Air Arm. He passed all the tests for both forces, but the BSAP was the first to offer him a position. Within days he had booked a passage on the *Edinburgh Castle* to Cape Town and then by train to Salisbury in Southern Rhodesia. His parents were far from happy about it because within a very short space of time both their children had left England. Trevor's sister Peggy, who was seven years older than he was, had recently married David Henderson who worked for the Chartered Bank and they had been posted to Malaya.

Trevor arrived at BSAP headquarters and duly underwent his training. With the BSAP being a mounted police force, each day began with stable parade. When he passed out of the training school he was able to look after himself and his horse on bush patrol for days and nights on end. For three years, he and an

African constable visited far-flung farms, mission stations and African villages in various parts of the country. Being a keen and good rugby player, he would conveniently be transferred to Salisbury during the rugby season so that he could play for the police. In 1941 the BSAP seconded an able group of young policemen to the Eritrea Police to help the British military administration re-establish law and order after the army had defeated and chased out the Italians. He spent three years in Eritrea before being moved to Somaliland, during which time he learnt to speak and write Italian and Arabic. His job was a very responsible one and often quite lonely. After six years he returned to Rhodesia to find he had in excess of six months' leave due to him, which he immediately requisitioned and got.

His notebook from his police training days contained instructions on a wide range of subjects, including how to shoe a horse, tell if a horse needed worming and cure mange on camels. Camels were used in northern Kenya but not in Rhodesia. This note must have been added when he found himself working with camels in Eritrea and Somaliland. He always said that camels were the most unfriendly animals and even if you had been riding one all day and it had carried you faithfully across an arid plain, when you got off the beast your instinct was to kick it, which of course he never did. They are not very loveable animals, for they spit and blow smelly bubbles at your face.

Interspersed in this large notebook (which is now in the BSAP section of the military museum in Chelsea) were various poems that meant a lot to Trevor. During those six years he had been the only European for many miles, so he read a lot and always carried his copy of the *Golden Treasury*. Trevor could recite many of his favourite poems and indeed recited them to me in tender moments.

When we met on the *Durban Castle*, we spent every morning playing deck tennis, but after lunch we would take our deck chairs to a quiet corner to talk and it was then that his love and knowledge of poetry became evident. I had just written my matric and one of my favourite subjects had been English literature, which of course included poetry, so I could keep up a little. Here are some of his favourite poems, which convey some idea of the kind of man he was — romantic without being sentimental, which I found terribly exciting.

'A Patriot' by William Wordsworth
I travelled among unknown men
In lands beyond the sea;
Nor, England! did I know till then
What love I bore to thee.
'Tis past that melancholy dream
Nor will I quit thy shore.
A second time; for still I seem
To love thee more and more.

'Wander Lust' by Gerald Gould
Beyond the East the sunrise, beyond the West the sea,
And East and West the wander thirst that will not let me be;
It works in me like madness, dear, to bid me say goodbye,
For the seas call and the stars call, and oh! The call of the sky.
I know not where the white road runs, not what the blue hills are,
But a man can have the sun for a friend, and for his guide a star,
And there's no end to voyaging, when once the voice is heard,
For the River calls and the road calls, and oh! The call of a bird!
Yonder the long horizon lies, and there by night and day
The old ships draw to home again, and young ships sail away;
And come I may, but go I must, and if man ask you why,
You may put the blame on the stars and the sun and the white road and the sky.

These two poems are not found in the *Golden Treasury* but he could recite them word for word. Another of his favourites was 'I vow to thee my country' by Cecil Spring Rice. He thought the words were very emotional and descriptive.

My retention of poetry was not nearly as profound; the 'Walrus and the Carpenter' was about as far as it went, but that did not stop me appreciating poetry. For Trevor's birthday I gave him a red leather bound copy of Kipling and in no time he had memorized reams.

Trevor had a great sense of humour and to illustrate it here are a couple of his favourite party pieces.

Careful Now
Starkle starkle little twink

The Early Years

Who the hell you are you think?
I'm not under the alcofluence of interhol
Though some thinkle peep I am.
I fool, so feelish
I don't know who is me
That the drunken I sit here
The longer I get.

Whisky Whisky

I had 12 bottles of whisky in my cellar, and my wife told me to empty the contents of each and every bottle down the sink — or else! So I said I would proceed with the unpleasant task. I withdrew the cork from the first bottle and poured the contents down the sink, with the exception of one glass, which I drank. I then withdrew the cork from the second bottle and did likewise, with the exception of one glass, which I drank. I then extracted the cork from the third bottle and emptied the good old booze down the sink except for one glass, which I drank. I pulled the cork from the fourth sink and poured the bottle down the glass, which I drank. I pulled the bottle from the cork for the next and drank one sink out of it and poured the rest down the glass. I pulled the sink out of the next glass and poured the cork down the bottle. I pulled the next cork out of my throat poured the sink out of the bottle and drank the glass, Then I corked the sink with the glass bottled the drink and drank the pour. When I had steadied everything, I emptied the house with one hand and then counted the bottles, corks, and glasses with the other. There were 29. To be sure I counted them again when they came by and I had 74 and as the house came by I counted then again and finally I had all the bottles, corks and glasses counted except one house, and one bottle which I drank.

* * *

So here I was at Cheltenham Ladies' College and due back in South Africa in August 1949 and Trevor was due back in Southern Rhodesia in October 1948. Ma agreed that on my return to South Africa we would somehow arrange a meeting and if we still felt the same way we would announce our engagement.

On seeing me into Cotswold House at Cheltenham Ma made her way to Southampton to board the *Athlone Castle* and return to South Africa. Trevor went to Southampton to see her off, much to her surprise, and also to ask her if he could marry me. Ma was taken aback and made last minute arrangements for my Uncle Charles, a retired banker, to check him out. A meeting was duly arranged and, needless to say, Trevor passed the test.

Meanwhile Trevor, who had applied to join the colonial police service a long time earlier but had heard nothing, received a letter of acceptance and an immediate posting to Singapore. The posting would be for two to three years. This was a personal blow, but a great advancement for Trevor's career.

On 28 September I received a letter from Trevor telling me about the Singapore posting and hinting that he would try and come down to Cheltenham to see me before he left. I never found out how he got around the strict rules, as only relatives were allowed to visit the young ladies. I suspect he charmed his way round dear Miss Parks-Davis, our housemistress. She called me to her office and told me that Trevor was coming to Cheltenham for the weekend and that I could go out with him on the Saturday *and* Sunday. I could not believe my luck. Here I was supposed to be a schoolgirl and yet I knew I was going to spend the next one and half days with the man I would marry. I was 17. We had a very happy time and the hours just flew by. We agreed to become engaged but not to announce it until I got back to South Africa. I was on cloud nine, but could only share my secret with Deb White (now Slater); the other girls were far too immature.

PD, as we called Miss Parks-Davis, had guessed what was happening and was very understanding of my situation. I received a telegram on 16 October to say that Trevor had arrived safely in Singapore. Our only means of communication was by letter and we wrote about twice a week and kept it up for three years. It was over this period that we laid down the foundations of our total trust in each other that led to our strong and lasting marriage. It was not worth even trying to telephone, for there was no satellite in those days. The only quick communication was by telegram, which we resorted to from time to time.

Eventually the year at Cheltenham Ladies' College came to an end and I received my diploma with distinction. I loathed the college, we were so limited in what we could and could not do. There were about a dozen of us in Cotswold House, which was a good-sized group with which to work. PD tried hard to make ladies out of us. She showed us how *not* to enter a room full of people, how *not* to introduce people, in fact the niceties of society.

I made one lifelong friend, Deb, and we became each other's salvation, for the other girls were so childish. Deb and I see each other from time to time and have regular telephone conversations to keep in touch.

Though DSG only had about 200 pupils, I was extremely lucky if I made the reserve for either the tennis or hockey teams, but at Cheltenham Ladies' College I was in the tennis and hockey teams and captain within five minutes. I still have my badge and this was at a school with more than 1000 girls. I was shocked by the low standards of tennis and hockey.

I was a bit of a rebel and got into all sorts of trouble. There were crazy rules, which I found tiresome. Some shoes could only be worn inside and some only outside and I invariably had the wrong ones on and the prefects delighted in hauling me in and sending me back. I had a terrific row one day with one of our domestic science teachers. She was very young and I suspect this was her first teaching post. She set us a task in the kitchen and I finished it, correctly, in a matter of minutes. She had not expected this as she had nothing planned for the rest of the lesson and she told me to get out all the aluminium saucepans and polish them with wire wool and a soft cloth. I exploded and told her my mother had not sent me to Cheltenham Ladies' College to polish perfectly clean saucepans. I was sent to our housemistress, who I suspect sided with me. I was a quick worker and resented having to get the lunch most days because the others were struggling with their blouses or buttonholes or whatever they were making. I felt I was being penalized for being efficient. The truth was that I was with 11 very immature girls and, although the same age, I was streets ahead of them mentally and physically. Thank goodness for dear Deb as she kept me sane, and I kept on thinking I have only got one year to put up with this. I must cope. I had lovely holidays with friends and relations, Christmas at Eyam in Derbyshire, a walking holiday in the Lake District at Easter and a few weeks in Kirkcudbright with an aunt, then at last it was July and I could go home. I set sail on the *Stirling Castle* on 4 August and Uncle Charles, who had not seen my father for about 30 years, decided to escort me. On 22 August I was back home on the farm and Ma and Pa decided to make my engagement official; an announcement was placed in the *Eastern Province Herald* and the *Midland News* on 24 August, Trevor's birthday.

I had only been home a couple of weeks when Miss Miller from DSG phoned to ask if I could help out in the junior boarding house as there was an epidemic of some illness among the housemistresses. I went on the understanding that I would help them through the crisis and possibly stay to the end of term, but I ended up staying nearly two years. It was great fun and I had lots of time off during the day to sew and generally prepare my trousseau. I went home in the holidays and, despite being engaged to be married, I had a wonderful social life with lots of dances, tennis parties, visits to friends and getting involved in local politics.

Politics was never far from the surface in any conversation in South Africa in the 1950s. The country was stunned when General Smuts lost the general election of 26 May 1948. Ma, Trevor and I were on the *Durban Castle* when the news broke and the mood on board was one of gloom and despair.

With Dr Malan as prime minister, the Nationalists seemed to be turning everything we knew on its head; for example members of the coloured community were removed from the voters' role, the parliament was made supreme over the appellate division of the courts, and there was detention without trial.

In 1951 I joined a protest group called Torch Commando, which consisted of a lively bunch of people opposed to the government's new laws. Sir de Villiers Graaff was our leader and many ex-servicemen and women who had fought to defend democracy in the Second World War joined. We went round the country holding meetings, which were always well attended, and attracting new members.

The Nationalists increased their majority in the 1953 general election and, although the Torch Commando did its best to stop the implementation of strict apartheid rules, we had very few MPs and sadly the Torch Commando folded. Then in 1955 the Black Sash was formed.

All this time Trevor and I corresponded by letter. Twice his date of departure from Singapore was delayed because he had been involved in quelling riots and had to remain for the inquiry, but eventually his leave was confirmed and he flew to Johannesburg in October 1951. He had sent me a cheque to buy an Austin A40 and I drove it up to meet him. We had a few days getting to know each other again in Vereeneging at the lovely Riviera Hotel on the Vaal River. One evening the manager offered us complimentary tickets to an Elizabeth Schwarzkopf concert at the Johannesburg City Hall. They were prime seats in the stalls and we spent a wonderful evening listening to her lovely voice. I shall never know why we were chosen when there were lots of other guests in the hotel.

We drove back to Mortimer via Natal and, on 10 November 1951, were married in the cathedral in Grahamstown. The Revd Joss Driver officiated and we had a full choir, with my old friend Professor Ronald Kirby playing the organ. It was a lovely service. The reception was held at Phyllis and Joss Driver's home, Holland House at St Andrew's College and it was a very happy day. We spent our honeymoon partly at the Hogsback, partly at Katberg but mostly on a tour of all the BSAP stations Trevor had known. We drove up to Rhodesia and Trevor met all his old friends in Bulawayo, Salisbury, Umtali, Marandellas and elsewhere. We then returned to South Africa for Christmas with Ma and Pa before sailing to England to meet each other's relations. Uncle Douglas arranged an amazing curry lunch at Veerasamys, Piccadilly for the Rice clan to which umpteen people turned up.

One of the first things we did on arriving in London was to go straight to a news theatre, and there was one at Piccadilly Circus on the corner near the Royal Overseas Club where we were staying. Being out of touch with news and events for some time this was the quickest way to catch up and perhaps catch up on what people were talking about. We had a radio in Africa, but usually with indifferent reception, and on the ship there was a daily newssheet, but here at the news theatre all the happenings were in pictures and the newsreel brought one up to date.

Soon after Trevor and I were married, and when Dick was in his final matric year at St Andrew's College, Ma and Pa decided it was time to retire. Many years before Ma had bought a nice little bungalow at our favourite seaside spot at Bonza Bay in East London, which had been let and been well looked after over the years. They sold the farm, Greenhalgh, embarked on a holiday in England and then, on returning, went to live at Bonza Bay, where Ma became actively involved with the Black Sash.

* * *

The Black Sash was formed in 1955 from the Women's League for the Defence of the Constitution, which had been set up to protest against the removal of coloureds from the voters' role in the Cape and against the Group Areas Act. This Act dictated by the colour of their skin where people could or could not live, irrespective of their family, history, traditions, trade or occupation. Indians, coloureds, Africans and Europeans were designated their 'Group Area'. This caused great sorrow and traumas in some families as brother and sister, husband and wife could be of different skin colours and made to live apart by this cruel law.

My mother, being a good Christian, joined the East London branch of this brave band of women. With new laws being introduced and old ones scrapped, the Black Sash was publicly mourning the emasculation of the Union as we then all knew it.

During important trials when political influences outweighed natural justice, the Black Sash women would stand in silent protest outside the courts wearing their black sashes and, they hoped, shaming the judiciary. They were regularly seen outside Parliament, council chambers, law courts and other places where meetings were held. Theirs was a peaceful demonstration. Their active work involved helping distressed people who had been driven from their homes, often also occasioning the split-up of their families. These persecuted people were in a state of shock and usually had nowhere to go.

Most white people were not threatened with the loss of their homes, but they rallied to assist their less fortunate non-white neighbours. Ma made many friends during these active years and did much good work, as did the other 10,000 members. Though their activities came to an end in 1994 when apartheid South Africa became the rainbow nation, the Black Sash has not been forgotten.

3

Singapore 1952–54:
New Life, New Continent

We sailed from Southampton for Singapore in the P & O liner *Canton*. Though the government paid our actual fares, we decided to pay for a nicer and larger cabin than the one we had had on the Union Castle line. The first part of the voyage was very rough and, for the first time in my life, I was seasick. We had a marvellous steward who took care of me and generally brought me back to life. There was a crisis on at Suez so we went through the canal under escort and in convoy with troops along the bank; it was very exciting. At Bombay I was not allowed on shore as I was still travelling on a South African passport — 'NO DOGS AND NO SOUTH AFRICANS' read the notice. We had a happy day at Colombo, Ceylon at the Galleface Hotel, where we met Sir Franklin and Lady Gimson, for whom Trevor had been ADC. The Gimsons were going on leave pending retirement. I was glad to meet them as they had been good to Trevor and he had loved being at Government House with them.

Singapore was the next stop and all Trevor's friends seemed to come down to the ship to meet us — probably to see who Trevor had married — Scott Lethart, Bill Cowan, Guy Matthews, Jeep Jepson and many others. There was no house for us and we were put into the Adelphi Hotel where we remained for six months; housing was short with the city still recovering from the Japanese occupation. It was not a happy time; I got bored cooped up in one room and wondered what I had let myself in for. Trevor had his work and was fine. I refused to play mahjong and bridge from 9.00 a.m. to 1.00 p.m. each day as most wives seemed to do. We were members of the Tanglin Club where I swam fairly regularly and made good use of its library; we played tennis either there or at the police mess. To relieve the monotony of the Adelphi Hotel menu we used to save up for a steak under the stars every Sunday evening at the Raffles Hotel Palm Court to the accompaniment of a military band. Later, when I became pregnant, a steak held less appeal, so I used to order a head of celery instead and eat the lot.

I was invited to teach riding at the Bukit Timah riding club, which I did for a few months. I was not paid a salary but in return could keep our horse there for free. El-Alamein, a retired racehorse from the Bukit Timah and Malaya circuit, was given to us as a hack and we had many happy times with him. Usually Trevor rode him and I borrowed a horse from the stables. The pupils were service children from the army or RAF and some Chinese ones. The ponies were all small animals from Java and all right in the ménage, but not ones I would have trusted out in the open.

We later moved to a nicer hotel called Chequers. It was out of town, overlooked the polo ground, and had a garden in which I could walk and even sit in the shade. Eventually we were offered a little house, which others ahead of us in the queue had turned down but which we took, mainly to get out of the hotel. It had been occupied by a Chinese family and was filthy. It was a bungalow on stilts with two bedrooms, two bathrooms, a dining room and sitting room. A covered concrete path connected the house to a building that housed the kitchen and servants' quarters; the garage was at the very end. We had a wild, dull garden that was all grass. An Indian squatter lived at our entrance, but nobody questioned his presence and in exchange he kept the grass cut.

The house stood between the Ghurkha Police lines and a Chinese temple, so if nothing was happening on one side it certainly was on the other. The Kalarati celebrations, which entailed cutting off a bull's head in one full swoop (a clean cut meant good luck for the year) were the highlight of the Ghurkha year. The Ghurkha Police were a fine bunch of men, thoroughly reliable and totally loyal to the British. Before the war the riot squad had been Sikh, but their loyalty changed so the Ghurkhas were installed after the war. The Chinese temple was a noisy place with much clanging of cymbals and, during the Chinese New Year the music went on day and night for two whole weeks.

By this time I was pregnant, so began to prepare for the arrival of our baby. I was lucky to be under Professor Shares, the pleasant Eurasian professor of gynaecology and obstetrics at Singapore University. On his advice, I took to relaxation with Grantly Dick Reed's book as my guide. Trevor had arranged for an opium raid on the night of 26 January 1953, the day I went into labour. Trevor was o/c of the narcotics branch of the CID and these raids took place every now and again, but on this occasion the timing did not please me.

These opium raids, or rather raids on people plundering opium, were carried out fairly frequently and Trevor always went with his men. They captured thousands of opium pipes and all the paraphernalia connected with the ritual of smoking the drug, not to mention vast quantities of opium in various forms.

When Trevor was out on these raids he always left me with a revolver under my pillow, but I was never nervous because I had been brought up with guns and had learnt how to respect and handle them correctly. There were a lot of armed house burglaries, so I may well have had to use the weapon, but thank goodness the occasion never arose. I was always pleased to see Trevor return home after these escapades unscathed.

As with all activities to do with illegal drugs, the protection rackets various gangs organized to shield the opium dealers from exposure of their evil trade involved the exchange of huge sums of money. With dealers devising increasingly sophisticated ways of trying to outdo the police, the police constantly had to introduce new methods and update or discard old ones, which could leave them in a vulnerable position. It sometimes became necessary to take a different route to the office each day, or drive in a different vehicle, or even change the car's number plates. Dogs were beginning to be brought in to sniff out opium. It has a very distinct smell, especially when the pipes are heated over a flame before being smoked, and, like all sniffer dogs, these dogs were marvellous; among other places, they found opium in hollow table legs and in hollow doors.

To return to the imminent arrival of our first baby, Trevor dropped me at the Kandang Kerdu Hospital on his way to the raid. I stayed there overnight and, on 27 January 1953, our daughter Merilyn was born in time for afternoon tea.

On my first day of motherhood I felt a strange sense of calm and relief that the birth was over, that all was well and that I had a lovely healthy baby. Visiting hours were fairly strict and suddenly Trevor appeared, the proud father, with a huge bunch of orchids. As it was not yet visiting time, I expected him to say that he had another opium raid and would not be able to visit us that evening. However, he had another excuse. The famous pathologist and fingerprint expert Professor Keith Simpson from Scotland Yard was delivering a series of lectures to the Singapore police and he naturally wanted to attend. The lectures clashed with visiting hours, but Trevor, being the man he was in the job he held, had no difficulty getting past the sister on duty.

When Trevor arrived I was holding Merilyn and getting used to this little person. He was obviously thrilled with his daughter and delighted to find that she had the right number of fingers and toes. He tickled her toes — she was very ticklish — and was quite intrigued and not a little infatuated. He said he had spent most of the morning sending telegrams all over the world to tell our relations and friends that we had a daughter.

I spent about four days in hospital and when we went home I had arranged for Sally, a highly recommended Chinese day nurse who had been employed by several friends, to help me cope for the first two weeks. Merilyn was as good as gold during the day, but the minute Sally went the trouble started.

Ma had sent me Dr Spock's book on child rearing, but the little I read went against the grain and I decided to trust my own instincts instead. There were several experienced mothers to whom I could turn for advice should I need it. There were no postnatal baby clinics, but I was lucky because the hospital had given my name to a nurse from Nestlé who arrived at the house one day to see if I needed any help. We chatted a bit and as I was breast-feeding with great success she could not sell me any of her powdered milk. She agreed to call once a week to weigh Merilyn and give me any general advice I needed. This was a good arrangement and lasted until Merilyn was six months old. I fed Merilyn for nine months and then put her on Nestogen milk, a special formula made by Nestlé for babies in the tropics. Merilyn seemed to like it and I kept her on it until we left Singapore.

As there were no baby clinics and I had thrown away Dr Spock's book, I took out a subscription to *Nursery World*, a monthly magazine that answered all my queries and helped me make a reasonable job of bringing up my daughter in hot and steamy Singapore. She never got prickly heat rash and slept 12 to 13 hours each night, having not slept a wink during the day.

When we were offered a new house at 29d Malcolm Road we could not believe our luck; it was so nice and clean. When we moved, we took on a new cook, an Indian, and arranged for Trevor's driver Ghani and his beautiful Malayan wife Sarah to live on the premises. I had insisted on having a washing machine from day one in Singapore — a Hoover Mark I — and taught Sarah how to use it. So she did all the washing and ironing while Ghani kept the car, a smart two-litre Sunbeam Talbot, clean and polished (along with our shoes). We were much happier in this smart little house surrounded by other smart little houses, all government property, and planned and planted a garden filled with gardenias, pawpaws, palms and cannas.

* * *

However, when an opportunity arose for us to go to Japan, we went. People said we were mad to take a nine-month-old baby with us, but it was now or never and we embarked on the Blue Funnel line's *Peleus*. We had two cabins linked by a bathroom that were very spacious and we appeared to be the only passengers. We first called at Manila in the Philippines and had to be in a convoy weaving our way between buoys and wrecks. The whole harbour was filled with sunken ships and the many masts showing above the water level were reminders of the recent naval battles. We were quite shocked at the price of everything in Manila and, from driving round the city, the very poor state of the country. The Dewar Boulevard on the seafront was not too bad, but all the streets behind it were full of potholes. The cathedral was a ruin, in and around which many squatters camped under tarpaulins. We then went to Hong Kong, which was totally different and a wonderful city. We knew many people in Hong Kong, but ended up staying with friends in Deep Water Bay. We left Merilyn with their trustworthy amah and went shopping, but to my despair, I was robbed. I did not know whether to be sick or cry, for I had just cashed travellers cheques to buy a camphor wood chest. At that time there was considerable rivalry between the Singapore and Hong Kong police, but, to give them their due, my wallet was returned within a couple of hours of losing it, minus the money of course, but everything else was there; they had found it in a dustbin.

We then went on to Japan. The *Peleus* was carrying Irish beef for the American army in Korea, where the war was still raging. Our first port of call was Otaru in Hokkaido, the most northern island. It was freezing. We dressed Merilyn up in her winter woollies, which she hated, for basically all she had ever worn in her life so far had been a pair of knickers. We had to tie her shoes on with string because she kept removing them and if we had not done that she would have got frostbite. We went ashore to one of the hotels and sampled sake wine, which did not impress me but it was hot and warming if nothing else. The island seemed primitive with its three-wheeled vehicles — similar to Indian taxis — and dogs and horses pulling carts. A huge coalmine dominated the town. On returning to the warmth of the ship we sailed down the east coast of Japan calling next at Yokohama (for Tokyo) then Osaka (for Kobe). We had some friends from Rhodesia in Tokyo and they took us to the best Japanese restaurants, where we sat on the floor. My friend spoke excellent Japanese, which was hardly surprising because her father had been posted to Japan as a diplomat and it was where she had been born, so we were lucky. We found Japan beautiful and the people friendly once they found out that we were not American and did not have any dollars. When we went into a restaurant with Merilyn, a highchair would arrive from nowhere with about six waiters eager to heat up baby food and/or bottles, or produce something else for the baby. With her blonde hair and blue eyes, Merilyn was the centre of attention and hordes of children would follow us wherever we went.

At Osaka we were again fortunate to have friends. He was in banking and was kind enough to arrange for a car and chauffeur to take us to the old capital, Kyoto, where we had a picnic at Nara Park and visited the largest buddha in the world.

In Kobe our friends took us to the King's Arms. Mr Courtney-Browne, who ran this pub, claimed that it was not a copy but the genuine thing. It certainly had the atmosphere, complete with beams and brasses, and served traditional English food like steak and kidney pudding, roast beef and Yorkshire pudding, with roast beef sandwiches its speciality. Visiting soldiers, sailors, statesmen, artists and film stars all went there. The pub was built in 1950 at a time when Japan was becoming increasingly integrated into the international community and there seemed a need for people of all nationalities to have somewhere to meet, drink and eat in comfortable surroundings; so CB, as he was known, fulfilled that need.

At Kobe the atmosphere changed dramatically when, instead of it being our own private ship, a rowdy bunch of American army wives on a shopping spree to Hong Kong came aboard. Naturally, we had been at the captain's table and now we were joined by a bunch of colonels' wives. You should have seen Trevor's face when they spread marmalade on their kippers. Though we had excellent food, some of these women would read through the enormous lunch or dinner menu and then ask for a sandwich — the steward's face was a study and it was an eye opener for us, for British colonels' wives behaved differently.

We spent a lovely holiday of about six weeks and it was a great experience to see Japan in 1953. The shops were rather sparsely filled by today's standards and we bought a few items at great expense; Japanese cameras and binoculars had not yet made their mark on the international scene.

* * *

The new governor, John Nicol, had invited Trevor to remain on as his honorary ADC, which involved helping at large functions or with VIP visitors. This he gladly did and we met some interesting people we would otherwise never have encountered. Singapore was a perfect stopping off place for people travelling between the east and west; in fact, it was the most convenient overnight stop on the flight from the UK to Australia. On one occasion, HE was unavailable, so he asked Trevor to go to the airport to meet Rab Butler, who was on his way to Australia. Trevor duly met him, brought him to Government House, gave him afternoon tea and asked him what he would like to do. He said that as the temperature was well into the eighties, he would like nothing better than a swim. Without batting an eyelid, Trevor said, 'Certainly Sir, just give me half an hour.' The reason for this was that the marble swimming pool at Government House had sprung a leak and was empty. Normally it took hours to refill, but Trevor resourcefully rang the fire brigade. It arrived almost immediately and with its power hoses filled the pool very quickly so that Rab Butler could have his swim. Rab Butler is often referred to as the finest prime minister we never had.

On another memorable occasion HE asked Trevor to go to the docks where an American freighter carrying the US Ambassador to the Samoa Islands had berthed and to invite him and his wife to lunch. Most people know that an invitation from HE is as good as a royal command, for the Governor is after all Her Majesty's representative. Trevor went on board, presented HE's compliments and handed him the gilt-edged invitation to lunch. The American read it, but declined the offer on the grounds that his wife was too busy shopping. Trevor was a bit taken aback, but in his diplomatic way pointed out the error of the Ambassador's ways. He then graciously accepted the invitation but for two days hence. A Government House car was sent to pick him up at the prearranged time and when the car arrived back at Government House only the Ambassador got out. He explained that his wife was shopping and would follow in a taxi. Taxis did not normally have access to Government House, so a message was given to the guard at the gate. We all then went in for the prescribed pre-lunch drink, or possibly two, and still there was no sign of Mrs Ambassador. HE was getting edgy and glaring at Trevor, as though it was his fault. At last a battered Ford Popular taxi arrived and Mrs Ambassador stepped out laden with shopping bags, including a very tatty old carpetbag. Trevor did his best to part her from all these bags and showed her to the powder room, but she refused to hand over her disreputable carpetbag and came out of the powder room as dusty and as untidy as she had been when she went in. The other guests at this lunch were dressed very smartly, but the American Ambassador's wife was in an ordinary very creased cheap cotton dress with sandals, not stockings like the rest of us were wearing in that heat, and her feet were filthy. We eventually sat down to lunch with HE looking very cross. When the Ambassador's wife declined the starter, the fish course and the main course, HE said to her, 'I notice you are not eating anything. Can I get you something else to your liking?' Her reply was snapped back, 'I would like a brandy as I have diarrhoea.' Without blinking an eyelid, Peter the steward immediately produced a brandy and soda and the meal continued with awkward pauses.

That was the downside, but the upside was the privilege of meeting HRH the Duchess of Kent Princess Marina. She had the most beautiful violet eyes I have ever seen and always wore at least something to match them — the flowers on her dress, her shoes, or a piece of jewellery. She had exquisite taste and elegance. I remember a magnificent Alexandrian brooch that was said to have come from a Russian tsarina's tiara and to be of a gemstone that is only found in the Ural Mountains of Russia.

There was a dinner party for her on 1 October 1952 and a ball on 3 October. I still have the invitation, complete with dance programme and attached pencil. I was noticeably pregnant by this time, so my dance programme was scantily filled. I do not think that the Duchesses of Kent had been properly briefed about just how hot and sticky it could get in Singapore and the poor lady suffered dreadfully with swollen ankles and feet. In that climate it is agony to wear heeled court shoes, and having to stand for hours during official functions could not have helped. One evening Trevor was dispatched to go out and buy her some flip-flops.

The coronation of Queen Elizabeth II was a grand occasion. Celebrations lasted for a week, with parades, children's parties, exhibitions, concerts, football matches, national dances, youth rallies and 'Beating the Retreat' by the First Battalion Yorkshire Regiment. On 2 June 1953 at 7.30 a.m. there was a parade on the Padang, with HE, flanked on the dais by all his ADCs, taking the salute. I was sitting just behind Trevor, standing rigidly to attention during the march past when, to my horror, out of nowhere the one and only bee in Singapore landed on Trevor's sweaty neck and stung him. Within minutes I saw his neck swell over and above his stiff collar. Luckily, the march past was nearly over, for the discipline of the occasion did not allow him to move. When we got into the car he was able to loosen his collar and as soon as we got home I applied blue bag and ice and anything else I could think of to get the swelling down for the ball in the evening. Trevor needed to be on duty at Government House in full mess kit and that meant another stiff collar. Trevor said my treatment was almost worse than the actual sting. The celebrations carried on all day. There were combined services of thanksgiving in St Andrew's Cathedral and in other churches, mosques, temples and synagogues and, in the evening, an illuminated procession ended up with the leaders being received by HE at Government House and the procession then disappearing in various parts of the town. Later in the evening there was a sea dragon procession and a fireworks display.

Shortly after it was announced that Edmund Hillary and Sherpa Tenzing Norgay had conquered Mount Everest, Lady Hillary went out to meet her husband to accompany him home and they too stopped off in Singapore. Trevor had the fun of meeting them at Kallang airport and taking the party to Government House.

It was both a great experience and a privilege to have lived the life we did in Singapore, for the Malays are lovely people. Abdul Rahman, one of Trevor's outstanding Malay officers, invited us to his kampong (village) on several occasions to meet his wife and enjoy a real Malay curry. Malay curries are particularly nice because they are made with lots of coconut and are not too hot. If an expatriate invited us to Sunday lunch, we knew we would have a delicious curry, often followed by a good snooze.

We also went to many Chinese dinners at which the food was very different from Chinese takeaways. It was always at a round table with a big plate or plates in the centre from which one helped oneself to as little or as much as one wanted. Sometimes there were 17 courses, but one did not have to eat all 17. The men were served whisky or beer (which they would down with a toast, *yam sing*) and the women were served cold tea, which was quite pleasant, with each course. At the end of the meal the waiter would come round with hot scented damp towels with which to wipe one's hot face and sweaty palms. Some women, to preserve their make up, would only daintily pat their faces and wipe their fingers. The towels were very small.

While Trevor and I thoroughly enjoyed Singapore, we both felt the pull of Africa. The writing was on the wall for Singapore's independence and there was the new and exciting prospect of a Central African Federation (CAF), so Trevor applied for and was granted a transfer. Then, about ten days before we left Singapore, Trevor's worthy and trusted inspector was shot dead. This was an awful shock for everyone and it intensified the danger for Trevor.

102

Just before we left HE gave us a very pleasant lunch party to which he invited all the full-time and other honorary ADCs. He told Trevor that he would like to give him a small present and asked him if he would like a suitably engraved silver cigarette box. Trevor was surprised at the choice of gift because he had never smoked, which just showed one how observant HE was. On hearing this, HE looked at a loss, so Trevor diplomatically suggested that he would appreciate a beer mug; a few days later HE produced a very nice engraved Georgian-shaped silver beer mug.

Soon after we first met John Nicol I accompanied Trevor to a lunch party at Government House. It was in the early stages of my pregnancy and it was a particularly hot day, at least 90 degrees, and there was no air conditioning. We were all standing round with our hot pre-lunch sherry when all of a sudden the room began to spin round. I quickly sat down and in so doing immediately blotted my copybook because HE, the Queen's representative, was still standing. The assembled company clearly frowned on me but I thought it was better than fainting. I recovered after a few minutes and then we all went in to lunch.

On another occasion, on 8 March 1954, shortly before leaving Singapore, we were invited to a dinner at Government House in honour of the Countess Mountbatten of Burma, CI, GBE, DCVO. I still have the programme and from this I see that I was taken into dinner on the arm of Mr Allington Kennard, whom I think was a journalist. The police band conducted by Nagindar Singh provided the music.

While we were thinking about what to take to Africa and what to leave behind, I said that we must take Merilyn's folding cot. With a change of scene every night and so much travel, she would be unable to understand the upheaval and her normal routine would be shattered. To give her some security, in my view, it was essential she had the comfort of sleeping in her own cot each night. 'Fiddlesticks' (or some equivalent), Trevor said, 'it would be far too much trouble.' It was the nearest we came to a full-scale row. I hastily wrote an airmail letter to *Nursery World* stating my dilemma and seeking their expert advice. My letter was published and the expert advice thoroughly endorsed my feelings. So, much to Trevor's annoyance, we took the collapsible drop-side cot and mattress on to the MV *Straat Makassa*; we then carried it on the roof rack of our Plymouth car every day for the 2000-mile journey from Bonza Bay to Lilongwe in Nyasaland. The exercise paid off, for she never had to face the problem of trying to sleep in a strange bed and wherever we went our hosts or the hotel were spared the nuisance of having to provide a cot for her. Mind you, when we finally settled into our house in Nyasaland, the cot needed to have a lot of remedial work done to it because it had taken quite a bashing on the roof rack, but it had been worth it.

4

Back to Africa

After many farewell parties and lunches, we managed to pack everything up and set sail for Africa on the Royal Inter Ocean Line's MV *Straat Makassa*. Realizing that our low-slung Sunbeam Talbot would be no use on African roads, we had sold it and bought an American Plymouth to take with us. The *Straat Makassa* was a freighter that could take 20 passengers, but once again we were lucky because there was only one other voyager — an elderly blue-rinse American widow who was travelling around the world on the proceeds of her legacy. One day she appeared in a very peculiar dress made from a material I had never seen before. I realized why when she explained that she had got all her friends to give her their laddered nylon stockings, which she had then cut into strips and knitted up into this dress. It looked terrible, but it was practical for travelling and washing she said.

Being only three passengers, we sat at the captain's table with the ship's officers and every dinner the American lady insisted we all have a liqueur; I recall hers was always a crème de cacao. The ship's doctor was a bit eccentric, for whatever one's ailment, he put you on a diet of rice water, his prescription for bunions to a stiff neck. The *Straat Makassa* was a very comfortable ship, built specially for travelling along the equator. The dining room and lounge were on the top deck and open both sides to catch the breeze. We had two communicating cabins and bathroom, so we were very comfortable. We did not call at any other ports, but just sailed due west for Durban. We were due to call in on Madagascar, but owing to a change of plan and no cargo to pick up there, we steamed on to Africa. In this lovely open-air dining room the most delectable food was served — I have in front of me a lunch and a dinner menu. Each was worth keeping just for its pictures, mainly eastern scenes and very beautiful.

Friends in Durban met us at the docks and took us to their home for the day. The next day, which was Easter, we arrived in East London to be met by Ma and Pa. They were thrilled to meet their first grandchild and luckily they took to each other — Merilyn was used to lots of different adults. We had a happy holiday with my parents who had now settled in Bonza Bay. My old nanny Elsie arrived to look after Merilyn, so I had quite a rest. Then the day came for us to embark on our 2000-mile drive to Nyasaland, so we loaded up the Plymouth, filled the boot and most of the back, made a sort of nest for Merilyn to play and sleep in and set off. We had a smooth drive and sped along the national roads in South Africa, which are very well built and graded and with hardly any traffic. In Potgietersrust in the Transvaal we stopped early one morning for petrol. We filled up the car, but when Trevor went to pay, the man refused to accept a traveller's cheque. When he saw that it had been issued in Singapore, he said, 'Gott man you've got communists there, I can't touch this!' A slight altercation took place during which Trevor stood his ground and refused to have the petrol siphoned out of the tank. We had to wait for the bank to open to cash another traveller's cheque — what a palaver. Trevor reported the incident to Shell (or whoever supplied the garage), for it could have proved very awkward. Bang went our early morning start! We were usually on the road by 6.00 a.m. and would travel for about 100 miles before having breakfast at a hotel *en route*. We would take a picnic lunch with us and drive until about 4.00 p.m. before finding a hotel for the night. This gave us ample time to exercise Merilyn and tire her out so that she would be ready to go to bed.

We broke our journey in Salisbury (Harare) where we met up with friends and relations. Meredith (who had by then retired from the Rhodesia Railways) and Ena kindly had us to stay. It was good to have a break and be able to unpack the car and have it serviced for the final part of our journey.

On leaving Salisbury, we headed east on the Mtoko road, Trevor's old hunting ground, for he had been stationed at Mtoko, on the border with Mozambique, and had done regular patrols on horseback in this remote part. We had no trouble with the customs, but the road deteriorated badly when we still had about 400 miles to travel and with only one town about halfway along the route. With a heavily laden car we had to go very carefully — there was no AA in these parts — and very slowly because we were driving on sand and the bottom of the car was scraping against the tops of the deep ruts in the road. Fortunately, there was hardly any traffic because it was quite difficult to get a set of wheels out of a rut to enable the other vehicle to pass. This was the only road to Nyasaland from Southern Rhodesia; the alternative, which was hundreds of miles longer, was via Northern Rhodesia. Our next hazard was the mighty Zambezi River. We knew there was no bridge but that the ferry was operating. At Tete we followed the signs to the ferry port and drove onto what seemed a rather precarious vessel; in fact it was a pontoon. The river was very wide and fast flowing, but we eventually reached the other side and continued on our sandy slow journey. We arrived at the Nyasaland border post very tired but thankful to have reached — or nearly reached — our destination. We spent the night at the Mwanza rest house.

The next day we arrived at the Zomba police headquarters. Driving through Mozambique it was dull and flat for most of the way, but on reaching Nyasaland the scenery changed and it became beautiful, with mountains, forests and streams. Arrangements had been made for us to stay at the 'Pig and the Whistle', the only pub in Zomba, at the foot of the majestic Zomba Mountain. Various police officers welcomed us and the deputy commissioner invited us to lunch the next day. We learnt later that the commissioner had not invited us because he disliked children. Nonetheless, we had a very pleasant meal and introduction to Zomba society. After a few days we packed up the car again having had it serviced — only to discover that the exhaust pipe was no longer cylindrical but squashed *flat* from having driven for 400 miles with the car scraping on sand all the way. We had to order a new one, which was sent up to Lilongwe and fitted there. We headed north and, after a few miles, took the Liwonde pontoon over the Shire River, which flows between Lake Nyasa and the Zambezi. David Livingstone in his day had also negotiated this ferry, which a gang of Africans pulls over with chains revolving round drums and singing, as they always do on such occasions. The road was still dusty, but the sand not so deep, so we made good time going through Ncheu (on the border with Mozambique), Dedza and eventually Lilongwe. We had been booked in at the Lilongwe Hotel and we stayed there for about a week waiting for our household belongings to catch up with us.

On about the second evening at this friendly little hotel, I had been to the kitchen to arrange for an early supper for Merilyn and, on walking back through the lounge, instantly recognized a figure lying prostrate on a sofa in *ulendo* (safari) kit as a special boyfriend from my school days. Michael Hall leapt up and we greeted each other warmly. 'What the hell are you doing here?' we asked in unison. Michael was an assistant district officer and though he knew that a new married policeman was coming, he had no idea it would be me. I took him along to meet Trevor, who looked surprised, and later asked me if we were likely to meet many more of my old boyfriends. We met Michael from time to time at the club (the centre of Lilongwe social and sporting life) and then, as we were posted to different places, rather lost contact. Sadly, he died of cancer as a relatively young man and I have met his widow at ex Nyasa functions. I fell in love with Michael when I heard him sing 'Oh, for the wings of a dove' as a choirboy at Grahamstown Cathedral (where his father was a canon). He was in the St Andrew's band and looked very handsome playing the bagpipes in a kilt and glengarry. He also played rugby, so there were several opportunities to view him from afar, and we danced together a lot at school dances. One never forgets one's first love.

The huge container with our worldly possessions was freighted from Singapore to Beira. It then came by railway to Nyasaland and at Salima, which was where the railway ended, a crane lifted it onto a flat-bed lorry, which brought it to the charming little house we had been allocated. There were no cranes in Lilongwe, so the lorry backed up to our veranda, which was about the right height, and with difficulty we unpacked from there. The lorry had to remain at the house for some time, for, charming though it was, the house was really too small. When we moved again it was into a brand new house about a mile away, but though I tried to make it as comfortable as possible, I never liked it. We were issued with the heavy furniture such as armchairs, dining table and chairs, sideboard, dressing table, chest of drawers and beds. Because of white ants, the floors were made of cement rather than wood and, as everyone knows, cement floors get very dusty. The remedy was to pour gallons of old sump oil (which was easily obtained from the one and only garage) over it until the cement reached saturation point; then with patience, perseverance, wax polish and elbow grease a nice shine would eventually appear on the black floor. Some people polished their floors with red polish, but that is hopeless with small children who spend most of their time on the floor. The next challenge was the garden. We made a vegetable garden at the back, a lawn at the front and planted lots of trees.

The Public Works Department (PWD) had bulldozed the whole area and removed most of the indigenous trees, which was shameful — we had one acacia left at the bottom of the drive. There were eight houses in a row, all exactly the same and all denuded of trees. It made it easier for the builders I suppose.

When the PWD built our house the foreman and inspector had not done their jobs properly because we had two narrow escapes. On the first occasion, when I went into my bedroom early one morning I noticed that what was meant to be an air brick had fallen out of the wall from high up near the ceiling and had landed on my pillow. The contraption on my pillow bore a closer resemblance to a rat-trap than an airbrick, for it consisted of some steel mesh squashed into a clumsy wooden frame. Had I been in bed at the time, if it hadn't killed me it would certainly have scarred or damaged me for life. The 'airbrick' had just been pushed into an aperture in the wall. It never occurred to us to sue the PWD, perhaps we should have; I was just thankful I had got up early.

The second escape was when the whole frame of a door leading from the hall to the bedroom passage just fell out one morning along with the door. Again, if my small daughter had been in the hall when it fell, she probably would have been killed. And again my chief reaction was relief that no one had been hurt. We never had it replaced — it was an unnecessary door anyway.

The third building disaster in that house was that the steel burglar bars on our bedroom window were fitted into a wooden frame that merely stood on the windowsill without being attached to the wall. Consequently, a burglar could easily have just pushed in the frame and climbed through the window.

So, when the old police house fell vacant and we were asked if we would like it, I jumped at the opportunity. As one of the oldest colonial-style houses in Lilongwe, it had deep shady verandas, high ceilings in all the rooms for coolness, a very big garden with lots of trees, and, very convenient for Trevor, it was within a stone's throw of the police station. This nice old house had a welcoming atmosphere and we settled in very quickly. The furniture was good and had been well looked after and the cement floors, having had the sump oil treatment many years before, were mature, beautifully shiny and really looked good.

If you look at a map of Nyasaland (Malawi) you will see that it is at the southern end of the rift valley, which is subject to earth plate movement. One night I was woken by the sound of the wardrobe and dressing table wobbling and making a noise like thunder in the distance. I was terrified and woke Trevor because I thought a burglar was trying to bash the door down. He knew immediately that it was an earth tremor and in a second or two it was all over. The only sign the next day was a crack in our bedroom floor.

In those days we were allowed to use prisoners (under a guard) to work in the garden and we soon had a highly productive vegetable patch and fruit from the indigenous mango, avocado and guava trees. We never had any problems with the water until one Saturday morning, when I was using our Hoover Mark I washing machine, the water ceased to run from the tap. At first I thought it was an airlock, which happened quite frequently, but it was more serious than that. I telephoned Trevor at the office and he got hold of the PWD water person who explained that new water mains were being installed in the town, but that we should not be affected. However, he came round to the house and, after inspecting this and that and our main stopcock, was very puzzled. To ensure that we were not left without water for the weekend, he installed a temporary pipe from the new mains to our house and at the same time fitted us with a water meter where the old and new pipes met. When Trevor came home at lunchtime and went to see how they had overcome the problem, he noticed that the water meter had two taps (valves), one on the new pipe and one on the old. He began to fiddle with the taps and found that when he opened the one on the old pipe, the meter went backwards. Up until then we had always paid a flat monthly rate for water of

£3.15s; but we then decided to 'adjust' the meter reading, irrespective of how much water we used in the garden, so that we continued to pay the same amount as before. We kept this up until we left the house to go on long leave. It was very naughty and we did not tell the people who took the house over from us about it. I wonder if anyone else made the same discovery?

At this time we acquired a liver coloured cocker spaniel puppy named Minnie — Merilyn adored her and it was good for her to have a pet. Minnie was very intelligent. One of her tricks was to go with Trevor to the office each morning and bring back the newspaper and any letters for me in her dry mouth. The Africans, who were astounded by this feat, would exclaim, 'Ah-Ah-Ah!'

Not long after we had moved into the house, we were woken one night by loud noises from a diesel engine and crashing gears, which appeared to be coming from the police station. Trevor put on some clothes and went down to see what it was all about (he was gone for ages). It turned out that an enormous lorry with a tarpaulin covering its load was backing up to a position next to the building. Trevor discovered, to his amazement, that it contained the monthly delivery of money (cash) to the Standard Bank, hundreds of boxes of coins. Being the beginning of the tobacco reaping season, more money was needed to pay extra labour, hence the huge amount of cash. Trevor had not been warned about a cash delivery, but here was this vehicle with no security and no escort being dumped at the police station, and the poor African constable being asked to sign for it. Trevor instructed him *not* to sign for it, for it was outrageous that he should be made to sign for so many thousands of pounds. Trevor telephoned Andrew, the bank manager, who took ages to come to the phone — he was not used to having his sleep disturbed. Trevor explained the situation and asked him to come down and sign for it, thereby exonerating the driver and taking responsibility now that the money was in Lilongwe. Andrew was most reluctant; he said the police had always dealt with it and they had never had a problem. 'Well things are going to change round here,' said Trevor. Andrew duly signed and Trevor put an extra guard or two on the lorry, which was not even closed or locked, and went back to bed. Andrew then complained to Trevor that he had not been able to get back to sleep again.

The money had been dispatched from Blantyre, railed to the railhead at Salima, then transferred onto a lorry and brought to Lilongwe.

Nyasaland was purported to be a policeman's paradise because there was hardly any crime in this beautiful country. However, since all good things come to an end and crime did begin to creep in, steps had to be taken to cope with it. Large amounts of money had to be dealt with in a responsible manner, for an insecure unescorted lorry presented too much of a temptation. Most Nyasas were honest. I remember one occasion when an old African walked into the police station with a very full mailbag on his back. He has seen it on the side of the road many miles out of Lilongwe, recognized it for what it was, carried it all the way and passed it into safe hands. I doubt if that would happen today. The post came to Lilongwe the same way as the money — by rail from Blantyre to Salima and then by road. This particular lorry had been carelessly loaded and I doubt if anyone had counted the bags at Salima because there had not been any report of a missing mailbag at the receiving end. Trevor had quite a job to get a reward sanctioned for this honest old African.

In 1955 Lilongwe was a small town in a largely agricultural area, with tobacco and maize being the main crops. The many expatriate farmers would visit the Lilongwe Club at weekends, when there was nearly always something going on in addition to the weekly cinema show. Trevor played rugby for Lilongwe and for the Central Province and the club arranged all manner of fixtures, including one entertaining South Africans versus the rest rugby match in which South Africa lost heavily. We both played a lot of tennis and the McClintoc Cup versus Fort Jameson (a town just over the border in Northern Rhodesia) was an annual fixture. There was a similar fixture for rugby. These events were taken very seriously — I played tennis for Lilongwe Club once or twice, which was good fun and very sociable.

The local battalion of the King's African Rifles (KAR) came and beat the retreat at the club and the children just loved it and followed the band out. (This was hardly Horse Guards' behaviour — but in central Africa you made the most of whatever entertainment there was.)

A group of us wives used to meet once a week to sew for the

Red Cross. We made simple little Viyella jackets, hemmed nappies and sheets and ran up pillowcases for the local hospital, for many African babies that were admitted had none of these things. We made blankets in the time-honoured way of everyone knitting squares and stitching them together.

Trevor's transfer from Singapore to Nyasaland did not count as leave, so we were given our six-month leave the following year. Consequently, we found it difficult to settle down because we had the feeling that our house was only temporary, which it was.

Wanting to make the most of being back in Africa, we arranged to spend a few days' local leave at the Luangwa game reserve in Northern Rhodesia. Camps were few and far between in the game reserve in 1954, so one had to book well in advance to get permits. I nearly upset the applecart by having a miscarriage a few days before we were due to go. Trevor was reluctant to cancel the booking and did not want to leave me and go on his own, but then I felt perfectly well so I went along with him.

Having piled the car up with tinned food, water and beer, we set off with Merilyn and a very efficient African nanny I had engaged. The camp provided beds, bedding, a cook and someone to do the laundry. We had to bring everything else, including flour and yeast, for the cook made superb bread and rolls. We slept in a grass hut with access to a concrete ablution block in which there was a good shower. Nsefu camp, our destination, was about 350 miles from Lilongwe and we had a trouble-free journey until we were actually in the camp, having had our papers and passports stamped at the gate. It was November, which is a hot month at the tail end of the dry season, and the clay clods in the riverbed we were negotiating had dried into hard very rutted blocks, not unlike concrete. Unfortunately, we scraped the bottom of the car on one of these clods while going very slowly up a slight incline. On changing into second gear the most ghastly banging noise emanated from the lower regions of the car, but we kept going because we were on our honour not to get out of the car or stop until we had reached Nsefu camp. In fact with lions, leopards and elephants around, we *had* to carry on, but were relieved that the noise ceased when we changed into third gear. However, when we arrived at the camp and changed into a lower gear, the noise started again. Trevor asked the Africans at the camp who were

113

helping us unload and put food and drinks in the paraffin fridge if any of them knew anything about cars. One volunteered to crawl under the car and see what the trouble was. He told us not to worry; there was a dent in the gearbox cover; he would take it off, hammer it out and we would be fine, and we were, what a relief.

Each morning we were woken with a cup of tea at 5.30 a.m. and when we had got up, the game guard would arrive with a heavy rifle and ammunition to ask what animals we wanted to see. Depending on our answer, we either walked to where they were or went some way by car and then walked. Between about 9.30 and 10.00 a.m. we would return to the camp for a huge breakfast, after which we would relax through the worst heat of the day, have lunch and then snooze before going out again to see the animals in the evening. On some days we walked about ten miles (leaving Merilyn and Nanny in the camp) and on others we would travel 100 miles before breakfast to see Thornicroft giraffe, which have markings that are darker and in a different pattern from those of most other giraffe. One morning we said we would particularly like to see as many birds as possible in a place where we could safely take Merilyn and Nanny. The game guard said he knew just the place, so we all got into the car, complete with our basket of drinks (one has to keep drinking in that dry heat to avoid dehydration). We understood from the accompanying armed guard that we were making for an island in the river, which we could reach by stepping-stones because the water was very low. We duly arrived and indeed there were hundreds of different species flying in for their early morning drink and bath. The most colourful were the bee-eaters, especially the little bee-eater, a beautiful green colour with a yellow throat and distinctive black-eyed streak, and the blue-breasted white-fronted bee-eater, which is mainly green with a mid-scarlet throat. We saw a malachite kingfisher in its brilliant plumage, finches galore and many others. Birds are one of the glories of Africa, for there are so many varieties and in such spectacular colours. We had been sitting very still, including Merilyn, which is a miracle for a toddler, when I asked the guard if I could get up to stretch my legs. He agreed and from behind a bush I saw an enormous cow elephant and calf purposefully wading towards 'our' island. There was no room for two families so we quickly gathered up our belongings and scrambled back to the safety of the car. Wow, what excitement! We really had a close-up view, but it just shows how vigilant one needs to be in a game park, especially when one is on foot.

With Nsefu being situated high up on the river bank, it was possible to sit in the shade of the camp and observe various animals coming down to the water to drink, elephants wading across the river and fish eagles calling. The next day I elected to remain in the camp and view the animals from my chair and I think I saw just as many as Trevor who had walked about 12 miles with the game guard and seen lion, giraffe, zebra, eland, puku, impala (antelopes) warthog and hippo. The following day we said we wanted to see rhino and the game guard fulfilled our wish; we got very close and it was thrilling. Our few days passed very quickly and we had an uneventful drive back to Lilongwe.

In case the reader thinks I was callous about my miscarriage, I can assure you I was not. As I was perfectly fit up to and after the event, I strongly believed then (and still do), that it was nature's way of telling me that all was not well with the foetus and it best be ejected. I have no way to prove this; there was no laboratory handy for an examination of the foetus and even if there had been I did not want to know. I also believe our trip to the Luangwa game reserve was just what I needed. It was something else to focus on in a positive way. As it turned out I was right. I also know how disappointed Trevor would have been had we cancelled, for we did not see another 'window' in his work cycle for perhaps years. He would not hear of going on his own, and anyway there would have been no point in leaving me moping on my own, brooding and being miserable. It is much better to get on with life. As it turned out, my instinctive reaction to the situation turned out for the best.

When Trevor and I discussed what size family we wished to have, I said four children and Trevor said 'Heavens no, two is quite enough.' Well, we ended up with three, for our sons are twins. Was that divine compensation for the one I lost? I shall never know.

* * *

In October 1955 we went on long leave. We started off by train to

Beira and then by Union Castle liner, the *Dunnotar Castle*, to Durban, where for some reason we transferred to the *Winchester Castle* and eventually disembarked at East London where Ma and Pa met us. We spent about a month at Bonza Bay where Merilyn had a happy time playing most days on the beach.

We sailed for England on the Ellerman Line's *City of Port Elizabeth* (how I miss sea travel, cruising is quite different and not nearly as pleasant). It was on this voyage that I remember the captain announcing that for the first time more people had flown the Atlantic than gone by sea and he reckoned that the writing was on the wall (or bulkhead for ocean liners). It was a very comfortable ship and it had an excellent nursery and children's nurse who would happily have looked after any child from dawn to dusk without the mother or father putting in an appearance; in fact, one mother did just that. I dressed Merilyn up as Little Miss Muffet, complete with a leather spider attached to her skirt by a thread, for the children's fancy dress competition and she won first prize. We docked at Tilbury (London) and the first thing we did was to buy a car, a little Ford 8 Popular — a basic car with no heating and it was the middle of winter. We spent Christmas in Wales at Aberaeron with Trevor's father and sister Peggy who had recently been widowed and was over from Australia.

Trevor had been selected for a course at the police college at Bramshill. It lasted from January to April and it was a very trying time for Merilyn and me. We had very little money, so could not stay for long at a hotel near Bramshill, but several friends in Derbyshire, Staffordshire and Sheffield were kind enough to invite us to stay. If the weather permitted Trevor would drive in the Ford Popular to wherever we were at the weekends.

While staying with a friend of Ma's in Sheffield, Merilyn developed German measles. This meant that she had to be kept in bed in a warm room, so we had to cancel our next move until the doctor gave her the OK to travel. It was a very cold winter and snow was thick on the ground. She was out of quarantine and allowed to circulate on her birthday, 27 January, and Trevor arrived for the weekend, which thrilled her and me no end. We were due to go to friends at Eyam Hall, but the road was closed over the moor, so we had to bide our time. It was the coldest day since 1895. The next weekend we were able to move to a decent hotel near Bramshill. Trevor came to see us most days and we could go for walks together, but Merilyn spoilt it all by becoming really ill with tonsillitis and I had to call the doctor twice — a sick child in a hotel is not much fun. Then Trevor became ill with influenza; he was marooned at Bramshill and we were marooned at Brandon Hall; it was not a happy time. Eventually, when Trevor got over his flu he collected us and we drove up to London to the Milton Court Hotel to say goodbye to Peggy who was sailing back to Australia on the P & O's *Oriana*.

Trevor took us down to a cousin in Westerham, Kent and I fell ill with flu. What a family! I felt awful not because I was ill but because I was in someone else's house. As soon as I was well enough, we moved to the White Lion at Hartley Wintney to be near Trevor at Bramshill, which incidentally is a magnificent Jacobean house and suitably imposing building for a police college.

We then went to stay with our close friends George and Margaret Hubert at Bredon's Norton. Merilyn was particularly badly behaved and refused to sleep. I was at the end of my tether, so I gave her half a Codis (without reading the instructions) and she was very ill. I had to call the doctor because I had poisoned the poor child. Imagine how guilty I felt! The doctor gave her an emetic and suggested I put her on a mild dose of phenobarbitone to calm her down. The doctor said that I should keep it up until we were back in Africa and in a proper routine because all this moving about was very unsettling for a young child of three. It was an unfortunate few months but we really had no choice.

At last it was time to return home to Nyasaland. We drove to Wales to say goodbye to Trevor's father and then up to London to the Belgravia Hotel. Trevor took our faithful little Ford Popular to Davy of Knightsbridge and they gave us £280 for it. I think we had only paid £250 five months previously.

We left the hotel on 12 April at 6.15 a.m. for Victoria air terminal and took off from London airport (Croydon) in an Argonaut BOAC plane, which was rather like a Pullman railway carriage. Being family we had a table and four seats. Now, looking back many thousands of air miles later, that first long flight went on forever. With no night flying in those days and frequent descents to fuel in outlandish places, the journey lasted for three days and nights.

117

Our first stop for fuel was at Marseilles, which had a very dirty terminal building, and we slept that night at the smart Phoenician Hotel in Malta. After an early start we had to land at Marsa Matrûh in North Africa for fuel and that night we spent in a floating hotel on the Nile at Wadi Halfa. The next morning we were called at 3.45 a.m. and our next fuel stop was at Khartoum, which was very hot, at 8.00 a.m. We came down again at Juba for fuel and then at last reached Nairobi where a friend from the Kenya police met us and took us to the new Stanley Hotel. Trevor went to have dinner with David and Jan Cracknell, but I could not leave Merilyn. When I thought she was asleep, I slipped out for some dinner, but when I came back to the bedroom, it was empty. Imagine my panic because this was Mau Mau time! However, to my relief, one of the hotel staff had found her wandering about in her pyjamas and had very sensibly sat down on the stairs and chatted to her until I arrived.

Next day was the final leg of the journey. We were given breakfast at the airport and then took off for Dar es Salaam and our last stop, Chileka airport, Blantyre. Jeff York met us and took us to the Shire Highlands Hotel in Limbe. Our troubles were not over. Merilyn woke and was very hot. I took her temperature and it was F105°. I panicked and called the doctor. She had swallowed some of her bath water, which had come straight from the filthy Nile at Wadi Halfa. Quick and appropriate medication had her fit in a day or two, and then we were able to drive over to Zomba police camp where Trevor had been posted as o/c Police Training Camp and promoted, so that was a good start.

We were allocated a house exactly like the new one we had in Lilongwe, but better built, so it did not take us long to get sorted out. It was quite nice living in the police camp as the children were free to roam among the houses and visit their friends without having to be taken. The only snag was that the unfriendly child-hating commissioner forbade the children and their nannies to watch the parades each day. In addition, an order went out from the commissioner's office that nannies and prams were not to be seen stationary — they must be on the move. Merilyn and her friends used to watch the parades from inside the hedge. We had several friends living in the camp and Trevor soon got into playing rugby again and I had a garden to sort out. Our lives were also quite hectic socially, which was enjoyable, and the police mess was handy for popping in for a drink or entertaining friends.

However, we began to think that it was about time we had another baby. Having had one miscarriage, I wanted everything to go perfectly, but babies do not generally come to order and it seemed to take ages before I eventually became pregnant. We kept the same cook/houseboy we had in Lilongwe, but I did not keep the nanny, who did not want to leave Lilongwe anyway. Then through Mrs Bartlett, who ran the nursery school Merilyn now attended and loved, I acquired the most marvellous African nanny — a large big-bosomed cuddly sort of person with a beaming smile. She was an ideal nanny and Merilyn took to her at once.

The postmaster general was due to go on leave and asked us if we would look after their spaniel Nickie for six months. I agreed, but had meanwhile arranged to have a spaniel puppy for Merilyn from the Achesons who lived on Zomba Mountain. Sadly, Minnie had been run over and killed while we were on leave. So from no dogs we now had two. The older dog got on quite well with the puppy, and Minnie II enjoyed his company.

At the same time we decided to have a chicken run so that we could have fresh eggs. One needed to test the eggs sold in the market by immersing them in water; if they sank you bought them. What finally decided us was that, having bought some local eggs without testing them in water, a chicken actually pecked its way through its shell in the fridge. We had quite a big garden and liked the idea of keeping chickens, so Trevor made a chicken run. We used to buy scrawny live chickens in the market and fatten them up for the pot and for laying.

My friend Daphne Coster, who had been my bridesmaid and was now headmistress of a school in Chingola on the Copperbelt (Northern Rhodesia), had sent a wire asking if she could come and stay and it was while she was with us that Merilyn had to have her tonsils out. She had had continual colds and a sore throat and ears for months and Dr Weir advised us that this was the way forward. We had a good little cottage hospital and on the appointed day we took Merilyn to the hospital and left her there. She seemed quite happy; I was the one who cried. She was due to come home on the third day, but could not because she had developed an enormous blister on her foot because a very hot hot-water bottle had been left in her bed when she was still unconscious. This was very bad nursing and the sisters were extremely upset — and so were we. Merilyn screamed the place down when she heard that she would not be allowed to go home and they would not let me stay with her. On hearing the commotion, an off-duty sister, Elma, came back to the ward and eventually managed to calm Merilyn down. Elma very sweetly remained with her until she was asleep and then looked after her the whole time until we were allowed to take her home. Elma married a police officer and I still get news of her from time to time — she was such a nice gentle person.

As luck would have it, Ma arrived to visit us on the same plane as the one on which Daph was leaving, so we only had to make one trip to Chileka airport. Though this was not her first visit to Nyasaland, for she had stayed with us briefly in Lilongwe, it was great fun having her with us. She was on her way back from Northern Rhodesia, where she had flown to see my brother, who had recently announced his engagement, and to meet her future daughter-in-law. Ma was worried about Dick because she thought his fiancée was unsuitable and quite wrong for him, but did not know what to do about it. She only stayed with us for a few days before returning to Pa at Bonza Bay.

While all this was going on Trevor was busy revolutionizing the police training school and keeping erratic hours organized round the shooting range, parades, lectures and trips round the province on recruiting drives. He also participated in police sports, at which he was very successful — he came fourth in the officers' race. Nonetheless, we both welcomed the weekends so that we could see more of each other and have some peace and quiet.

When we first arrived in Lilongwe in 1954, Trevor had asked at the police station when all men were present for a volunteer orderly/batman. Lloyd stepped forward and turned out to be a real treasure. He became one of the family and we all loved him.

Lloyd belonged to the old school in the Nyasaland Police — he was barely literate so could not be promoted under the new policy, but being the salt of the earth was too valuable to dismiss. He looked after Trevor's uniforms. I used to wash Trevor's shorts, bush shirt and socks in the washing machine, but he did all his starching, ironing and shoe and button polishing. We abandoned starched khaki when Terylene came on the market, for it was much cooler, softer and smarter. The iron with which Lloyd did most of his ironing was heavy, made of cast iron and heated with charcoal. Unless one was very careful, little bits of red-hot charcoal would burn small holes in the garments. To get the charcoal to glow and be really hot, Lloyd would fan it or swing it over his head.

Lloyd used to do all sorts of things for me, which he was not really supposed to do. He would go to the market and buy meat, vegetables and fruit much more cheaply than I could. The meat at the market was almost alive it was so freshly slain, so I would need to keep it in the fridge for at least a week before use; otherwise it would be too tough. The local fish, *chambo*, was readily available from the market and delicious — versatile, yet tasty on its own, and it did not collapse when cooked.

Lloyd had two wives, but he only had one at a time living with him. His second wife was considerably younger than his first and he had a total of 19 children. His second wife had a farm at Kota Kota on the lake and she used to bring me gifts of rice she had grown when she came to stay with Lloyd.

Lloyd was fond of our little spaniel Minnie and loved taking her for her weekly dip. The vet had a dip, which he encouraged all dogs to use once a week to kill off the ticks. As rabies was endemic, we had many scares; Minnie was injected annually for distemper and rabies and had a certificate to prove it. When a rabid dog was about — we were all ordered to tie up our dogs and keep them indoors until the scare was over or the rabid dog had been shot. I shall never forget one day when something made me go and see if the children were all right playing on the veranda. To my horror I saw an obviously rabid dog weaving its way across the garden and making straight for my open front door. I called the children and they came in immediately and I shut the door. There must have been a degree of urgency in my voice for the children to come in at once. I telephoned Trevor and then the vet, who arrived shortly afterwards and shot the dog at the back door.

I remember another rabies incident in the police camp when the vicar was calling on the deputy commissioner's wife. She went into her kitchen, found a rabid dog there, called for help, and the vicar dashed in. Meanwhile, poor Mrs Helliwell was bitten on her ankle and the vicar on his wrist, but he managed to get the dog out of the kitchen. There was much ribaldry afterwards about the vicar's hand on Mrs H's ankle. The dog was duly destroyed and the horrid injections administered to the bitten couple. The rabid dogs came in from African villages, but it was a rare happening.

In addition to running the police training school and bringing things up to date with one man and a dog, Trevor had to pass language and law exams to qualify for his annual increment. This was standard procedure and those who had any ambition met the challenge. Twice a week a teacher would come to the house to give him a lesson in Chinyanja, the local Bantu language. Trevor firmly believed that one should be able to speak the local language of one's area. He had a gift for languages — perhaps it was the Welsh in him — and in his early days had learnt Arabic and Italian. In Singapore he had learnt Malay (again a language teacher came to the house twice a week until he had passed the exam) and now he was adding another language to his repertoire. But that was not all. If you did not know the law, you were not much use as a policeman and law exams were taken annually until one reached a senior rank. All this was very hard work and Trevor certainly earned his six-month leave every two-and-a-half to three years. A change was also important for one's health. On the whole Nyasaland had an agreeable climate, but it got very hot in October until the rains broke. October was often called suicide month.

With Government House in Zomba, we received several invitations over the years from Sir Robert Armitage (a handsome man who looked splendid in his full dress uniform and feathered cocked hat) and Lady Armitage, who were hospitable and kind. We held a Red Cross fête in the Government House garden, which was a great success, and on another occasion Lady Armitage gave a party for the Corona Club (the colonial club to which most colonial wives belonged) at which we all had to wear a special hat and were judged accordingly — some were quite outrageous and some of course were quite beautiful.

The official invitations went out for the annual police ball and preparations were hectic. We had a wonderful night, with friends coming from Blantyre (including Alison from my childhood in Mortimer who was a very good horsewoman). I remember getting home at 4.00 a.m., with hideously swollen feet because I was pregnant. Trevor made me rest in bed for the whole of the next day.

At this time we moved house. With a new baby coming we needed more room and were allocated a bigger and nicer house in a different part of the police camp, near a gate that was guarded day and night; we once saw a lion outside the gate. We now had three decent sized bedrooms, so I prepared one as a nursery, one for Merilyn and one for Trevor and me. As if we did not have enough to do, 20 day-old chicks arrived — sweet little puffball Australorps bred on a nearby farm. It was also the shooting season for geese and duck and Trevor loved shooting. He would get up at 4.00 a.m. or earlier and drive to his favourite spot to shoot a few birds on the dawn flight. Spur wing geese and wild duck always made good eating and were very welcome in the larder.

My feet never really recovered from the police ball so Trevor insisted I saw a doctor. Unfortunately the only doctor was new and I took an instant dislike to him. He told me to rest, pummelled my stomach and said, 'you are very big, but it's not twins as I can only hear one heartbeat. Rest as much as you can.' The baby was due at the end of January, but by mid-November I was too large to drive. If I put the seat back to accommodate my tummy I could not reach the pedals, which was a blow.

Meanwhile, I convinced myself that I was carrying twins as there was so much activity going on inside me. If one baby was asleep the other was exercising, and I quietly prepared for two, making two of everything, but I did not buy a double lot of nappies — just in case. I did, in fact we all did, a lot of sewing in Nyasaland. I made all my own cotton frocks, evening gowns, tennis skirts and dresses, and all the children's clothes. The latter were not very complicated for they only needed a blouse or shirt and shorts, or sometimes a dress. I loved smocking and Merilyn always wore a smock for better occasions. Their shoes were flip flops or Bata canvas slip-ons, which were a godsend because most of the time we went barefoot — very good for our feet and bare feet on nice cool cement floors in the hot weather was bliss.

I often wonder how our grandmothers and great grandmothers coped in hot places like Africa and India with their corsets, umpteen petticoats, mutton chop sleeves, stockings, and buttoned-up shoes and boots. They did not even have fans let alone cool loose clothes. We are very soft by comparison.

These pioneering women lived in appalling conditions. They had no fridges and no cold drinks. They cooled their water by hanging it in canvas bags under trees to catch the breeze. (On long car journeys when the children were small and always wanting a drink, we always hung a canvas water bag on the front bumper as a precaution against running out.) I feel not enough recognition has been given to the pioneering women of the early colonial era. There are a few books about them, but they deserve a lot more attention and admiration. The men mostly went out by choice or through a sense of adventure, but the women mostly went because it was the only way they could be with their husbands. I am sure if some had known what conditions they were to meet, they would have chosen not to go.

I feel we owe them all a great debt of gratitude for making the way easier for us later. I felt privileged to be a colonial wife. In some ways being brought up in South Africa made the transition easier, for I was used to the climate, though to move from Singapore with all the modern conveniences of the 1950s to Nyasaland, which had not yet caught up with the contemporary world, seemed slightly ridiculous. But what Nyasaland lacked in material comforts it made up for with beautiful scenery and, by offering a simple healthy life with few distractions and a well-balanced outlook on the world, it was an ideal place to bring up children.

Grocery shopping was difficult. We had one general store owned by the African Lakes Company (ALC), a firm that dates back to David Livingstone's days, which is known throughout Nyasaland as Mandala, the Chinyanja word for glasses. (The first man to open an ALC shop apparently wore glasses and the name stuck.) Mandala had very little fresh food other than spasmodic local supplies. When the occasional consignment of fresh English sausages arrived, the news spread like wildfire (bush wireless) and everybody would rush down to buy their pound or two, which they would cook with the utmost care. Mandala did its best, but when a co-op started up in Blantyre, we all joined and I used to have a monthly order, for it was a much cheaper way of shopping for non-perishables. A large trunk like box with a padlock (we had one key and the co-op had the other) would be transported to and from Blantyre on a Land Rover or lorry to be filled or emptied either end with products such as soap powder, flour, sugar and tea. When we were first in Lilongwe, our fresh milk was delivered by bicycle in a whisky bottle with a dry corncob as a cork. This milk had to be boiled, and Merilyn grew up hating milk. When she got to school in England she was amazed at how nice the milk was when delivered in proper bottles from a properly run dairy. Those who subscribed to the *Daily Telegraph* could barter it for eggs, vegetables or fruit — and the Africans found the airmail edition ideal for rolling their own cigarettes.

Apart from my enormous size, I seemed to be coping well with my pregnancy. I made and iced a Christmas cake and made mince-meat for dozens of mince pies. I took Merilyn to various children's Christmas parties at her nursery school, the police mess and the club. It was all very jolly. Then one of Trevor's young policemen fell ill and we took him to the cottage hospital, where he was put into an iron lung straight away — he had polio. Trevor stayed with him until about 11.00 p.m. and at 1.00 a.m. he died.

It was a great shock — so sudden and fierce, so sad. But life carried on. It was Christmas and parties had been arranged. I did not go to the next party as my feet were so swollen and so were my legs, right up to my bottom. I had toxaemia but the silly young doctor did not realize and just told me to rest. Then Trevor's other young officer became ill and was taken to hospital — but thank goodness it was not polio and he recovered in a day or two. A few days later there were three cases of polio, one European and two Africans. The children's Christmas party at the club was cancelled and an air of gloom set in. The staff at the training school held their Christmas party and although I was invited I really did not feel up to it. Trevor went and I went to bed.

At 3.00 a.m. I woke up to realize that I was in labour about six weeks early. I woke Trevor and he could hardly believe me. He dressed, called the nanny to be with Merilyn and took me up to the hospital, which was situated on the slopes of Zomba Mountain with a view over Zomba town and the valley beyond.

The sisters made me very comfortable and at 11.45 a.m. Simon was born and at 12.15 p.m. on 23 December Christopher made his entry into the world. The horrid doctor I disliked so much for-tunately did not arrive in time and Alice, the dear old African midwife, delivered my babies with the help of Sister Mason. It was such a shock for Trevor to have *two* sons at once. Merilyn was thrilled and bragged to her friends at nursery school 'My mummy has had two babies and your mummy only has one.' She has always been able to turn things to her advantage.

Soon after the boys were born I was back in my ward and a nice doctor and senior sister came to talk. I thought they looked rather serious and my first thought was that something was wrong with one of my babies. No, they were perfect except for one thing. They were premature and there were no facilities for premature babies in Zomba and anyway they did not want me stay with two vulnerable little babies in the same cottage hospital as a polio patient in an iron lung. The premature babies would need special nursing and the polio patient needed special nursing and the nurses should not swap from one special case to another. Simon weighed 5 lbs 4 oz and Christopher 4 lbs and it was he about whom they were particularly concerned. They wanted me to go to Blantyre hospital, 40 miles away, where I would be away from the polio and the babies could be looked after properly. (There was no such thing then as a special care baby unit.) They suggested it would be more comfortable if Trevor drove us in our car rather than the not very comfortable ambulance. Trevor was summoned and the situation explained and at 11.00 a.m. the next morning the babies (not yet 24 hours old) and I were bundled into the Plymouth. Simon in my carrycot with hot-water bottles and another carrycot, also lined with hot-water bottles, appeared from somewhere for Christopher; one of the sisters accompanied us and we set off. I sat in front with Merilyn on my lap and the sister on the back seat with a carrycot either each side, making sure my babies came to no harm.

On arrival at Blantyre hospital (the old one not the posh new Queen Elizabeth) they were astonished to see these two tiny little babies, for they had not been told that the babies were premature, only that I was being sent over with my twins because of the polio. It was action stations! The hospital could only produce one incubator and it was decided that Christopher should be put in it immediately. Luckily for me there were no other babies in the baby ward, so they made it as warm and comfortable as possible for Simon. I was given a single ward about two doors down the passage. The next drama was that I could not produce a drop of milk. I was crying with disappointment and being made to drink gallons of water, juice and Guinness, but no milk came. Now I know that is was because of my toxaemia and that if that silly doctor had had any idea of how to treat me, it would not have happened. My disappointment turned rapidly to anxiety, for both boys were losing more weight than was good for them, there was no wet nurse (when Merilyn was born I fed about four little Asian babies by pump) and the bottle feed recommended by the doctor did not seem to be doing much good. Then, to my delight, a new sister just out from the Great Ormond Street Hospital came to me and said 'With your permission I would like to alter your babies' feed as I can get them to gain weight. Will you back me against the doctor because I am going to ignore his instructions?' I told her to go ahead and do whatever was necessary to make my babies thrive and I would cope with the doctor (an old friend from early Lilongwe days who drove round in a yellow and black Rolls Royce). I had total confidence in this sister and she changed their feed to ordinary sticky sweet Nestlé condensed milk, suitably diluted. Simon and Christopher never looked back. What a relief.

It was quite fun in the hospital after that. I was made a great fuss of and received lots of visitors; the only snag was that the hospital would not allow Merilyn in to see me. So when Trevor visited he brought Merilyn and Nanny and I would sneak out to the car to see her. The first time I did this, she looked at me in an unbelieving sort of way and said 'Are you really my mummy?' This broke my heart, one is weepy anyway after having given birth; I burst into tears, hugged her and told her 'of course I'm your mummy and always will be.'

Trevor and I had only vaguely discussed names. If Merilyn had been a boy, he would have been Jeremy and we had a few ideas, but nothing definite. The sisters said 'you must have names; we can't go on calling them Bevan Baby I and Baby Bevan II.' I rather liked the name Ben (strong Rice family connections) but Trevor did not — but that made me think of Bill and Ben the flowerpot men on BBC television and, being skinny little premature babies, they did rather resemble flowerpot men. So their temporary names became Bill and Ben to satisfy the sisters. Eventually Bill became Simon and Ben became Christopher.

As I was unable to feed my babies and my swollen limbs had returned to normal I began to think of going home. But home was a long way from Blantyre hospital and I was loath to leave my babies behind. The next day when Trevor came to see me, to my amazement and pleasure, Ma was with him. He had sent her a telegram saying 'TWO MALES ARRIVED UNEXPECTEDLY, YOUR HELP URGENTLY REQUIRED' and Ma arranged for everyone in Bonza Bay to look after Pa so she could fly up to Blantyre to cope. She was speechless with joy when she was shown her two grandsons.

On New Year's Day 1957 I was allowed to go home, but I felt as though I were leaving part of myself behind, which I was. I had an unreal feeling, which is difficult to describe. It was lovely having Ma to stay and I was rather spoilt. I was waited on hand and foot, had breakfast in bed and in no time was back to normal, seeing lots of friends and wallowing in congratulations and gifts. The oddest gift of all was a tea chest of baby clothes and bottles from Save the Children Fund (SCF). I was a bit taken aback, as I had ample clothes and Trevor had bought a second set of nappies. At the bottom of the chest I found a dozen Pyrex feeding bottles, which I kept, but returned all the clothes because there were many mothers in far greater need than I was. The bottles were a godsend, for they were difficult to buy locally, but I did return all 12 when Simon and Christopher had grown out of bottle feeds.

There were no more polio cases and the two hospitals thought it would be safe to bring the babies back to Zomba as they were no longer on the critical list and doing well on condensed milk. I had telephoned each day to hear how they were. So, about the middle of February, we went to Blantyre to fetch our sons. This time I was in the back with the two babies and Ma and Merilyn in front with Trevor. It rained cats and dogs — a real tropical downpour and Trevor had quite an anxious drive. We got the boys safely to Zomba hospital and it was nice having them nearer and being able to feed them and get used to a routine — they were doing well. Simon came home after ten days and was fine; Christopher took a little longer to reach the desired weight of 5 lbs before he was allowed home at the end of February.

Everything in the nursery bedroom was now doubled up — the PWD had produced *two* side-drop cots without even being asked and as I already had Merilyn's old one and one other, I had the luxury of two cots in their bedroom and two on the *khonde* (veranda) for their daytime naps. Because Simon and Christopher are identical twins, when their body weights equalled, they were very much alike to look at. I claim I never made a mistake, but Trevor had great difficulty telling them apart when they were small and threatened to brand their bottoms.

They may be alike (and still are) in looks but different in temperament and character. Simon bellowed the minute he woke up to signal that he needed feeding instantly. Christopher would just lie there when he woke up and let Simon do the bellowing. At about ten months they both showed signs of thumb sucking. As Merilyn sucked her two fingers, I could not bear the idea of them all going round sucking their thumbs and fingers, so reluctantly I introduced dummies to the boys, but only let them use them when they were in their cots and ready to go to sleep. They both soon got the message. When they began to walk I gritted my teeth and took their dummies away. Simon stood at the bottom of his cot and screamed with rage (shaking the cot) for about two hours. Christopher just gave me a withering look and put his thumb straight back in his mouth and went to sleep. Simon went to sleep the next day quietly and has *never* sucked his thumb or fingers.

They grew into beautiful babies and when Nanny took them out in their side-by-side pushchair, they caused quite a stir. Nanny adored them and was very proud of her charges. She was excellent with Merilyn too, so we were so lucky to have someone like her.

Ma had helped me enormously when the babies were allowed home and as they were still very small and hungry we were feeding them two or three times during the night. Although Ma loved being with her baby grandsons she began to fret about leaving Pa by himself for so long. Once she was home in Bonza Bay she would not want to fly back again too quickly for their christening, so we decided to have the christening before Ma returned to Pa.

A friend of Ma's had given me a beautiful length of really old lace and I had not known what to do with it, but now it came into its own and I made an 'instant heirloom' christening robe. Unfortunately, there was not enough for two robes, but we were able to borrow a second one. Ma made a magnificent christening cake and a private christening was organized in St George's church, Zomba — a dear little church with a not so dear vicar. However, we could not change him, so the christening went ahead. It was quite a feat finding enough godparents, for there were precious few who could be at the service. When the vicar would not allow us to have our oldest and nearest friends in Nyasaland, a Roman Catholic couple (we are Church of England), as godparents, we were furious — so much for ecumenical movement. (This would not happen today, I am sure.) There was one other snag. It rained like only a tropical rainstorm can and there was quite a long pathway from the car park to the church and I was concerned about the babies getting damp and cold. Anyway, despite the vicar and the weather we had a happy service and no crying babies. We then all went home to christening cake, champagne and tea, with the main objective of having Ma present having been achieved.

When the boys had doubled their birth weight and were making good progress, the sister who had advised Nestlé condensed milk now suggested changing to Lactogen milk powder. This we did and the prescribed formula did not seem to satisfy Simon or Christopher — so I was advised to increase the powder to the same amount of water, until they did seem satisfied and did not bellow between meals. I learnt the hard way and eventually I found I had to double the prescribed amount per bottle before these two hungry little boys were satisfied. Life was a lot easier then and easier still when they began to take solids. I am not going to bore my readers with a detailed account of raising premature twin babies in the outback, but just to say that having twins who were developing at different paces was utterly fascinating. From about five months they became individual characters and were happy and well. Simon mastered rolling over, crawling and walking a little ahead of Christopher and when Christopher began to crawl, Simon was *terribly* thrilled and shrieked with delight. Up to then Simon had usually very sweetly brought toys to Christopher so that he was not left out.

In 1957 Her Majesty the Queen Mother and HRH the Princess Margaret visited Nyasaland and of course stayed at Government House in Zomba. To cope with the extra police guard and escort duties during the royal tour, Trevor was roped in to help. This was an exciting time for us all, for with so few expatriates we all had really good close-up views of the royal party. It goes without saying that everyone loved the Queen Mother. Whenever there was a break in her official schedule, she would ask to go up Zomba Mountain to pick flowers. She has a collection of wild flowers, which she presses. The road up Zomba Mountain was steep and twisty and, about halfway up, became one way. Traffic went up on the half hour and down on the hour and there were large clocks standing on the roadside displaying this regulation. But this was abandoned for the Queen Mother and the road was cleared and closed to the public. Most of the wild flowers on Zomba Mountain are protected, so who better to pick them than the Queen Mother? Many of these flowers only grow at high altitudes, so are rare species. Flame lilies, arum lilies, orchids, gladioli, red sesame, cannas and many other varieties grow here on a well-wooded plateau 4000 feet above sea level. This must have been a welcome break for the Queen Mother, free from protocol and endless handshakes.

* * *

In October 1957 we faced another move, this time to Limbe in the Southern Province near Blantyre. Limbe was the main railway depot for Nyasaland and from there the line went as far as Chipoka on the lake; then a branch line continued to Salima in the Central Province. With tobacco being Nyasaland's main export and very important to its economy, Limbe was also famous for its tobacco auction floors, and Imperial Tobacco, Gallagher and some smaller companies had their headquarters there. The town had a thriving club and golf course, was well wooded and was a pleasant place in which to live. Because the house we were allocated had been built on a steep slope and was starting to slide down into the Cholo Road below, which had been cut through a forest of gum trees, the PWD had built three substantial flying buttresses (as you see on cathedrals) to keep it in position. The floors in the two front bedrooms had been levelled shortly before we moved in, but the previous occupants had gone to sleep with their beds next to the inside walls and woken up under the windows of the outside walls. I suspect that the problem was more than just subsidence and that the foundations were too shallow. Anyway, we moved in and settled down to life in Limbe.

We knew quite a few people in Limbe and Blantyre, so had a fairly full social life with tennis at the club and the usual round of drinks parties, dinners and dances.

When the boys were about 16 months' old, we decided to take a family holiday at Lake Nyasa. Several people owned holiday cottages on the lake's western shore between Fort Johnstone and Salima and some even right up to the north of the lake some 400 miles away. We had friends with a nice cottage between Fort Johnstone and Monkey Bay and they agreed to let it to us for three weeks in May 1958. Organizing the logistics for such a holiday took some doing. We had to borrow a paraffin fridge and a lorry in which to transport everything we needed — tinned and dry food, tea, coffee, drinks, water filter, bedding, pots and pans, two cots, two highchairs and double rations of baby food. We also took Nanny and William, along with all their paraphernalia. All this planning was well worth it as we had one of the most relaxing holidays I can ever remember. The cottage was only a few yards from the water and we spent the whole of every day on the beach — all wearing hats and smothered in Nivea Cream, which was the only cream available. The three children were in their element splashing in the lake's warm water and it was, I remember, where Chris learnt to walk. We lived a simple life going to bed soon after dark (we only had paraffin lamps) and rising early. Trevor did quite a lot of fishing, so fresh fish was often on the menu.

The nextdoor cottage belonged to the Peterkins — a long-established, well-respected couple who lived outside Limbe on the Cholo Road and who ran a herd of pedigree Jersey cows. We overlapped with them for a week, which was very enjoyable. They invited us to pick fruit from their highly productive citrus orchard (and there is nothing nicer than fresh lemon with fresh fish) and Mr Peterkin took Trevor out fishing on the lake in his motorboat, which he thoroughly enjoyed.

One day we drove up the unspeakably bad lakeside road to Cape McClear where a swanky hotel had been built to cater for the Imperial Airways (forerunner to BOAC and BA) flying boat service, which touched down there *en route* between Lake Victoria and the Vaal River near Johannesburg. This wonderful form of travel did not last long and the hotel rapidly deteriorated. Trevor said that a flying boat was a really 'classy' way to travel and the most comfortable.

It was time for Merilyn to begin proper school and, on asking around Limbe, La Sargesse convent seemed to be the most suitable choice. So we made arrangements to go and meet the Reverend

Mother and have a look around. I made the appointment over the phone and spoke to the Reverend Mother.

When we arrived, a nun whom I presumed was the Reverend Mother met us in a very austere waiting room. Meanwhile, unbeknown to me, Trevor had met the Reverend Mother in the course of his duties. So here I was on my best behaviour saying 'Yes Reverend Mother, No Reverend Mother'. I thought Trevor was behaving rather strangely, for he kept appearing from behind a pillar or door and mouthing something at me and pointing to the nun who was showing us round. I could not lipread, but what he was trying to get across to me was, 'Say yes Sister, not Reverend Mother.' As this was not the Reverend Mother showing us round I was made to feel I had blotted my copybook. When the penny dropped and I apologized to the Sister, she laughed and said that she did not mind being called Reverend Mother.

I made Merilyn's school uniform, a blue checked gingham dress with royal blue bolero and navy blue felt hat. She already knew a few children at the school, so it was less of a shock than it might otherwise have been, and she started the day after her fifth birthday party on 27 January 1959.

Before I took on Africans to work in the house or garden I always sent them to the hospital for a checkup in case they were carrying a disease that could be passed on to the children or to Trevor and me. Although I did most of the cooking myself, I took on Julius to help prepare vegetables, wash up and, in particular, to refuel the Dover stove mini range regularly with logs to keep up the temperature. So, when Julius came back from the hospital with a clean bill of health, I confirmed his appointment. Soon afterwards Simon and Christopher began to develop runny tummies with occasional vomiting. This happened too often for comfort, but their specimens did not seem to reveal anything untoward. Then, when Julius said he felt unwell and did not turn up for work on several occasions, we arranged for him to go back to the hospital for more tests. He turned out to have amoebic dysentery, for which he was given medication. However, since he was not very good about washing his hands, was not taking his medicine regularly and the babies were still getting bouts of runny tummy, I decided he must leave. I suggested he follow his medical instructions properly somewhere else, for he was too much of a risk to my family, and when he was clear I would give him a reference for a job. He went back to his village and we lost contact, but Simon and Christopher did not have any more tummy troubles.

Endemic diseases run rife among Africans and I felt that if people were in my house handling my children and our food, I needed to be sure that they were fit. It was the least I owed to my family. Many colleagues did not take these precautions and thought I was being very harsh, but I disagreed. The treatment was free and it was surely in the African's interest to be rid of diseases.

Malaria, bilharzia, dengue fever and measles presented enough of a danger without introducing extra hazards. We protected ourselves from malaria with prophylactics and nets, avoided bilharzia by not swimming in stagnant water or walking through tall wet grass, and fortunately never contracted dengue fever, a violent mosquito-borne disease. But it was important to keep fit and to eat a balanced diet with lots of fresh fruit, vegetables, fish and meat.

One night a burglar decided to relieve us of about six of our laying hens and had trussed them all up in a sack ready to remove. He then decided to break into the kitchen for some food. He took a bite out of the butter pat in the fridge — leaving his tooth marks to prove it — and removed several other items to eat later. He then went to the pantry, where Trevor kept his photograph developing and printing paraphernalia, and took a swig of fixing lotion. Being a clear liquid in a large bottle, he obviously thought it was gin and it made him violently sick. So, abandoning his loot, including the bag of trussed-up hens, he fled out of the backdoor and down the drive leaving a trail of vomit in his wake. We slept throughout and so did our watchdog Minnie.

Our friend Frank Scot, who lived on a farm, asked if we had ordered our Christmas turkey yet and when we said we hadn't, he said 'don't. I'll send you one'. A few nights before Christmas a battered taxi drew up in the pouring rain and pitch dark with two bedraggled turkeys in a basket strapped to the roof rack. We got the birds down and put them into the outside kitchen to dry out. It might have been kinder to slaughter them then and there, but I did not feel like being a butcher in the dead of night. They were dispatched and plucked the following day — and good eating they were too. We had one and gave the other to Nanny, William and Lloyd, for there were no deepfreezes yet.

But we had moved forward. The PWD had installed an electric cooker and that really was progress. I could now dispense with a stoker for the cooker. With the Dover stove now redundant, the outside kitchen became a dumping ground for all manner of items, including two very wet turkeys.

With my new Belling cooker, meals could be far more varied and exciting. Cakes turned out reliably and we even had a grill. The oven kept an even temperature and we could have cheese soufflé for supper. At last my domestic science cooking training was coming into its own. A large heavy-based cast aluminium saucepan, a smaller one and a large family-sized heavy-based frying pan were supplied with the cooker, which would be unheard of these days. I have recently (40 years later) given the two saucepans to my daughter to use on her Aga stove, for they are just the same as the old Aga cast aluminium ones.

One feature of having twin boys is that if one child hurts himself, as sure as eggs are eggs the other will get hurt in more or less the same way shortly afterwards. Once, when all three children had measles at the same time and Trevor had just left for the office, I was putting Simon into his highchair for his breakfast porridge (Nanny was doing the same for Christopher) and for some unknown reason I turned round to reach for his bib before I had strapped him in. In a flash he had leapt out of his highchair and fallen head first on the cross bands of Chris's chair and cut his eye just below his eyebrow, obviously seriously because his eye was drooping. I held Simon (who was screaming blue murder) while Nanny fetched a face flannel rinsed in cold water, held it on Simon's face and took him from me. I phoned Trevor who came straight back to take us to the casualty department at the Queen Elizabeth Hospital, leaving Nanny to cope with Chris and Merilyn. When we arrived, the doctor took us to the theatre, where he administered a local injection and stitched Simon up. Simon had a very swollen and bruised face for a number of days, but on the whole was very good. About eight days later he had the stitches out and the wound had healed beautifully. It took some time to lose the redness and for many years afterwards, whenever he got very hot, the scar showed. As an adult his eyebrows began to spread and you cannot see anything now, but at that stage it made it easy to tell the twins apart. There was more to follow.

Trevor had put up a swing in the garden for the children. Merilyn had been practising her latest trick, which was to 'fly' off the swing while it was still quite high, and had landed beautifully and walked off with the swing still swinging on its own. At that moment Chris happened to walk past and, bang, the swing caught him on the bridge of his nose and cut him quite badly. Thank God it missed his eyes. There was another rush to the hospital for a stitch or two, but this time it was late afternoon so Trevor was home. So here we were with two little boys both with scars on their faces — strangers now had to remember which scar was which child's, for Simon's solo identification had not lasted long.

We did not own a cine camera — Trevor preferred stills and doing his own developing and printing. However, we thought it would be nice for Ma and Pa to have moving pictures of their grandchildren, so we asked Jo and Alison (my childhood friend who now lived in Blantyre and still kept horses and rode every day) if they would come and take a film of the children playing in the garden if we bought the cine film (super 8). They readily agreed and we arranged a day for filming. Luckily it was a nice sunny afternoon and all went well with Nanny, Minnie, Merilyn, the boys and occasionally Trevor and me all filmed for posterity. It was a great success and many years later, long after Ma and Pa had died, I had the cine film adapted to a video and I play it now sometimes — and am filled with nostalgia.

Apart from the social round of cocktail parties, dinners and lunches, we had regular weekly entertainment, either a film or amateur play, at the Limbe Club. Some productions were excellent and there were several very talented and dedicated people around. Trevor once took part in a production of Terence Rattigan's *See How They Run* at the Lilongwe Club in the early days, which, given the circumstances, including a makeshift stage, was an enormous achievement.

While we were in Limbe, we often drove into the country on Sundays for a picnic at Mlanje or tea with the Ward family at Mikalongwe. Ken was livestock improvement officer and his job entailed introducing suitable and proven cattle strains to the local indigenous cattle breeds to increase their fertility and to produce better beef and more milk. This was a Colonial Office initiative and another officer was doing the same for chickens. All this tied in with efforts to improve farming, crops and yields on the Mikalongwe Estate and generally to teach correct husbandry and stock management. Africans in Nyasaland were natural farmers, but were loath to cull because numbers equalled wealth. Consequently, far too many weedy unproductive animals overstocked the grazing. The Ward children (two girls and two boys) and my children are still friends (I stayed with Felicity and Mike in Botswana in 1997). When Jo was due in 1958 Beryl decided that, as it was her fourth baby, she had no need to go to Blantyre hospital and would be happier nearer home. She chose the rather poorly equipped Ngaludi mission hospital and I remember her taking out her needle and thread to mend the holes in her mosquito net. Jo was born without any hitches and Beryl returned to Mikalongwe within a couple days. Beryl said the only thing that stopped her having another child was the thought of reading all those Noddy books for the fifth time.

Between Limbe/Blantyre and Zomba the lie of the land was reasonably flat, but to the east of the road, about 12 miles from Limbe, Chiradzula Mountain stood out as a landmark. There was a police post, a district commissioner and not much else, but on this Sunday in mid-October there was a most horrific air crash with no survivors. Trevor was alerted and immediately collected as many men as he could to rush out to Chiradzula. Chileka airport was due west of Chiradzula and the plane took off due east for Mozambique. With a heat haze and smoke from burning grass, visibility was poor and the plane just flew into the mountain. Debris was scattered everywhere. It was a Portuguese plane that had just refuelled at Chileka and nobody seemed to know much about it, or even how many people had been on board. Communications in those days (1958) were not very good. This was the first time we had been directly involved in a plane crash and it was not a nice feeling. Trevor and others had to bag up bits of bodies to be repatriated for identification; it was gruesome work.

* * *

With political unrest sweeping across Africa after Macmillan's 'Wind of Change' speech in Cape Town, Dr Banda was being hailed as the Messiah to lead Nyasaland to freedom. He was a qualified doctor and, on his return from London, he opened a surgery in Limbe. Because he chose to live and work there, the political hotheads in Limbe were constantly agitating, holding meetings and paying him visits. Trevor got to know him quite well. Banda became a well-known figure in his black homburg, three-piece suit and walking stick/fly whisk. He was a dapper man.

At about this time we decided to escape for a few days in an attempt to repeat the happy time we had had at the lake as a family. We took a different cottage, at Nkudzi Bay, on the same stretch of beach between Fort Johnstone (Palm Beach) and Cape McClear, but it was a disaster from the minute we arrived. The place was absolutely filthy and almost uninhabitable. People had been sick (and more) without making any attempt to clean up. The mattresses stank and it was awful. We cleaned and tidied up a bit, so that at least we could sleep that night. It was November and extremely hot, and the huge ironstone rocks that enclosed Nkudzi Bay gave off even more heat. The sand was so hot at midday that we got blisters on our feet from running between the house and the water. Then, when the boys seemed poorly, we decided to cut our losses and pack up and leave. It took the children three to four days to recover — they had picked up some bug despite my attempts to clean up — and even Trevor was not 100 per cent for a few days. It was a catastrophic holiday.

* * *

One of the highlights of the year was the ball given by the KAR at its mess in Zomba. Colonel Pat Lewis and the officers of the regiment had sent us an invitation, so we arranged for Nanny to sleep in the house with the children while Trevor and I went to the ball. Trevor looked very smart in his mess kit with monkey jacket, miniature medals, gabardine overalls (shaped trousers with one-and-a-half-inch braid down each side seam), shiny patent leather mess boots and spurs. He was entitled to wear spurs because he had served in a mounted unit (BSAP) and I felt very proud of him.

We joined other police friends to make up a jolly party. It was, as always, a splendid evening and the KAR band excelled itself. There were numerous beautifully decorated bars; there was a champagne bar, several beer bars, a wine bar and a black velvet bar. This was Trevor's favourite party drink (half Guinness half champagne) and towards midnight I lost him. When I found him again he was mixing black velvet in a bucket and serving it with a soup ladle and thoroughly enjoying himself, as was everyone else. At dawn we were served mulligatawny soup, and eggs and bacon and the hard core, which included Trevor, tucked into this feast. Eventually, it really was time to leave, so we lined up to shake Colonel Lewis's hand and to thank him for a delightful night. For some reason, Trevor had been in front of me to say his goodbyes. I saw him put one foot (still with spurs) on the top rung of a flight of about 20 narrow steps and then, to my horror, collapse in a heap and roll down to the bottom; his spurs had tripped him up. Once I realized that he was not hurt, I decided to pretend not to know him as I made my departure in as dignified and ladylike a manner as I could manage. We made our way to the car and he was in no fit state to drive, but he insisted on driving out of the car park and past the mess in case anyone saw him *not* at the wheel. As one might imagine, in his state it took a long time to manoeuvre safely through the mass of cars. I was very patient and did not utter a word; he managed to drive shakily past the mess and, as soon as we were out of sight, he stopped, climbed into the back seat and instantly fell asleep. I then drove back to Limbe in brilliant sunshine. As I pulled up at the back door, which we tended to use more than the front one because it was on the same level as the drive, William met me and asked 'Where is the *bwana?*' Trevor was still fast asleep on the back seat and carried on sleeping for most of that day. I couldn't indulge in such a luxury because I felt it was only fair to give Nanny the day off, but I went to bed with the children at about 6.00 p.m.

Christmas was fast approaching and my usual culinary preparations were going well. My old governess, who was now housemistress at Whitestones Preparatory School near Bulawayo, was coming to spend Christmas with us. My brother Dick arrived at the same time. He was still in Northern Rhodesia, but had detached himself from the fiancée of whom Ma so disapproved and had come to us for a bit of a break.

✳ ✳ ✳

Politically, things were heating up. There were frequent unruly gatherings, disturbances and some arrests, and it began to get very unpleasant. Although the Central African Federation of Southern Rhodesia, Northern Rhodesia and Nyasaland still held, the writing was on the wall for independence and for the break-up of the federation. Southern Rhodesia had been a self-governing colony since 1923 and self supporting financially, it had never had a penny from the British government, whereas Northern Rhodesia and Nyasaland were heavily dependent on financial support from HMG, especially Nyasaland, which could not sustain itself on its tobacco and tea exports. Northern Rhodesia had the wealth of the copper mines, so for as long as the world price of copper held up, it was in a far stronger position to become independent.

Because Dr Banda lived in Limbe we had more than our fair share of disturbances and crowd problems, which meant a lot of extra work for Trevor. Having had to cope with similar situations in Mogadishu in Somaliland in the early 1940s and again in Singapore in the late 1940s, Trevor was more experienced than most of his colleagues in this type of policing. Several people noted how calm Trevor's police districts and stations were during tricky (riot) situations because everybody knew exactly what to do and Trevor was always there in the control room overseeing everything. But we saw less and less of him at home. He frequently did not get home until 11.00 p.m. or midnight and was up and off as early as 6.30 most mornings. The children were missing not having him around in the afternoons and evenings, which was when he used to play with them. I remember Merilyn asking 'When am I going to see my daddy?' He left the house each morning before they were awake and returned when they were fast asleep in bed.

To make things easier for the police because they had limited numbers, a curfew was imposed. This made it safer for the likes of us, for the police then knew where we were. It was also decided that all European wives and children in outlying districts, on farms and in isolated DC *bomas* should be collected and put in one place for their own protection. A notice was sent round to all the families that a vehicle would come at a stated time to collect them and a few vital items — there would be no room for grand pianos. The plan was duly put into operation and my friend Helen York (Police, Cholo) was collected. When all the women and children were deposited at their safe address, they began to unpack and compare experiences. When Helen unpacked she was dismayed to find that she had brought a hammer, a pair of plastic overshoes and not much else. We laughed so much when she told us this after peace had returned. She said she just could not think straight. Some took their jewels and others their wills.

With Southern Rhodesia having experienced similar troubles and civil disobedience, and our police and army too small to maintain law and order, as soon as the manpower could be spared a contingent of BSAP was sent to Nyasaland to help. It was quite exciting to watch the BSAP arriving with armoured cars coming up the Cholo Road past our house.

Ma, who had come to stay with us during February, was intrigued by the goings on. She had never seen or been near anything like such a situation in her quiet sheltered life and found the arrival of the BSAP convoy particularly exciting. Ma had a friend on a farm outside Limbe who ran a dairy herd and supplied us, among others, with fresh TT (TB-tested) milk delivered daily. We had agreed that Mary Good could collect Ma the following day and take her to her farm for a few days. Trevor had said that he would be much happier if we postponed her visit and that it was not a good idea to move about unnecessarily (we had about two hours of non-curfew time for shopping and taking children to school), but Ma seemed reluctant to accept his advice. I thought there must be something in the wind, but knew better than to ask.

Trevor's policy was to tell me things *after* the event. He knew that if outsiders quizzed me (which they frequently did) I could then honestly say that I did not know.

✳ ✳ ✳

Next morning, 3 March 1959, Trevor mysteriously left home at 2.00 a.m. I did not ask any questions. A car drew up to collect him and I peeped through the bedroom curtains. It was not a police car, but I recognized Mr Peterkin who was a special constable. I knew he was reliable and wondered what they were up to. On leaving, Trevor told me to listen to the 7.00 a.m. news. Ma and I then learnt that Dr Banda had been arrested in his pyjamas, taken to Chileka airport and put on a plane for Southern Rhodesia. We

141

learnt later that his destination was Gwelo prison. There was a great commotion among his African supporters, with roadblocks and riots. Trevor came home eventually, very late and very tired.

Now I knew why Trevor had been reluctant to allow Ma to go to Mary's farm. There was a strict curfew that day, with no milk delivery and no school. We received instructions from the radio. There was much unrest, burning of the *boma* at Rumpi and riots at Karonga right up at the northern end of the lake, so the troubles were widespread. Many arrests were made and on one day 249 people were detained. Trevor was working at full stretch, as were all the security forces, and I see from my diary that Trevor was home for breakfast, lunch and supper, which was once since heaven knows when. He used mostly to return home at 10.00 or 11.00 p.m. with other officers, some local, some BSAP, and they would have a few beers to relax. I must have made dozens of omelettes at midnight. Thank goodness we had chickens.

To add to the drama, our neighbours Mary and Jon Dennison were expecting their first child and Jon, who was one of Trevor's better officers (ex-BSAP) and spoke the local lingo perfectly, was being sent to Mlanje because of the manpower shortage. He was very upset about it, for his daughter was born in the middle of the troubles while he was away. Anyway, Mary coped; we all helped and did her shopping. The situation calmed down with the main ringleaders in custody and life began to return to normal. The children went back to school with an escort for the normal school run and guards round the school buildings. Jon was able to return to Limbe and meet his daughter, much to his and Mary's relief.

During the curfew I knitted about six jerseys, for I had to do something. Ma decided it was time she went back to Bonza Bay and to Pa. Of course she dined out for weeks on her experiences in Nyasaland during the troubles.

The BSAP was still helping out, swelling the security numbers and we managed to get about six of them to dinner one evening. It was a great party. There is something special about BSAP men; they have all got that extra something. The social round soon sprang back to life — drinks parties, dinners, cinema at the club, friends to lunch, and tennis. We were back to normal and began to think about our six-month leave.

1. Granny Rice in her wedding veil, 22 July 1868.

2. Merilyn wearing Granny Rice's veil at her own wedding, 12 May 1979.

3. *(right)* Author (in Granny Rice's veil) and Trevor at their wedding, 10 November 1951.
4. *(below)* All loaded up for the game reserve.

5. *(above)* Trevor, Sir Edmund Hillary, Lady Hillary and Hunt at Singapore airport.
6. *(below)* Rab Butler and Trevor at Singapore airport.

7. *(above)* Sir Robert Armitage and Trevor, Limbe tobacco auction floor.
8. *(below)* Chris, Nanny and Simon, Limbe.

* * *

With photographs, passport renewals and children's inoculations up to date, in the middle of May we flew out of Chileka airport bound for England. As we were on an overnight flight to London, I had previously asked our doctor for a knockout drug to give to Simon and Chris on the plane. He was reluctant at first, but I eventually convinced him that it was bad enough to have one baby crying all the time in a plane, but *two* was more than I was prepared to tolerate. He gave me some liquid and I gave them each a teaspoon after our evening meal and they slept the whole night. I put Chris on the floor and Simon and I (with the arm rests down) shared the three seats. Merilyn and Trevor were across the aisle. When we got on the plane (BOAC) there were two dinky cars in Simon and Chris's seats. That was travelling! All three were given BOAC Junior Jet Club logbooks and tins of sweets and all three kept up their logbooks until they left school and ceased flying to distant lands for their holidays. These contained the date of the flight, the flight number, departure and destination places, and number of hours and statute miles flown, and was signed by the captain of the flight. When the miles flown reached 25,000 they were given badges and on each flight there was a large tin of sweets in their seats. The last flight recorded in Simon and Christopher's logbook was to Malta when they were RAF cadets at school. They have a complete record of the total statute miles flown from their first flight in 1959 to their last BOAC Junior Jet Club flight in August 1974.

Shortly before we were due to go on leave, Trevor's foot was so painful that he could hardly put it on the ground and it seemed to be worse when he was overworked and tired, which could have been nature's way of telling him to slow down. Though variously diagnosed as arthritis, rheumatism, sprained tendon and ligament damage, the doctors seemed unable to help. While at home one day on his bed in great pain, I walked into the room with a cup of tea when he admonished me for shaking the bed and adding to his difficulties. I was quite shocked as, remember, the floors were solid cement, so there was no give and I could not have shaken the bed by walking across the room. I thought, right, I've had enough of this and walked (stormed) two houses up the road to where the doctor lived (Trevor had always insisted on going to the doctor on his own) and blew my top. The doctor was taken aback at my fury and at being accused of not doing anything for Trevor; he and a colleague arrived at the house shortly afterwards to find Trevor in some distress. They took away an enormous amount of blood under the direction of the Polish doctor and said they would let me know as soon as possible what they found. They did and to Trevor's mortification the condition was diagnosed as gout and Butazolidine was prescribed. (I discovered later that unscrupulous owners give this to their horses to make them jump higher.) Anyway, it calmed down the crisis and Trevor felt in control. When the painful spell was over he was put on Zyloric, which kept the gout manageable and he never had any more bad attacks.

Some weeks before leaving we had ordered and paid for a 403 Peugeot estate car to be at London airport to meet us. As we stepped into the arrival hall, we heard, 'Will Mr Bevan from BOAC flight 312 please come to the information desk.' Great, we thought, it must be to collect the keys of our new car. But no, it was to say that the car had been lost. The agent had received notice that it had left the French factory and had been dispatched to Gatwick airport as arranged. What were we to do? We took a taxi to our hotel in East Grinstead and sent the bill to the car agent. Our destination was a hotel in Blindley Heath, used by dozens of Nyasaland families on leave. The management were marvellous with children and would take complete care of them for a whole day to enable one to go up to London to shop in peace. Trevor and I took advantage of this service to collect our new car, which had now been found. (It had been shunted to a siding somewhere in northern France and forgotten.) We drove back to Blindley Heath delighted with our huge car — just the job for three kids and all their *katundu* (Chinanga for luggage).

Trevor needed rest and this we were able to have right away. Family friends had a holiday cottage near Rye on Camber Sands where we hibernated for a month. Trevor's sister was in England and came to live with us for a bit, but she wasn't used to children and there were some tense moments. The only cooking facility at the cottage was a Baby Belling and I had to cook for six. I was quite proud of my achievement and spent more time in front of the Baby Belling than on the beach.

Our month at Camber came to an end and we arranged to tour England and Scotland seeing friends and relations. It was a lot to ask friends to have five extra people to stay, so many visits were day trips, but good friends George and Margaret Hubert, who farmed at Bredon's Norton, had a big enough house to cope. They are godparents to Simon and we are godparents to their daughter Ellen. We had a lovely time on the farm, though Simon and Christopher disturbed the routine one afternoon by letting the pigs out of their sties. We had never heard such a row as pigs squealed, and directions and expletives were shouted, but at last peace and quiet was restored and the pigs were put back in their sties. I thought we would never be asked again. Margaret's father Bap, Sir Raymond Priestley, also lived with George and Margaret. He was an authority on the Antarctic and had been on both the Shackleton and Scott expeditions to the South Pole. Bap had been struggling with a geology thesis as an undergraduate at Clare College Cambridge when someone asked if he would like to join the Antarctic expedition. He said 'anything would be better than writing this thesis' and was taken on. This was on the *Terra Nova* between 1901 and 1904. Shackleton was on this exploration and Bap then accompanied him on the 1907–9 search of the South Pole on the *Endurance*. He was now an old man, a widower, and living quietly. He was marvellous with children and told them endless stories of his harrowing experiences. Unfortunately, though enthralled at the time, my children were too young to remember any detail, which is a pity because it was a privilege to hear these experiences at first hand. He was a lovely old man.

I remember one funny story in particular. When Prince Philip was on a world tour on the *Britannia*, Bap was asked to join him for the Antarctic leg — he was about the only person still living who had been with Scott and Shackleton and was considered to be an expert on the South Pole. Bap delighted in being called out of retirement to go back to the Antarctic. On walking along a beach one day, the party of men met thousands of penguins marching towards them — penguins have no fear of man. All of a sudden, when they were quite close, to a bird they turned round in an orderly way and waddled off. Prince Philip then said, 'They must have recognized you Bap and said, "good Lord, there's that b— man Bap again," and turned round.'

It was marvellous being on leave in the UK at that time and being able to make the most of the long hot summer of 1959. While paying a duty visit to Trevor's father in Wales, we stayed at a very pleasant country hotel at Llanrhystad in Cardigan Bay. The best thing about the hotel was that the children's bedroom still had blackout curtains from the war, which were perfect for blocking out the summer sun at 7.00 p.m. Another hangover from a bygone age was that we were charged a shilling (5p) for a bath.

We then drove further north to the Lake District and stayed at a B & B at Elterwater near Ambleside to break our journey to Kirkcudbright in Scotland. Aunt Puss had loaned us the use of her charming little cottage for a few weeks. Being next to the ruins of Kirkcudbright Castle was a source of great wonder to three small children who had read about ruined castles in their storybooks. The Preston bypass (M6) had recently been opened and we travelled its entire length. It was exciting because it was the first motorway to be built and the children were thrilled by its speed. The lovely hot summer continued and we spent many hours on the beach at Carrick, which was the nearest one to Kirkcudbright.

Trevor's boss from Singapore days had retired nearby, so we contacted him and were invited over for the day. It was good to see him and his wife again. Sayde McClean was one of the very few senior police wives I admired, for she was always caring and thoughtful towards us younger wives and Iain, I knew, thought very highly of Trevor and gave him every encouragement.

We then began our journey back to London calling on friends in Yorkshire and staying with old family friends at Eyam Hall in Derbyshire. Ma had grown up with Charles and Irene Wright, who lived in the seventeenth-century manor house, and the banns for Ma's marriage had been read at Eyam church in 1929 when Charles's father was the incumbent.

Eyam is known as the 'plague village' because of an outbreak there in 1665/6. London was riddled with plague at the time and a parcel of old clothes was sent from there to the local tailor, who caught the disease from the infected clothes and died. His cottage near the manor house and church is still known as plague cottage. To prevent the disease spreading, the rector sealed off the village. Food was left at an arranged spot outside the boundary and by October 1666 the village was clear of the plague.

146

While we were there we went to the Bakewell Show and saw Pat Smythe jumping, which I found very exciting because I had only ever seen pictures of her before. We also watched proper Bakewell tarts being made. While we were in Sheffield we called on Robert Haley's parents in Whitely Woods. Robert looks exactly like his father who grew magnificent roses, which we were duly shown. They gave us a warm welcome and we in turn were able to give them first-hand news of Robert and Lorna and their two girls Anne and Susan back in Nyasaland.

Our next stop was the Morton Court Hotel in London for last minute shopping and farewells to friends before embarking for South Africa from Tilbury docks on the *City of Durban*. There were only 99 passengers, so we had a pleasant voyage and the nursery, our main reason for choosing the Ellerman Line, was first class. There were 14 children, of whom 11 were under four. The approach to Cape Town was rough — the Atlantic rollers lived up to their name — and all three children were seasick and very miserable. My godmother Aunty Ba (Aileen de Villiers) met us at Cape Town docks and our precious Peugeot 403 was the third car out of 30 to be taken off the ship. We loaded up and drove to Fish Hoek to spend a few days with Aunty Ba and her daughter Roccoleen. We took two days to drive to Ma and Pa in Bonza Bay, spending the night at the Wilderness Hotel and making good time on South Africa's magnificent national roads. Having ample space in the car made travelling vast distances with three small children much easier. The boys were in the back and they slept, played or fought with each other; Merilyn had half the back seat to herself and her toys; Trevor and I sat in front; and our luggage was on the roof rack. We travelled thousands of miles this way. Apart from lots to drink, we always carried slabs of plain chocolate and ginger biscuits — and none of us was ever carsick. I read recently that ginger helped many people overcome travel sickness, but it was preference and luck as far as we were concerned.

We spent two enjoyable, relaxing and happy months with Ma and Pa in Bonza Bay with, weather permitting, every available hour spent on the beach. However, we felt that Merilyn was missing rather too much schooling, so we arranged for her to attend the local village state school. She knew several of the neighbours' children and quite enjoyed it. The amusing part of it was that, as a family, we all spoke with a colonial English accent, but since this little school had a strong Afrikaans influence, Merilyn spoke with a marked Afrikaans accent from Monday to Friday and with a colonial English accent at weekends.

Pa still kept up his riding and he and Elizabeth, who ran the nearby riding school, became great pals and Pa could go over and have a ride whenever he liked. I enjoyed being able to join him and we rode two to three times a week and had lovely gallops on the beach. When King George VI, Queen Elizabeth and the two princesses visited East London in 1947, it was from Elizabeth's stables that horses were chosen for the princesses to ride on Bonza Bay beach. Indeed, the main road through Bonza Bay was named 'Princess Drive' after this historic event. The royal family lived on the royal train the whole time they were in South Africa. For the East London leg, a special siding was constructed in a quiet picturesque spot at Bonza Bay where the train remained for several days to give the very poorly king a few days' rest, peace and quiet.

Soon it was time to pack up the car again and head north on our 2000-plus-mile journey back to Nyasaland. The journey was uneventful and we made good time. In Salisbury (Harare) we spent two nights with Angela (a Rice cousin) and Rosemary, who was later to become my sister-in-law. Trevor rushed round to see as many of his BSAP pals as he could before we set off on the last lap. On the afternoon of our departure from Southern Rhodesia we drove to Mtoko on the Mozambique border, where Trevor had been stationed in his BSAP days. We spent the night at the Mtoko hotel so that we could leave early and have the whole day to drive through Mozambique and negotiate the ferry at Tete over the Zambezi. This we did. The only snag was that a bee stung Merilyn on her nose on the ferry. Who would have believed it?

Another memory I have of Tete ferry was that among the African workers and beggars milling around while we waited for the ferry to reach our side was a woman (and I saw her more than once) with no hands, not because of leprosy but because they had been cut off. I don't know whether her crime had been theft or adultery, but she was an old woman and wore a cloth bag round her neck into which one put money, food or whatever. I am glad to say that this form of punishment was not practised in the British colonies.

Trevor had been posted as second in command in the Southern Province to live in Blantyre and, not for the first time, our house was not ready, so we were stuck in the Ryalls Hotel. Nanny and William turned up and I was very pleased to see them. The children were overjoyed to see Nanny again and there were hugs and smiles all round. Peter, the o/c Southern Province, suggested we move into his large house until our house was ready because it would be better for the children. When we did this, Nanny and William came too and life became much easier.

William had come to work for us in Limbe and had turned out to be a real treasure. He could do anything, was of the old school, and was as loyal and hard working as you would ever find in Africa. He had a special brand of English, which he spoke very well on the whole. If Simon and Christopher were fooling around, say, under a table or whatever, he used to say to them 'mind you will bang your headache'. Another was if I went out of the kitchen for something after having put a cake or batch of biscuits in the oven, when he thought they were ready he would call, 'Madam, I hear smelling.' Also, like all really good servants, he was a snob. If I said, 'William, we are just going to Mr and Mrs so and so for a sundowner and will be back for supper at 8.00 p.m.,' he would mumble something like, 'I don't know, always out and I never have an early evening off,' which I would ignore. But if I said, 'we are going to a cocktail party at Government House, he would say, 'that's all right madam, enjoy yourself. Don't worry about the children. Nanny and I will be here until you get back.'

With two such excellent servants and Lloyd the orderly, I was not very good at locking up my storeroom and sometimes if I had locked it I could not find the keys. If this happened, I would ask William and he always knew where they were. He would say 'look on the bookcase, hall table or wherever' and there they would be.

Just before we went on leave a memo came through to say that Lloyd was overdue for retirement and would Trevor see that PC Lloyd Finjani was pensioned off. Trevor called Lloyd into his office and explained the situation. Lloyd was furious. He said 'I only retire when you do, Sir, I'll refuse to retire before,' so Trevor of course kept him on as Lloyd was now part of our family.

The reaction at headquarters (or it may have been at the London Colonial Office) was that only the commissioner and assistant

149

commissioner were permitted to have orderlies and that the privilege was to be withdrawn from all ranks below. Trevor ignored the order and Lloyd saw us through to the end; his last job was semi-legitimate because Trevor was to become assistant commissioner. The children would have been heartbroken to lose him.

He was a real character. Since we had to do a certain amount of formal entertaining, in the early days we once asked him to help serve drinks at a cocktail party. As he carried the tray round, he stopped and chatted to each guest, enquiring about their children, latest car or whatever, and the drinks hardly got circulated — it really was very funny. He treated all our guests as his friends.

On another occasion a huge crowd had assembled to meet a VIP visiting Lilongwe. When the time came to go home, a traffic jam built up at a crossroads with huge transport lorries and visitors' cars wedged together. Because the normal volume of traffic was low, there were no traffic lights or give way signs. Trevor saw what was happening and, since Lloyd was with him, he sent him on to a road junction to divert the cars to another route, thus avoiding the jam. This actually made matters worse because Lloyd insisted on having a personal chat with every driver he recognized before waving them on to the diversion. Eventually, the traffic sorted itself out and everyone was very good-natured about it.

After a week of enjoying Peter and Gwenda Long's hospitality we moved to our new house. It was exactly the same design as the one we had left six months before in Limbe, but this one was on the flat with a really nice established garden (a vet had had it for the three previous years and had done wonders).

While we had been on leave Penny and Humphrey Courtenay, who lived quite near our new Blantyre house, had been kind enough to look after our spaniel Minnie. When we fetched her she seemed glad to see us, but kept disappearing back to Penny. After a week or two of dual loyalty she realized she was only going to be fed by me, so settled down and stopped roaming.

Life assumed a regular routine around Trevor's office hours and Merilyn's school commitments. Police work quietened down and, with all the hotheads in detention, things went more or less back to normal. Merilyn was now at St Andrew's School in Blantyre and the police families took it in turns to do the school run. Later we had a bus.

Before we knew what was happening, Christmas was upon us. The children's Christmas party at the police mess in Zombe had been arranged on the twins' third birthday, 23 December, so I was spared having to hold a children's birthday party. What a relief!

As we had only recently come back from our long leave, our friends made sure that we did not miss out on any Christmas festivities. We had 11.00 a.m. drinks with one family in Limbe, Christmas lunch at Mikalongwe with Ken and Beryl and their four children, and dinner in the evening with Helen and Jay York. All in all it was a jolly good Christmas. The twins were now old enough to appreciate Christmas and Merilyn loved it as much as ever. It was a lovely day to look back on — one of our happiest — 1959 had been such an eventful year.

The year 1960 started well. Trevor was awarded the Colonial Police Medal (gazetted in the New Year's Honours' List) and I was thrilled for him, for it was so richly deserved. The house was a running stream of friends coming in all day long to offer their congratulations. It had been a very exciting New Year's Day.

For my birthday on 7 January Trevor gave me a return air ticket to Salisbury for my brother's wedding on the 9th. Ma had flown up from East London (Pa said he was too old to move, which disappointed Dick) and she and Dick met me. There was a party that evening and, at 10.30 the next morning, Dick and Rosemary were married at Avondale church. A friend of mine from Grahamstown days conducted the service. When I knew him, Revd David Jenkins (not the Bishop of Durham), an outstanding man and an excellent priest, had been a student at St Paul's Theological College. The reception was at the George Hotel over a magnificent lunch. The bride and groom left for the Leopard Rock Hotel in the Vumba and Rosemary's parents got to the races at Borrowdale in time for the 3.30 — Rosemary's Uncle Hamish Rodger-Campbell had a horse running in that race. Ma and I went to see various old friends and the next day I flew back to Blantyre.

Simon and Christopher had each been given a large fairly robust lorry for Christmas in which they could sit and push each other round. While we were in South Africa, Ma and Pa then produced two more superb vehicles for them. They were not actually toys; they were models of a JCB with a grader blade and hydraulic dumper truck. There were levers and handles to move the grader blade and scoop and the hydraulics actually worked. Provided sand (or mud) was available these two little boys spent hours and hours with these exceptional toys. The lorries were less robust than the JCB and dumper truck and soon began to disintegrate. Our friend Robert, who ran a transport business with enormous lorries and trailers, offered to mend Simon and Christopher's lorries in his workshop. So, much to the twins' delight, their beloved lorries were welded together and were as right as rain for another few weeks. I lost count of the number of times Robert was handed two broken lorries, for the twins knew he would weld them together again. The lorries ended up stronger than they began, for there was more weld than lorry. We still have the JCB 40 years on. Simon has it in his flat in Chiswick and only very special children who visit are allowed to play with it.

The next big excitement for January was the arrival of Harold Macmillan, Prime Minister of the UK. We all duly lined up at Chileka airport as the welcoming crowd — I took the three children and we watched the great man inspect the Guard of Honour and meet the local African chiefs and toffs.

Because Merilyn had been to so many birthday parties, I arranged a very large party for her birthday on 27 January. Trevor had planned to be with me to help, but sadly a riot and its aftermath prevented him from being there. The previous day a big lunch had been laid on for Macmillan and hundreds of Africans had decided to gather outside Ryalls Hotel where the lunch was being held. The hotheads were demanding all manner of things, tempers boiled over and the police had a hard job controlling the mob. The *Daily Mirror*, *Daily Express*, *Daily Telegraph* and many other UK papers trailing Macmillan sent back to London widely exaggerated stories of the so-called Ryalls riot. They accused certain policemen of having stamped on an African's foot and drawn blood and of using heavy-handed tactics in restraining the mob. These irresponsible accounts raised alarm in the UK and heated telegrams and telephone calls flew between Blantyre and London. There were calls for an inquiry into what had gone wrong and into the 'over reaction' of the police, which was not true. So, with this hullabaloo going on, Trevor was unable to attend his daughter's birthday party. Ken and Robert, who had brought their children to the party, stayed to help me and it turned out to be a quite successful, if exhausting, children's party, with endless games to keep the little dears happy.

Patricia (a Rice cousin) and Jim turned up for a week. Jim was a commercial traveller, so he put up at the hotel with all his goods, and Tricia stayed with us, which was nice. It was her old father who had come to Greenhalgh to regain his health in 1946.

Then Dick Arrowsmith, a friend from Trevor's school days in Chingford, Essex, came to visit us. He was now living in Salisbury and was a senior manager in the tobacco trade, and had come to Nyasaland to assess the tobacco crop there. It was nice to see him and be able to return a little hospitality. On leaving school Trevor and Dick had both joined the Artists' Rifles (Territorials) and had had wonderful times together at annual camps and in general training. They both went out to Southern Rhodesia in 1938 — Trevor to the BSAP and Dick to go gold mining. During the war they went their separate ways but never lost touch; indeed I stayed with them in Harare in 1997.

Secretary of State for the Colonies Iain Macleod arrived to see the situation in Nyasaland for himself. There was great agitation to release Dr Banda, to prepare for the break-up of the federation and to plan for independence. Macleod was a wise man and some said he had the best brain in the Tory Cabinet (1960).

Meanwhile, we had the four Haleys staying with us. They had decided to return to the UK and give their girls a good education, also Robert's company had been bought by Lonrho and they felt the situation was too unsettled to start something new. In talking one evening, Trevor quietly said to Robert and Lorna 'I think you've made a wise choice and this is a good time to leave.' We did not think any more about it, *but* the next day Dr Banda was released. Trevor knew what was due to happen and Macleod was still there to take full responsibility. That was the Friday and on the Saturday we took the Haleys to Chileka airport and bid them Godspeed on their flight to England.

Simon and Christopher were going to miss Robert more than they knew. Our house had a steep drive and they would drag their large Tonka lorries up, get in and whiz down the hill at breakneck speed. Tonka toys are fairly robust, but they were not built for this kind of treatment and frequently came to pieces — Robert's workshop and welding gear was no longer available.

Some months before, Robert had appeared one morning with a gang of labourers and an old Citröen car body for Simon and Christopher to play in. Having manoeuvred it to a suitable place in the garden, Robert and Trevor fitted a second steering wheel and pedals so that it had dual controls. The car had no wheels but Nanny, the dog and the cat were all loaded into it and driven many imaginary miles by two very happy little boys. When we left the house for transfer to Lilongwe, we neither took the static car with us nor had it removed. I believe that some years later, new occupants objected to the piece of junk in their garden and had it taken away to a scrap yard.

There was a great buzz of excitement among the African population over Banda's release, but otherwise all was quiet and life seemed fairly normal.

A little Morris Minor car drew up one evening and there was my cousin Angela Rice (her father had been chief engineer on Southern Rhodesia Railways) and her friend Betty Vincent (whom I had known at school). They had just driven up from Salisbury. Two women in a very small car had covered 450 miles from Salisbury to Blantyre without turning a hair. We were delighted to see them and admired their spirit. They stayed a few days and then went on to the lake for a short holiday.

In 1954, we had the privilege of meeting His Grace the Archbishop of Canterbury, Revd Dr Fisher, in Lilongwe. It had been a real thrill to meet the man who had crowned the Queen just the year before, and now we had the good fortune to meet the Archbishop of York, Dr Ramsey (the one with the eyebrows). The contrast between the two archbishops was very noticeable. Dr Fisher was a warm person, interested in everything, obviously enjoyed life and had a twinkle in his eye. Dr Ramsey, on the other hand, seemed bored by the reception and rather looked down his nose at us; we were not on the same intellectual level. Living in these outposts of empire, we got to meet some interesting and influential people. Dr Fisher had been able to visit Likoma Island, the headquarters of the United Mission to Central Africa (UMCA), to see the great cathedral there, but Lake Nyasa can produce violent storms and one such storm prevented Dr Ramsey from getting there. The island has since been abandoned as the UMCA's headquarters and the mission now has its headquarters in Blantyre.

A number of eminent journalists also visited Nyasaland from time to time and O'Driscoll from the *Daily Telegraph* once invited Trevor and me to dine with him at Ryalls Hotel, where we spent a very interesting evening. The press was still obsessed with the so-called 'Ryalls riot' during Macmillan's visit to Blantyre.

Many changes were now taking place and there was talk of posting Trevor to Mzuzu in the Northern Province. Mzuzu was then quite remote and a long way from anywhere. I knew I could cope with the situation, but would have to learn to make our own bread, for there was no baker there. I had a few false beginnings but soon got the hang of it; eventually the family enjoyed the home bake so much that I was forever making bread. Then guess what? Headquarters changed its mind and we were posted to good old Lilongwe again. This time Trevor was promoted to be in charge of the Central Province.

Before we moved to Lilongwe, the Queen Mother, who was purported to love coming to Nyasaland, paid us another royal visit. We were invited to the royal garden party and got quite close to her several times. Her Majesty had been in Lilongwe and our good friends Mike and Mary Sharpe had to vacate their house (the Provincial Commission) so that she could stay there. Mary had great fun getting it ready and no expense was spared to ensure that everything was perfect. Mary is a very capable and well-organized person; the only mild snag was that her cat very nearly had kittens on the Queen Mother's bed, but was discovered and removed within seconds of the first kitten's birth. The main purpose of the royal visit was to open our big, bright, cheerful, new hospital at Blantyre, which the Queen Mother duly did and royally named the Queen Elizabeth Hospital. We all then rushed to Chileka to wave goodbye to the gracious and lovely lady.

While staying with Peter and Gwenda before moving into our house in Blantyre, Merilyn learnt to ride a bicycle in the garden on Sherida's small bright pink bike. Soon after this, the bike was stolen. Then, one day during the Queen Mother's visit, Peter was in the escort car driving at a good speed (the Queen Mother did not like being driven slowly) down the Cholo road when, lo and behold, he spotted a small pink bicycle leaning against a house in one of the roadside villages. He could hardly halt a royal entourage to claim his daughter's bicycle, so radio messages flew through the air and a vehicle at the tail end of the royal convoy was detailed to capture a small pink bicycle. I am sure the Queen Mother would not have minded if he had stopped the royal convoy to retrieve his daughter's bicycle.

Since the police were still smarting over the inaccurate reports in the UK press of the Ryalls' incident, they decided to have a big dinner at Ryalls to put the matter to rest once and for all. The day duly arrived and the men (it was a men's only evening) turned up in full evening dress and unanimously decided that any policeman on duty at Ryalls that infamous lunchtime was to award himself the 'Order of the Mustard Spoon'. The inquiry into the Ryalls incident brought the events into perspective by declaring that the amount of blood shed would hardly fill a mustard spoon. So, numerous mustard spoons with a safety pin welded on the back and anointed with a drop of bright red nail polish were distributed and the 'Order' worn whenever medals and decorations were called for — I have the spoon in front of me as I write. After that, as a joke Trevor always wore the spoon along with his other medals at the annual police dinner. The dinner launching the 'Order of the Mustard Spoon' attracted a lot of attention and was even mentioned in a federal news broadcast.

On 11 June 1960, the annual Queen's Birthday parade was held in Zomba. Trevor was due to be presented with his CPM at the investiture and the Governor, Sir Robert Armitage, was to do the honours. Two days before, Merilyn went down with chickenpox and the boys were immediately in quarantine. We therefore had to leave Nanny and William in charge of the children (a kind neighbour dropped in at lunchtime to see if all was well) while Trevor and I went off to Zomba, I too glow in the reward given to Trevor for all his hard and successful work. It was a very happy day and a good parade. We were then invited to a sherry reception at Government House, followed by lunch with the Commissioner of Police Mullen. We returned home to Blantyre to find the children, pox and all, fine but very disappointed to have missed seeing their father on parade having a medal pinned to his chest (ouch). This memorable day was also Pa's eightieth birthday, so of course we sent him a telegram.

A few days later Simon and Christopher developed high temperatures and then chickenpox; it was inevitable, but something one had to go through with small children. (I had it as an adult not long before I was married and was very ill, not to mention exceedingly worried about my skin being restored to its natural clarity by the wedding.) When the boys were well again, we packed up everything, loaded the lorry and left for Lilongwe. It was July 1960.

* * *

We spent a couple of nights at the Lilongwe hotel where Dave Elder was still the manager. We were offered a house, which I refused to accept because it was filthy and too small. We were then offered a much nicer bigger one nearer the school, but it was just as dirty. I was getting fed up with dirty houses. I always left a clean house and expected decent people to do the same, but I was nearly always disappointed by other people's low standards. After making myself thoroughly unpopular with the PWD and demanding they come and clean, paint and do whatever was necessary to make the house habitable (in my opinion) they reluctantly agreed and I had a gang scraping, cleaning, rubbing down and painting for what seemed like weeks. They were slow workers and I made them carry out the work to a high standard, which took time. They did one room at a time, which was the only way we could live in the house at the same time as having a complete redecoration. Trevor and I were on camp beds in the sitting room for about four nights while our bedroom was being done. It was winter and the fire in the sitting room compensated for having to sleep on camp beds, for we were nice and warm.

There was an extensive area laughingly called the garden, about two acres of long grass with a fragment of wild hedge at the bottom, so, when the house was decorated to my satisfaction, I decided to tackle this with the help of a gang of prison labourers. I marked out the flowerbeds, a swing area for the children and a vegetable garden, and planted a hedge all round the boundary to provide some privacy. Provided one chooses the right plants, shrubs and trees, growth in that climate is rapid and in no time we had a Tacoma hedge round the boundary and a thick mulberry hedge next to the house. It really looked quite good in a short time. Also, being one house away from the Bishop Mackenzie

School, it was ideal for the children. The vegetable garden was soon productive and we began to feel at home and settled; we hoped we would be allowed to stay there for the rest of our tour.

Lilongwe Club was the setting for the flower show, a very important annual event followed by a ball. The flowers, especially the dahlias as I remember, were magnificent. The show was always well supported and attracted people from the surrounding districts, including Dowa, Dedza and Kasungu.

Trevor was delighted to be back in the Central Province, especially as it was the duck and geese-shooting season. An old-timer Theo Bradshaw (Braddy) used to take him and others camping for a day or two at the Bua River to shoot game birds — spurwing geese and duck — Trevor never came back empty handed. There is nothing like the flavour of wild duck, though it took me a while to learn how to cook a spurwing goose. With no fat on the bird, one either has to cover it in fatty bacon or, the method I preferred, place at least half a pound of butter inside it before a long slow roasting. It was no good stuffing the carcass, for that only seemed to dry out the meat even more. If Trevor brought back too many birds, Dave Elder at the hotel was good enough to keep them in his very cold room for us. We had a fridge, but no freezer.

One would not normally have expected an Elizabeth Arden consultant in Lilongwe, but we had one and she gave very helpful tips on how to prevent one's skin ending up like dried parchment. We paid for the creams, of course, but there was no consultation fee and it was a marvellous service, especially given the climatic conditions and our limited resources. Her consultations were held in a curtained off corner of the London & Blantyre Trading Company, the general store in which we got our main groceries. We also had a Mandala store (as in Zomba, Limbe and Blantyre) and the Limbe Trading Company (LTC), which the children called 'I'll Tell See'.

A delightful family from Salisbury lived a couple of doors away from us and we became firm friends. Geoff Mills was a postal engineer and he had come to Nyasaland to help modernize its communications system. Jean was a very good friend, a great cook, a clever needlewoman and an excellent gardener — she taught me a lot — and both were tennis players. They had two children, Mike and Jenny. Sadly, Mike had cystic fibrosis and we all admired the way he coped and the tremendous amount of support he received from his parents. It was due to their determined and continual supervision through good times and bad that Mike lived right into his twenties, which was unheard of in the 1960s. Jean taught him at home from a correspondence course — he was a highly intelligent boy — and when they returned to Salisbury he was able to go to university there. Merilyn and Jenny were great friends and were always together, either at their house or ours. Mike was not able to visit every house to which he was invited because the tiniest cold, should he catch one, was really dangerous for him. His immune system did not function properly and Jean had to be very careful. However, he often came to our house provided we had no colds.

Banda was holding meetings all over the country to which it was quite usual for 15,000 people to turn up. No building could accommodate these numbers so they were held at the old airport or football field. On one occasion, the police commissioner's wife, Mrs Mullen, and her three children popped in for a coffee on their way to the lakeshore, where they had rented a cottage. Trevor was horrified that the commissioner was allowing his wife, three children and a police driver to travel on that particular day. The roads were chock-a-block with buses — all packed to the hilt and in various stages of disintegration — en route to see Dr Banda (Kamuzu, the Messiah) and everybody in a high state of excitement. Trevor persuaded Mrs Mullen to spend the best part of the day with us and go to the lakeshore at Salima when the excitement had died down and the roads were empty. To let his family drive off like that, the commissioner must either have been totally ignorant of Banda's movements, not realized the numbers involved, or had complete faith in Trevor's policing of the province.

Merilyn had been saying she wanted a cat. I am not a lover of ordinary cats, but I like Siamese and, as luck would have it, we acquired a dear little female kitten we unimaginatively named Puss. She was much loved and grew into a very handsome cat. She was a great hunter and often came back with mice, shrews and rats. The mice she ate, but shrews have a bitter taste, so she would just play with the wretched animals for hours and then get bored; it would be left to us to catch and release them. One disappeared under the bath and lived there for ages before we finally got it out.

We used to keep a window open at night so that she could come and go as she pleased; it was open just enough for her to get in and out. One night Puss woke me with the most awful caterwauling, thumping and growling noise as she tried to get a cane rat through the aperture. The cane rat was bigger than she was, so I got out of bed and let her in through the door — she was determined to show me her prize and then proceeded to crunch it up under my bed.

When she was in season we borrowed rather a handsome king Siamese called Titus, shut them up together and hoped for the best. However, Puss would not let him get near her and fought him at every move (we kept a watch through the window). He gave up and we returned the frustrated tom. After a little while, to our surprise, Puss produced a litter of enormous black kittens. We kept two and they turned out to be more like dogs. Puss had obviously mated with a wild cat and these ferocious kittens took some handling. When challenged they would charge at any dog and their tails used to bush out, which made them look quite stunning. After this experience we had Puss spayed. Her other spirited pastime was to try and catch snakes, usually spitting cobras. She would go hunting in the bush and come back screaming with pain, half blind and her eyes swollen and running (cobras direct their venom straight into their enemies' eyes). The only cure was to pour as much milk as possible into the eyes and put the cat in a dark cupboard, and then repeat the procedure until the swelling went down. Puss never learnt and I lost count of the number of times we had to administer the milk treatment.

Compared with salaries today we were desperately badly paid. Though we paid no rent and our heavy furniture was provided, we hardly ever had any money to spare at the end of the month. Our expectations were simple and temptations to spend were limited. The climate favoured informal simple clothes for most of the year and we were happy. All our friends and colleagues were in the same boat, so there was very little if any pressure to keep up with the Joneses. I kept my housekeeping account book from Nyasaland and this is a typical month's spending:

LTC (including two wedding presents)	£3.4s.10d.
Electricity	£6.4s.5d.

Bakery	£1.18s.9d.
London & Blantyre (groceries)	£1.0s.5d.
Milk	£12.0s.0d.
Meat (plus groceries)	£24.0s.0d.
Miscellaneous	£2.19s.10d.
Wages	£15.0s.0d.
Vet	7s.0d.
Water Board	£2.1s.3d.
Pharmacy	£2.11s.6d.
Dress material	£1.13s.6d.

This adds up to £72.5s.5d. I now spend more than that a week for one person and this was for a family of five, three servants, one dog and a cat. We always had a productive fruit and vegetable garden, which we supplemented with items from the local African market. We were also all very generous with our neighbours. If we had a surplus of avocado pears, we would swap some of them for cabbages, mangoes, guavas, peaches or pawpaws. Nothing was wasted and we were all very healthy. I do not have a record of what it cost to run the car, but I know it had to be serviced once a month. Trevor must have paid for items like club subscriptions and contributions to the church. I made most of my clothes and an everyday cotton frock would cost me between £2 and £3 with the material bought from a local Indian store, which always had the best selection of cottons. I purchased the occasional smart garment and of course decent shoes when we were on leave. Otherwise, we lived in sandals, canvas Bata slip-on shoes and flip-flops. Bata shoes only cost a few shillings. When Merilyn was little I smocked all her dresses; I loved smocking and think there is nothing nicer on a little girl, and I always made pants to match (though I did not smock those). When the boys came along I made all their buster suits, a shirt and bloomers buttoned together to hide the baby's nappy — very sweet and very neat. It was quite a relief to reach the end of the second set of eight or ten buttonholes. Trevor then gave me a wonderful gadget that screwed onto my Singer sewing machine and that made buttonholes — it was great. When Simon and Christopher were out of nappies, making shorts was very easy, for there were no flies, just elastic round the waist. I made all their pyjamas and my nighties. Trevor always wore a sarong instead of pyjamas and that did not take long to make. There was a great system of hand-me-down clothes from one family to the next, which helped enormously and even maternity clothes did the rounds. I made several outfits for myself that were used by at least three other expectant mums. Some of us were better seamstresses than others, but we all helped one another. I was thankful I had a domestic science, needlework and dressmaking training and I sewed with some confidence. One lesson I learnt very early on was always to buy good-quality material; it made a better garment and kept its shape. If you put the same amount of work into cheap and indifferent material, it looked homemade and soon lost its shape and fell to pieces, so was not worth doing. Miss Crossley, who so influenced my sewing at the Cheltenham Ladies' College never allowed us to take short cuts; we had to finish off our seams properly and neatly. These habits never left me and paid dividends.

Trevor used to go on *ulendo* for a few days at a time to check up on the more remote corners of the Central Province. Lloyd always went with him and knew some basic cooking as well as how to perform the drill with his valise. The valise, which was made of canvas, was rolled up and buckled to keep the dust out. If the weather were too hot for a normal sleeping bag, it would be unbuckled, rolled out and made up as a bed ready to climb into and go to sleep under the stars. The valise, which dated from BSAP Somaliland days, was a well-worn piece of equipment.

In one village Trevor helped an old chief and to show his gratitude the chief presented Trevor with a lamb. In his best and most polite Nanja Trevor explained that he was not allowed to accept gifts. 'Then take it for your children,' the chief said, so he did. The Nanja word for sheep is *kosa*, so Kosa became the sheep's name. His behaviour was very unlike that of a sheep — he thought he was a dog. He used to love being with the children and would graze quite happily near wherever they were playing in the garden. He frequently followed them into the house with disastrous results; his little cloven hooves would slide all over the polished cement floors and he could hardly remain upright; he would look so embarrassed. Kosa was a marvellous jumper and thought nothing of leaping right over my carefully constructed hedge into the vegetable garden to gobble up a row of lettuces or beans. It wasn't as if he were hungry, for he had his grain, hay and grass. Another favourite nibble of his was geraniums, especially the scented ones, and he would eat the whole plant right down to the root and then dig that out with his hoof. A leopard would have had Kosa if we did not stable him at night, so we made a nice bed for him in a leopard proof corner of the garage, but he would only go in if one of the children led him in, usually by the ear. He would not allow an African to touch him — we never knew why. The poor gardener would spend ages and get quite exhausted trying to get him to bed if we were not at home. He eventually had to wait for us to get back so that one of the children could put Kosa safely inside. He was quite a character and frequently bit off, or at least undid, visitors' shoelaces. When we went on leave at the end of our three-year stint, Kosa went to the abattoir and into Dave Elder's freezer. We ate him on our return and very tasty he was too — Trevor was amazed that he didn't taste of geraniums.

One day during her morning break, Merilyn appeared from school very agitated asking if she could please have 2/6d. 'Whatever for?' I asked. An African had appeared in the playground with two very small leverets and she wanted them. I gave her the money and went to fetch the tiny bundles of fluff. I had heard how difficult it was to raise hares for all sorts of reasons and had no idea where to begin, so I asked the vet who suggested diluted milk and ABDEC vitamin drops. The gardener quickly made a cage with sleeping quarters and feeding area from an old packing case and small-mesh wire netting. He fed the tiny creatures drop by drop with a fountain-pen filler and, to our amazement, they thrived and grew quite big. The children collected dandelions and other delicacies for the little hares, which had become quite tame, and we had to stroke their tummies for a motion. We left their cage outside at night thinking they were perfectly safe because a leopard would not dare come close to the house and tear the cage to pieces. But, sadly, one morning we found the wire netting ripped to shreds and no hares in the cage. We never found out exactly who or what had caused the damage and taken our hares.

An English cousin of mine came to stay with us over Christmas 1960. Douglas Rice had just left Bedford School and in his 'gap' year had come to Nyasaland under the British Voluntary Service Overseas scheme to teach English at Dedza secondary school. We were delighted to have him with us and during his year in Nyasaland we saw him change from a boy to a man in the nicest possible way. He palled up with some other volunteers and between them they bought an old Opel car, with which they had great fun and in which they were able to get around and see Nyasaland.

Douglas later went to Cambridge, did well and for many years taught English at Blundells School, Tiverton, Devon, where he is now head of the English department, having produced three sons with the help of his delightful wife Alison. His one son Benjamin is a poet and has won poetry prizes; I am delighted we have another Benjamin Rice to carry on the name. For the Christmas Douglas spent with us we had a normal Christmas day with church in the morning, but in the evening the Barrons of the Mbabzi estate had invited us to a party where we had a lovely Christmas meal and then played silly games in the traditional English way. We all thoroughly enjoyed ourselves and Douglas said he had never had a Christmas like it. Douglas's father was one of the first chiropractors to practise in England and his wife Zillah was a successful author of children's books, including *The Canal Children*, so it is easy to see from where Douglas acquired his love of English.

One of the problems of living in an outpost of empire is how to get a haircut when there are no hairdressers. Luckily, one police wife, Kay Williams, was a trained hairdresser and she kindly used to come to my house to cut and set my hair. This was a relief because I had been struggling on my own, but clearly without much success, for Trevor forbade me to carry on cutting my own hair — it must have been *awful* for him to comment. An Indian barber was contracted to cut all the policemen's hair and he came to the house regularly to cut Trevor's, but I was not allowed to ask him to cut Simon's and Christopher's. I had to take them to Bicycle, an African who had worked in Milward's garage as a mechanic but had had a horrible accident when a car fell off the jack onto his leg. It was so badly broken that he was left with one leg much shorter than the other and, as compensation, he was allowed to use a small corner of Milward's garage showroom as his barbershop. Simon and Christopher hated going there and would scream, squirm and wriggle. Bicycle's eyesight was failing and he wore glasses, but one lens was cracked, he squinted through the other and his customers saw their reflections through a contorted and wobbly mirror. I only discovered quite how bad it had been when I took the boys for a proper haircut while we were on leave in the UK. At first they were very apprehensive, but once the operation began they relaxed and were all smiles; I could hardly believe what I was seeing. They said 'Mum, it didn't hurt one bit!' I then realized that Bicycle was not only half blind but also used blunt scissors, which must have been agony.

Political agitators, who were continually trying to fuel dissent, persuaded the embryonic trade unions to call a strike of all domestic staff. The organizers of the strike were calling for an all round domestic wage way below what we were paying our own staff, but then we had always considered good servants worthy of a decent wage and had paid them well.

Trevor called in our servants and explained that they could be targets but that, as they were paid well above the wage the agitators were demanding, he expected them not to go on strike. He said that if they felt vulnerable he would provide them with police protection, for we valued them as servants and as loyal friends. They said, very bravely because they knew of the intimidation, that they had no intention of striking and would work as normal, but that it would be a comfort to have police protection. The day came, we had no trouble and everything carried on as normal, so normal in fact that Trevor felt confident enough to fly down to Zomba for a police meeting.

Many families panicked and many domestics did not turn up for work, whether they were paid over the odds or not; there was a lot of ill feeling, but no damage or fighting. The next day I went with Lloyd to the local African market to top up on meat, vegetables and fruit and to show that all was back to normal on the domestic front.

When the usual teacher went on leave, I was asked to run the Sunday school and, seeing that I had three children attending it, I felt I should agree so long as I could do it *my way*. Attendance had dwindled, but in no time we had 60 children coming every Sunday morning to the gathering we held in the Bishop Mackenzie School hall. I cannot play the piano and could not find a pianist, so I just played the hymns with one finger and we got on fine. We read stories, played games and acted out biblical stories, which the children seemed to enjoy. Then, one Easter, I felt ambitious and decided to write a play, which we arranged to perform at the simple little interdenominational church on Easter Sunday. Someone painted an enormous cardboard circle to resemble the rock that was rolled away from the cave where the body of Jesus had been laid and I frantically made Roman togas in cotton khaki and helmets from cardboard sprayed with gold paint. We had a beautiful angel and all the mothers came up trumps with their children's costumes. We found someone to play the harmonium and everything went smoothly. The children enjoyed it and to some, I hope, it brought home the meaning of Easter. I felt quite elated.

Dr Banda was born at Kasungu, northwest of Lilongwe, where he went to a mission school before walking to South Africa to attend Fort Hare University. From there he travelled to the USA and later to Edinburgh to train as a medical doctor. Though now living in Blantyre, he decided to throw a big party at Kasungu, to which Trevor, for whom he seemed to have a growing regard, was invited.

One would have thought that Trevor had enough to do, but he still found time for relaxation and we both played tennis two or three times a week. I had team practice every Thursday afternoon, a match or tournament on Saturdays and social tennis on Sundays. Trevor had always enjoyed amateur theatricals and took part in a production of *White Sheep of the Family* to which I took Merilyn on the first night. This was her first grown-up play and she loved it. It all took place on the usual makeshift stage at the club.

The Church of the Province of Central Africa decided that the Lilongwe congregation now merited a resident priest and we all engaged in frantic fund raising activities to equip his house. The diocese paid for the house itself and we all donated something towards its contents, whether an item of furniture, a blanket or a teapot. Once this was achieved, we held a fête in the churchyard to raise funds for running expenses. I organized the cake stall and was pleased to have sold every last biscuit and to have made a tidy sum of £25. The whole fête raised £202, which was a huge sum for our little community.

The great day arrived to welcome our very own priest, for whom we had laid on a tea party at the new vicarage and all went well. Up until then we had relied on visiting priests — either someone from a mission station, someone who had driven up from Zomba or Blantyre, or a layman had taken the service.

166

I was asked to serve on the church council and, thinking I may be able to contribute something, I accepted, but soon fell out with our new priest. He came from a poor area in Sheffield and had what were to me strange ideas about Africa; his domestic servants were fleecing him left and right and we, the small congregation, had to pay for it. I spoke out about his attitude, which did not go down very well. He thought that everybody with a white face had an endless supply of money and should give most of it to the Africans, whether they deserved it or not. I objected and resigned; life was a little easier without that hassle.

My hay fever, blocked nose, headaches, sneezing and coughing were getting me down and the nose drops our GP had prescribed did not seem to be helping, so it was decided I should see an ENT specialist in Salisbury. This was easier said than done. We decided to drive to Salisbury and take Nanny, who had never been out of Nyasaland, with us. Because it was the rainy season, we could not drive through Mozambique and had to take the much longer journey via Lusaka in Zambia, spending the first night at the resthouse at Kachalola in Northern Rhodesia. There are 100 miles of escarpment at Kachalola — 50 miles of hairpin bends down to the Luangwa River and 50 miles up the other side made for a very tiring and very hot journey. Cars used this narrow road during the day and lorries at night, so heavily laden lorries winding up and down the road could disturb one's sleep. We left early next morning and arrived at Lusaka at noon. A few miles into Northern Rhodesia there is (or was) a notice on the road saying 'CATTLE CROSSING FOR THE NEXT 400 MILES'. I always meant to stop and take a photo of it, but never did. When we arrived at Salisbury that evening, we went straight to the Bourdillons (my brother Dick's parents-in-law) at Borrowdale and they made us feel most welcome. Mrs Bourdillon ran a flower farm and a flower stall (which she supplied daily) in Cecil Square; she was a knowledgeable and gifted flower grower. The next day we left Nanny and the three children with the Bourdillons while Trevor took me to see Mr Campbell, the ENT consultant. He told me that the nose drops had destroyed the membranes of my inner nose and he then proceeded to cauterize it. After having pushed about five yards of wadding up my nose, he said he could not allow me to return to Nyasaland by road because of the dust (only a few miles of the road was tarred) and that I must fly back. So we went and booked a flight on the new sky bus. The next day I felt fine (complete with wadding) and, since the car needed a service, we took it into town and borrowed cousin Angela's Morris Minor to rush round and shop for the long list of items that were not available in Nyasaland. When we got our estate car back that afternoon we returned to Borrowdale, packed up and drove north on a tarred road to Sinoia to spend the night with Dick and Rosemary. I spent two further days with them while Trevor drove the three children and Nanny back to Nyasaland via Kariba and Lusaka. The Kariba Dam had recently been completed and one road into Northern Rhodesia was along the dam wall. Kariba was then one of the biggest man-made lakes in the world and an impressive sight. Since an African legend holds that the great Zambezi River's flow will never be stopped, Nanny could not believe that she was driving along the dam wall and that the river had indeed been tamed; she said she was dreaming.

Building the Kariba Dam displaced the entire Tonga tribe and this caused a considerable amount of resentment. Hundreds of head of game were also affected and the wardens became quite famous for their pioneering methods of saving the animals — their techniques were recorded in films and documentaries and books were written about them. A huge valley was flooded and the electricity the hydroelectric power produced serviced the people of Zimbabwe and, to a lesser extent, of Zambia — the southern generators seemed to have been better managed and used to capacity. To have a constant and reasonably priced source of power was considered to be a wonderful asset for industry and agriculture throughout the country (at least that was the theory).

Many see the legendary story of the river god Nyaminyami as an attempt to reconcile tradition with the reality of modern life, but Nanny was having none of it — it was a dream.

After a short sojourn with my brother and the removal of five yards of wadding — I boarded the sky bus for Nyasaland. We stopped in Chileka to change to an old Dakota and just as I was about to sit down the hostess came along and said 'I wouldn't sit there if I were you, there's a hole in the floor and it's draughty,' so I moved and arrived in one piece at Lilongwe where my family, after a careful if tiring drive back from Salisbury, met me.

Living in the Central Province meant that we saw many people from the Northern Province (Mzuzu) on their way south and visa versa. We always enjoyed having them to lunch or for the night and it was good to pick up news and gossip first hand whether from the north or south. One such visitor was Paul Thirsk, the dashing district commissioner to whom my friend Daph, who had been my bridesmaid and was now headmistress of Chingola School in Northern Rhodesia, had become engaged. Paul, who was on the staff of Lord Apthorp, the governor general of the Central African Federation based in Salisbury, was paying an official visit to the Central Province provincial commissioner, Mike. Daph had written to say that if we wanted to meet her 'intended' he would be in Lilongwe in July, so he came to supper one evening and we were quite charmed by him. We were to meet at intervals in the UK much later after he and Daph had retired. His last posting was as deputy governor of Guyana in South America.

A colony of agricultural experts (an agronomist, various tea, tobacco and animal husbandry specialists, and a resident vet) at Chitedzi, a busy HMG-funded agricultural research station outside Lilongwe, aimed to improve crops and livestock and to teach practical and proven methods to African farmers. This highly successful venture produced some very good African farmers. The station also organized an agricultural show at Lilongwe to which the world and its wife went. I took some exhibits, but arrived too late to have them judged. In one ring event, Ken demonstrated how to pack a donkey for a week or two *ulendo* in the bush or in other remote areas, for donkeys can get to parts that vehicles, including bicycles, cannot reach.

September 1961 saw a big change in our family's lifestyle. With Simon and Christopher now of school age they joined Merilyn at Bishop Mackenzie. We lived within a stone's throw of the school and all three went off quite happily but with some anticipation and excitement on the first morning. They met the next morning with less enthusiasm. Christopher had decided that he did not like school and Merilyn was called out of her class to come and calm him down more than once. I am not a great believer in nursery school for all children. Merilyn enjoyed the companionship and games, but it was different for Simon and Christopher; being twins they felt complete in themselves and had no desire to mix socially or share their toys with anyone else. They knew that if children of their age came to our house they had to share their toys and be reasonable and when such children arrived they would each solemnly hand the visitor a toy or something and then disappear to the bottom of the garden to get on with their own game. We therefore decided not to send them to nursery school until the term before they were due to start school proper at the age of five. Simon accepted the change and joined in at nursery school, but Christopher hated it and spent the first three weeks sitting under a table sucking his thumb and refusing point blank to participate in anything. When I was consulted about this, I suggested they just ignore him and that in due course he would join in, which is what eventually happened. So, by the time they went to school proper they had some idea of how they should behave and, indeed, by the end of the first term the boys were playing an active — if not altogether constructive — part in school life.

My daily life altered too, for I too now went to school. With a considerable expansion in education during the years of the Central African Federation, new schools had been built for both African and European children, as well as schools for children for whom English was not a first language. A serious shortage of teachers ensued, so unqualified people were being recruited into the profession and I was taken on as a general subject teacher at an Asian primary school. The children were mostly Muslim boys and girls of Indian parentage, but there were also a few Afrikaans-speaking coloured children whose parents had come from South Africa. Some of the Indian children had older brothers at public schools in England or India and their fathers were mostly rich merchants who wore beautiful clothes, drove Mercedes and had huge houses. The majority of children were Gujarati speaking, intelligent and well behaved. I had mostly seven and eight-year-olds in my class, but also a few nine and ten year-olds who had started late for some reason. Though my brief was to teach in English, one little coloured girl who only spoke Afrikaans and Nanja seemed so miserable that I used to take her aside and speak to her in Afrikaans. I had 25 in my class and they were on the whole a very nice group of children. School lasted from 7.30 a.m. to noon and on some afternoons there were games between 2.30 and 3.30 p.m. My own children had the same school hours and

Nanny always fetched them from school at noon. This was fortunate because, with the schools two miles apart, I clearly could not be in two places at once and Trevor was often away at midday in another part of the province. The pay was quite good and, thanks to Kokhri School, we were able to have a superb six-week holiday one Christmas and New Year at Bonza Bay with Ma and Pa.

Although I still taught Sunday school at Bishop Mackenzie, I now had Elma to help me out, which was marvellous. On Remembrance Sundays, instead of Sunday school, a parade would be held at the *boma*, which most of the town would attend. We had an annual Sunday school prize giving on the last Sunday of the term with Bibles as prizes and carols to round off the year.

The school term ended on Friday and on Saturday we left for South Africa. Having called on various friends in Zomba *en route*, we spent the first night with the Wards at Mikalongwe. We left them at 4.00 a.m. hoping to drive straight to Salisbury in one go. We did well and called in on Bill Hayes at Mrewa in Southern Rhodesia. Bill was an ex-BSAP pal of Trevor's whom we had last seen on our honeymoon in 1951 when he was living in three African huts with his wife and father-in-law. They had bought a good tobacco farm and Bill had worked hard in the interim. Now they were in a beautiful large brick house with a thatched roofed house and lovely tranquil garden filled with shady trees. What a change!

After a little shopping in Salisbury the next day, we spent the night at the Elephant and Lion on the Beit Bridge road, a famous stopping place for Rhodesian travellers with lots of zebra skin rugs on the floor. We were on the road at 6.15 a.m. the next day and, despite the customs rigmarole at Beit Bridge, drove right through to Parys on the Vaal River in South Africa, over 400 miles. We bypassed Johannesburg by going through Krugersdorp and Randfontein, for unless one drove through Johannesburg very early in the morning there were always hold-ups. The next morning we arrived exhausted at Bonza Bay. It was a long journey, but the children had been very good; it got so cold round Aliwal North (5000 feet above sea level) that we had had to unpack extra blankets for the children to sleep under. Bonza Bay was also unseasonably cold and wet for a few days, but soon picked up.

The nicest surprise then happened. My old school friend Jenny Hirst arrived next door from London. Her parents had also retired from farming and had come to live in Bonza Bay, which was great.

We took the children to a pantomime in East London and when the weather picked up we resumed our normal Bonza Bay routine of spending as much time as possible on the beach. Arthur Lawford also took the children out on the lagoon in his little boat with an outboard motor. Our old maid Elsie was sent for and readily took over my three children — and I just sat back. We had a happy family Christmas Day and the fact that it was wet passed unnoticed with all the excitement, presents and feasting. As Simon and Christopher did not really know any Bonza Bay children, we had not given them a party on the 23rd, just a special cake each for tea, so we decided to concentrate more on Christmas.

When Simon and Christopher were very small, between the ages of one and five, we would have their birthday party in June or July, for there was so much else going on at Christmas and they got excited enough over that. This worked well until they started proper school and found out their correct date of birth. They were furious, so from then on 23 December has always been celebrated.

The Grand Prix was on Boxing Day and we were invited to join Jack and Rosemary Marston's party to see this exciting race in which both Stirling Moss and Tom Clark were competing. We went in one car from Bonza Bay to the East London circuit where Jack had arranged for a large lorry to back up against the fence protecting the crowd from the racetrack; with chairs, cold boxes and beer on the flat bed of the lorry, we had a mini grandstand view. I enjoyed the novelty and thrill of seeing my first Grand Prix, with cars whizzing round then disappearing from view, but the noise was deafening. Stirling Moss came second, but for some reason was hailed as the hero and fêted all over East London.

Bonza Bay was a very sociable place and, in 1962, it was still only a village. We received numerous invitations to sundowners and suppers and having Elsie there to look after the children allowed us to have a great holiday. I went riding with Pa two or three times a week, Trevor took the children to the beach and everybody had a good time.

On leaving Bonza Bay we took five days to drive back to Nyasaland in our Peugeot estate. As there had been heavy rains we were advised in Salisbury to go via Lusaka rather than risk the roads through Mozambique, which lorries had churned up into a sea of mud. This added several hundred more miles to our journey but was quicker in the long run. We spent one night *en route* with Dick and Rosemary at Sinoia and broke the journey in Lusaka briefly to see friends before an early start to tackle once again the dreary 400 miles to Kachalola. After one night at the guesthouse at the base of the escarpment of the Luangwa River valley to let the children exercise, the next stop was Lilongwe.

Several friends dropped in that afternoon and evening to welcome us back and to bring us up to date on local gossip and news.

Mike and Mary invited us to drinks one evening when Sir John Glyn Jones and Lady Jones were staying with them in Lilongwe. This was the first time I had met the new governor, who was quite different from his predecessor Sir Robert Armitage.

School term was about to begin and for us all to resume the hectic school routine. We now seriously had to consider a school in England for Merilyn. We were due to go on long leave in September, so after many deliberations and discussions, we wrote to the PNEU headquarters in Ambleside for a list of suitable boarding schools for girls in southern England. They were very helpful and we chose Burgess Hill School in Sussex. We wanted a middle of the road school; we did not want anything too fancy, too posh or too big. It was a difficult decision to make blind, as it were, but we did as much research as we could and felt fairly confident that we had made a reasonable choice.

Our next excitement was the annual flower show at the club. Merilyn entered for her age group and to her delight won the Countess Dalhousie Cup. She was thrilled and had the honour of presenting the bouquet to Mrs Nicholson who distributed the prizes. I won third prize for an arrangement.

All over the world, the women's day of prayer is usually held on the second Friday in Lent. Our little ecumenical church in Lilongwe always held a service to mark the occasion and it became my lot to take some prayers. The church was quite full and some formidable women, whom I had never seen before, were there to represent the various mission stations, the Dutch Reformed Church at Mkhoma, the Seventh Day Adventists and the Baptists. I, however, had made a determined effort to ensure that the Anglicans were well represented.

173

Huge crowds always followed Banda wherever he went, so Trevor always had a hectic few days whenever he came to Kasungu or Lilongwe. With thousands of people coming from miles around Trevor was responsible for a lot of careful planning, organization and delegation.

I was delighted when Alison from my Mortimer childhood days came to visit us with her new husband Doug Collings. He had to see some business associates about cotton growing in the Chitwali area, so they stayed for several days, giving Alison and me lots of time to chat; it was good to see her so happy. She still kept horses and had come into her own more than ever because Doug, who was building himself a reputation for designing three-day event courses and show jumping circuits, was just as keen. The general interest in horses and riding was growing in Nyasaland.

A young assistant district officer, Peter Swan, kept his horse in a garage to which he had attached a small paddock. Peter rode most evenings and at weekends, but one morning the horse came back without him with stirrups flapping and in an excitable state. Peter's house and garden backed onto ours and I noticed the riderless horse in the lane. Since no one had any idea where Peter might be, once the horse was caught, unsaddled and stabled, a search party set out to find him. With African bush wireless in action he was found in no time at all, but being quite badly concussed and with broken ribs he was taken to the cottage hospital. When I went to see him, he asked me to exercise his horse daily while he was in hospital. I was not keen because I thought the horse had been poorly schooled and I did not wish to be thrown in the middle of the bush somewhere. However, I did take him round the school football field a few times on the grounds that if he got stroppy and threw me, at least someone would see where I was.

We tried to spend one weekend a month at the lake. Our friends Bruce and Doreen Barron had a cottage on the lakeshore at Salima, which they kindly allowed us to use. It was a marvellous break for Trevor and the children just loved the beach and water. Since Trevor usually had some work to do in the vicinity, he would go ahead in his Land Rover with the food and bedding box while William (sometimes Lloyd) and I would take the car with the children, Nanny and perishables. Trevor would then meet us at the cottage.

9. *(above)* Sir Robert Armitage, the Queen Mother and Major Imray, Blantyre, 1960.

10. *(below)* Farewell dinner, Shire Highlands Hotel, Limbe. From left to right: Gwenda Long, Trevor, Cyril and author.

11. *(above)* 4 July American Beach Barbecue invaded by the Brits. Trevor as Boadicea and landrover complete with cannon that fired blanks.

12. *(above)* Author (top left) as lone woman at Manama Rifle meeting.

13. *(below)* Pirate towers along Ras al-Khaima coast, later adopted as police badge.

14. *(above)* Hammerhead sharks (with their hammers removed) laid out on fish quay, Ras al-Khaima.

15. *(right)* House on the rock, Yemen.

16. *(right)* Ras al-Khaima fort, which served as police headquarters, gaol, court and barracks between 1967 and 1972.

On one particular visit it had been raining very heavily; the lake level was up; all the little streams had become raging torrents and the puddles had become lakes. I used to park the car near the cottage and had never noticed that the spot was in a dip. By midday the water was almost over the top of the wheels, so before the car floated away I waded out, attached a hosepipe to the exhaust, got Christopher to hold it up by leaning out of the back window of the car and started the engine. I then backed the car slowly out of the lake onto the highest bit of ground I could find. If Trevor had been there, he would have done the same, but he had left the cottage early in the Land Rover to meet some people further up the coast to take a boat to a remote village.

I had not given Trevor's venture a second thought. Because the road to the particular place to which he was heading was so bad, a boat trip seemed to be the simplest mode of transport, irrespective of whether or not it were raining. However, when late afternoon came and went, sundown came and went, and nine o'clock came and went I began to get worried. Neither Trevor nor I had any means of communication. By midnight I was a total wreck. I was convinced that I was a widow and that Trevor had drowned or that a hippo had attacked his boat. All sorts of horror pictures were going through my mind. Luckily, the children were asleep and, as Trevor often came home long after their bedtime, they knew no difference. When William and Nanny came into the cottage from their house and saw the state I was in, they managed to calm me a little with their presence and I agreed to lie down on my bed. There was nothing I could do and they said they would stay in the house with me until the *bwana* returned. I must have dozed off, for at about 3.30 a.m. Trevor appeared, very bedraggled and exhausted, but thank God he was all right. They had been shipwrecked. They had carried out their visit to the remote village as planned, but on the return voyage the wind force increased, there were huge waves and the boat disintegrated. Fortunately, these craft never venture far out into the lake, so when it became evident that the boat was sinking, Trevor and the others did not have to swim far — in fact he said that he could touch the bottom with his feet from the moment they left the boat and started to fight their way ashore. Their only torch had had a thorough soaking, so it failed to work. Though still raining and blowing a gale, they somehow slid and staggered along the lakeshore in the pitch dark until one of the Africans gained his bearings and managed to guide them to a path that eventually led to the road, then safely back to the Land Rover and then, thank goodness, back to the cottage. Storms on Lake Nyasa can blow up very quickly and become most alarming, but I never want to go through that again.

We were still playing lots of tennis, both tournaments and social tennis. If we were invited to play at Mbabzi, I would take Nanny and the children, for she and the Mbabzi nanny Sarah and her two charges all got on well together. The bank manager's wife Pam Stevens was my usual partner for ladies' doubles and tournaments, and Ralph or sometimes Bruce were my male partners in the mixed games. It was great fun and it kept us fit. We sometimes played the Dutch Reformed mission station at Mkhoma, which had good teams and they were very hospitable.

Pam's husband had been brought up in Cradock and he and his two brothers had been a well-known trio and not exactly for being shrinking violets. It was strange that I should meet up with Steve in Lilongwe of all places, and he was terrified that I would talk about some of his youthful escapades, which were incompatible with his image as a sedate bank manager. He had no need to worry because I would not have dreamt of letting him down.

An old settler called Frank decided to organize a dining club exclusively for men. Sometimes they met at the Lilongwe Hotel, where Dave did them proud, and sometimes they met at Frank's place in the country for a booze-up — there would be no work that afternoon. They met once a month and I think it was a jolly good idea for the men to get together to blow off steam; we all need a vent pipe from time to time. The nice thing was that if the party had been too excessive, I usually received a bunch of flowers from Trevor the next day.

By June 1962 I had had enough of teaching at Kokhri School and handed in my resignation. When I asked Trevor to check the suitability of my resignation letter, he said I must sign it 'your obedient servant', which I refused to do, for I was *not* a civil servant and had no intention of signing a false statement. We had quite an argument, but it was my letter and my resignation, so I won. I planned to leave the school at the end of the winter term, for I needed time to get everything organized for our long leave.

Having carried my saddles and bridles round with me for years, I reluctantly decided to sell them rather than use them only occasionally and lend them out. Gwen Wallace, who knew the saddles, came round immediately and bought them both. She certainly got a bargain when you see the price of English hunting saddles today. I wonder if her son Simon still has them?

Ma, who loved coming to Nyasaland, decided to fly up and spend a few weeks with us before we departed on leave. She specially enjoyed the small aeroplane that brought her from Chileka airport to Lilongwe. It was usually a five-seater Beaver or Islander. She enjoyed the casualness of the experience and used to say that she could never get over the pilot, while tearing down the runway about to take off, offering her a boiled sweet and asking, 'by the way, is your door shut tight?' She really felt she was flying. Her friends called her the 'Flying Rice'.

It was time for the Lilongwe annual show once again and Ken spent the night with us prior to demonstrating his donkey on *ulendo* in the show ring. I entered some flowers, cakes, buns and biscuits. Though I got nothing for my flowers, I won prizes for my cookery, including my lemon curd.

Prior to the show ball, we had a large and successful dinner party as well as a lunch to which we invited the bandmaster, Mateyo Numero. William disapproved and I was very embarrassed when he almost threw a plate in front of Mateyo and very pointedly collected his plate last. William ticked me off afterwards for having an African eat at my table. He said he did not know what we were thinking, that it was wrong and that he thought the *bwana* was losing his touch.

We had written to Burgess Hill School and I now had the school clothes list. I made as many of the garments as was practical, like casual dresses and pyjamas, but we had to buy the rest in Brighton/Hove when we got to the UK. I then began to pack up the house. I had numbered boxes for items such as books and linen, for I had done it so often that it had become routine.

We always spent the last two or three nights before leaving at a hotel so that I could leave the house empty and clean and ensure that all the boxes were properly closed for storage. We used to get a small 'disturbance' allowance for moving; it never covered the total cost but went some way towards paying the hotel bill.

We piled into the Beaver aircraft at 10.15 a.m. on Friday 14 (the five Bevans filled the aircraft) to a great sendoff from our special friends at Lilongwe airport. At Chileka we transferred to a Viscount that flew us to Brazzaville and then we carried on in a French airline to Paris. After collecting yet another Peugeot 403 saloon, we drove to Le Touquet airport where we boarded a Silver City air freighter with our car and flew to Lydd in Kent. The children enjoyed the novelty of flying in four aeroplanes in 24 hours. As we were driving away from Lydd towards Brighton, a VW Beetle car overturned in front of us. It appeared to wander from the left-hand side of the road, so the driver must have over-compensated the steering. We of course stopped and Trevor got out to help. No one was killed but one woman was badly shaken, so Trevor got her out of the VW and brought her to our car and we sat her in the front and revived her somewhat. A little voice from the back of our car said, 'Is she dead Daddy?' She was in shock and very floppy. Soon the police and ambulance arrived and took over, so we could leave the scene and continue on our way to the house we had rented in Middleton-on-Sea outside Bognor Regis. We bought the rest of Merilyn's school uniform on the Monday and had two days in which to sew on all the nametapes.

We lost no time in getting Simon and Christopher into the little local village school. Luckily, it was a church school and it turned out to be very good. They too had to have a uniform.

On the Thursday we drove over to Burgess Hill to take Merilyn to her new school. I was dreading this moment and did my best not to show it. Merilyn's emotions up to then were a mixture of excitement and apprehension. It was almost cruel to leave her in a totally strange environment not knowing a soul. I felt awful leaving her on her new bed in her new dormitory surrounded by piles of knickers and socks waiting to be checked to see if she had brought the correct number of everything. I fled to our car and wept buckets — such partings really were the downside of colonial life. However, Merilyn was a brave little girl (and still is a very brave woman) and she knuckled down. She did not enjoy the strangeness, but she made some good friends with whom she still keeps in touch. One of the reasons we chose a PNEU school was because there would be children boarding there from various parts of the world, which could give them something in common and lead to friendship. One of Merilyn's friends was from Argentina and another's father was in the RAF and serving in the Far East, so she was not an entirely different species.

One evening Merilyn and a friend named Cathy Rankin were sitting on Merilyn's bed looking at her photos and Cathy said 'I've got an Aunty Puss living in Scotland too.' It turned out that they were cousins and that made a great difference to Merilyn — she had a link and was not alone. But she was bullied and never told me about it until she had left school, which is why I said she was brave. She had a different upbringing from most of the other girls and because of this she was bullied and suffered some cruel blows. Can you imagine how awful I felt when she eventually told me? When I asked her why she had not told me at the time or even later, she said, 'You had returned to Nyasaland by then Mum. If I had told you, what could you have done 5000 miles away? And anyway, it would have been too late to do anything.' We had brought our children up to be independent, but Merilyn certainly gained this mantle at an early stage.

On this leave Trevor decided to take a correspondence course to improve his prospects when the time came for us to leave Nyasaland (as independence was obviously getting nearer and nearer). He did a business management course with something called the Rapid Results College and, having taken Simon and Christopher to the school bus, he would lock himself away all morning in the dining room. I would meet the boys back at 3.30 and walk them home. They loved being on the bus by themselves, aged six. The school put them on the public bus with the others and we met them in the village, so they were quite safe. The novelty of (a) being on a bus and (b) being on a bus by themselves counted for a lot. The little school they went to was somewhat archaic. Being winter there was a huge cast-iron anthracite (or coke) fire in the middle of the classroom with railings round it so that the little dears did not get burnt. We paid 1/– (5p) each for their school dinner and it was a very good meal.

Having got the children into schools, during this leave we told our English friends and relations that if they wanted to see us they would have to come to Middleton. There would always be a meal and a bed. Several came, including the Haley family, who drove over from Wales, and we had a good time. The Haleys were now settled back in the UK with the two girls at school at Howells in Cardiff and Robert running a transport business. The weekend they came happened to coincide with both the Brighton veteran car run and Merilyn's half term. We collected Merilyn (it was good for the three girls to be together again), loaded up an enormous picnic and set off to see the veteran cars. Robert is a veteran car enthusiast and there is very little he does not know about them. We found a suitable spot on Pyehill from which to chant the gallant old vehicles on and had a lovely day. Robert, now retired, restores old cars and partakes in veteran rallies here in the UK, in the USA and once in New Zealand and in France.

Before we left Nyasaland our dentist in Lilongwe was concerned about Merilyn's protruding upper front teeth (and so were we), so he referred us to an orthodontist in Hove who advised a brace, which over the years did its job and her teeth were pushed into shape. But the school was unhappy about her regular visits to the specialist. Children were expected to have their dental needs seen to in the holidays, but under the circumstances Miss Hill (Merilyn's housemistress) eventually agreed to escort her to her appointments, for which I am grateful — there is nothing worse for a girl than to grow up with ugly teeth and I could never understand how parents allowed their children to go through life with misshapen jaws and crooked teeth, especially as the treatment was free.

Simon and Christopher were well settled at their little school but seemed to be having endless colds, coughs, sore throats and earache. The local doctor referred them to an ENT consultant who said that their tonsils and adenoids should be removed, for their tonsils in particular were enormous. The date set for their operations at the little hospital had to be cancelled when they both developed another horrid cold and they were then booked in for the Tuesday of the following week. By then it had turned very cold — this was the famous winter of 1962/3 — but we duly deposited them at the appointed hour on the evening before the operations. It was not very nice, but at least there were two of them so they were not entirely alone. The hospital had asked us *not* to go in on the day of the operations, but said we would be welcome the following day. When we went along they seemed remarkably well, though Christopher looked a bit more post-operative than Simon did, and all the nurses and some of the patients were dancing attendance on those 'two dear little boys'. The doctor was a little worried about letting them go home too soon in such intense cold and asked if we had a warm house. The answer was that we did not have a warm house, the heating was very old-fashioned, but that we would move their bedroom into the dining room on the ground floor. With an extra radiator and by leaving the doors open between the dining room and the kitchen (which housed an old Ideal boiler) on the one side and the sitting room (where we kept a roaring open fire going) on the other, we managed to get their room warm enough to bring them home before any more snow fell and the roads got too difficult. This solution worked very well and we gave them a long-handled broom with which to bang on the ceiling should they need us at night.

If we were in England in December, we always made a point of going to the Varsity rugby match at Twickenham, where we would meet a crown of ex-Singapore and various other friends. However, I decided not to go to this particular Varsity match, it was too complicated with Simon and Christopher being at day school, so Trevor went up on his own by train, met the usual crowd and had a great time. I was not particularly worried about him getting home from Bognor station, for I assumed there would always be a taxi there, so I went to bed. At some unearthly hour in the night the telephone rang, 'I am at Bognor station. I came in on the milk train and there are no taxis. Can you come and fetch me?' My answer was 'No, I can't leave Simon and Christopher on their own. What if they should wake and find no one here? Sorry, you will have to walk.' The three-mile walk clearly did him good, for when he arrived home at about 4.30 a.m. he was stone cold sober.

When term ended we arranged to take Merilyn and the boys to a proper pantomime in London. My friend Jenny insisted we stay in her flat, which she shared with a friend who would not be there, and we took sleeping bags. The children slept on the floor and we did all the traditional things in London. We went to the Bertram Mills Circus, saw *Puss in Boots* with Frankie Vaughan, which was great, and on Simon and Christopher's birthday we went to see them changing guard at Buckingham Palace (just like Alice). Then Christopher suddenly began to cry because, though we were all well wrapped up, he was cold and seemed to think that he was never going to be warm again. We left London and drove back to

Middleton; I was convinced that the heater in the car was not working because it got colder and colder the further south we went and our house was like an icebox. The Ideal boiler had of course gone out, but luckily no pipes had frozen. As soon as we had unpacked the car, the boys put themselves to bed fully dressed with hot-water bottles — it was *freezing*. Trevor hosed the car down because of all the salt on the roads and as he ran the water it froze on the car. I kept my big coat on until I went to bed and very nearly went to bed in it. The next morning there were icicles inside the bedroom windows.

What a terrible winter that was! Pneumatic drills were used to get carrots out of the ground and even the sea froze at Middleton — people came to gawp at the unusual phenomenon. While Simon and Christopher's return to school was postponed because the school had frozen up, we managed to drive Merilyn safely back to Burgess Hill complete with flannelette sheets. This term she was in a smaller dormitory in which a gas fire was burning happily; it was unusual to have a fire in a dormitory. During this extreme weather we had power cuts and when we did not have power cuts the voltage and gas pressure were very low.

Towards the end of February Merilyn had an exeat weekend and we drove over to fetch her through what seemed like tunnels of snow. Snow banked high on either side of the road had frozen and it just stayed that way for weeks. This would be our last weekend with Merilyn before we endured another parting and returned to Nyasaland.

The time came to pack up in Middleton and send our heavy luggage (trunks) to Southampton docks, from where we were later to embark. After leaving the house we spent the first night with former Singapore friends *en route* and the next with ex-Bonza Bay friends near Southampton. A snowman the children made in the garden at Middleton on Boxing Day was still there when we left on 1 March. It was the only thing I did not tidy up when we left.

On the Saturday morning we drove through frozen cliffs of snow to the appointed quay at Southampton where there was no one about and no ship — we had booked on the Dutch liner MV *Randfontein*. When the AA man eventually appeared to claim our car, we unpacked it, put our luggage in a safe place in the customs' hall, and walked to a nearby hotel for a coffee.

At 10.00 a.m. the MV *Randfontein* appeared and docked without the aid of tugs — there were none about. The ship's derrick lifted and manoeuvred our car on board and down into a hold. We were the only passengers being picked up at Southampton, which seems incredible by today's standards. We had chosen the Dutch line because it was good with children and I needed a rest. With two comfortable adjoining cabins and our own bathroom we were set for a good two-week voyage. The children's nursery, which was on the top deck, included a caged-in part of the dock that allowed them to be out in the fresh air without escaping and to see the other passengers playing deck games. There were the usual fancy dress and sports competitions for children and adults. I dressed Simon and Christopher up as Bill and Ben the flowerpot men and they won a prize, much to everyone's amusement. Trevor and I went to the fancy headdress evening as the 'heavenly twins'. The chief officer was mystified when we asked him for a picture of the heavens, stars and constellations. With wire, pipe cleaners, foil and cardboard we rigged up a model of the Great Bear and Southern Cross constellations, which we wore with great aplomb. We won first prize.

Friends we had met in the Luangwa game reserve, who had insisted we stay with them when we returned from our UK leave, met us when we docked at Cape Town. Having sent our heavy trunks by freight to Nyasaland to lighten the burden in the car, we drove on a spectacular road out of Cape Town to Somerset West, an attractive town with mountains in the backdrop set in the heart of the fruit and wine growing area. In fact our friends were involved in the fruit export industry.

The next day we drove along the famous Garden Route to Knysna, where we stayed with my cousins Meredith and Ena Rice. Meredith had a house up on a hill overlooking The Heads, the treacherous outlet to the Indian Ocean, and the Knysna lagoon. Meredith and Ena's daughter Margaret was there with her *two* sets of twins, a pair of girls and a pair of boys, and there was awed silence as the three sets all glared at each other as they weighed up the situation. I cannot remember where we all slept; the house must have had elastic sides. Meredith, who had now retired from the Southern Rhodesia Railways, was one of my favourite cousins.

Our next stop was Bonza Bay. Sadly, we only spent a few days there this time, for we were due back in Nyasaland.

The now familiar routine of our 2000-mile drive home passed uneventfully as far as Salisbury where we stayed with Jean and Geoff Mills in Borrowdale. They had completed their stint in Nyasaland, so Geoff was back on home territory where they had built a comfortable and spacious home and made a most attractive garden. Most of the houses in and around Salisbury were spacious with lovely gardens.

After this brief and pleasant respite in Salisbury, during which we got the car serviced, we continued via Northern Rhodesia because the roads were still bad in Mozambique. I just had time to buy a new Dunlop Maxply tennis racquet for £8.8s.0d. We aimed to sleep that night at Makuti, about 30 miles from the Northern Rhodesian border, but were running late so we telephoned them from Sinoia to say that we still needed the accommodation but would be late. We arrived at the Makuti Motel to the sound of tom-tom drums, the dinner gong. We had a very nice meal and very comfortable rooms, a carport, two double bedrooms and bathroom along with fitted carpets, clean mosquito nets without holes and nice hot water for a bath. Simple requirements, one might think, but it was wonderful for weary travellers to find such comfort in the bush. It cost us all of £5.10s.0d.

We left at 6.00 a.m. and were amused to see road signs warning us of elephants, for their presence was unmistakable from the huge piles of their dung. The road dropped down to the Zambezi River valley, characterized by numerous baobab trees (which only grow at low altitudes) and by a distinct landmark of central African lowlands, a tsetse-fly control shed. This entailed driving into the shed, giving one's name and car registration number and closing the car windows while an attendant pumped anti-tsetse fly insecticide under your car and round the wheels. The Chirundu Bridge straddling what was then a very angry and very full Zambezi River is a most impressive sight. We then moved on to the next big river, the Kafue, which was also running in spate. In fact, there was a watch on the bridge because, with so many odds and ends being swept down by the raging torrent, a build up of debris on and around the bridge pillars could cause great damage. We had a good breakfast in Lusaka and filled up with petrol. We also took the precaution of filling a jerry can, for there is no petrol station on the Great Eastern Road for 377 miles between Kachalola (193 miles away) and Fort Jameson. The road was so much in need of restoration that we had to slow down to 20, sometimes 10, miles an hour. The dust in places was ghastly but luckily we did not pass too many vehicles. We arrived at the Kachalola guesthouse exhausted at 4.00 p.m. to find that the swimming pool contained only a few inches of water. However, it looked clean enough to allow us to let Simon and Christopher have a nice long play in it to expend some of their excess energy.

The next day, 27 March 1963, is one I shall never forget. We set off as usual at 6.00 a.m. After all the rain the countryside was looking superb, the lush green grass so tall that it almost formed an arch over certain stretches of the Great Eastern Road. There were lots of bird around, hornbills, bishop birds and many others. The black soil on this road can get very slippery when wet, so the PWD had scattered gravel on the incline to give tyres a better grip; it certainly helped.

Much of the transport in central Africa is by heavy lorry and African buses and these vehicles break down fairly frequently. To warn oncoming traffic, it is customary to place a fairly large branch of a tree in the road. There were several of these about, but since there were no vehicles anywhere, we merely thought that the vehicles had been mended and driven on without removing the warning signs. However, on rounding a bend and seeing maize fields on either side of the road, it became apparent that we were approaching a village.

We then came to a roadblock, with huge stones right across the road and between 20 and 30 excited Africans wielding pickaxes, pangas and knives, and some brandishing knobkerries and spears. There were two or three slightly older men in the group who appeared to be in control. We had no option but to stop. Trevor quietly said, 'wind up your windows and lock your door and don't speak.' We always travelled with the back doors locked anyway. For once the boys did as they were told and we sat very still. Trevor wound down his window to speak to one of the older men, but kept the engine running and his foot on the accelerator. The leader, who was wearing a bright blue shirt and battered trilby hat, had widely spaced teeth and a very shiny intelligent face. His mates were clambering all over the bonnet on my side of the car, which I found very threatening. Trevor kept his cool and spoke politely and quietly. 'No, we had not got our United National Independence Party membership cards, for we lived and worked in Nyasaland and were on our way home.' Northern Rhodesia was further from independence than Nyasaland, but these people were acting as if they were already in power. The leader discussed independence with Trevor and demanded we pay him to drive through Northern Rhodesia. Trevor said he could not do that as it was against government regulations and anyway he worked for Dr Banda and he would be very upset if he knew that his fellow Africans were holding us up on our journey. An older man now appeared to do the talking and he queried Trevor about Dr Banda and the association he claimed. Trevor said, 'Here is Dr Banda's private telephone number. Ring him up and ask him about me.' The man was taken aback and one could almost see him wondering whether this *bwana* was perhaps a friend of Dr Banda's. The spokesman then said that even if we did not pay we should have got permission in Lusaka to drive through his territory. Trevor said that the next time we drove that way he would ensure that he had the necessary permission and that he would bring a personal letter from Dr Banda to cover us. At this point an even older man in dungarees, leather belt and much worn felt hat edged his way forward and said 'Morni *bwana*'. He then shooed the younger men away from our car and ordered them to roll away the rocks and drums blocking the road so that we could proceed. He was one of the old decent Africans who recognized and respected authority. We said goodbye as politely as we could and Trevor drove slowly on, only to find another boulder or two across the road just round the corner.

Here a European in a PWD Land Rover told us that he had just removed another roadblock about 150 yards up the road. His men then rolled the rocks away and a huge lorry and trailer that had been behind us went through. Trevor remained behind to ask the PWD man where he could find the nearest DC or police station. We followed his instructions to the DC's *boma* about 20 miles away at a place called Petauke. The DC expressed his concern and asked Trevor to accompany him back to our ambush spot to see if they could identify some of the hooligans. The twins and I were duly dumped on the DC's charming Swiss wife, who was very kind and understanding about our traumatic experience. She and her husband had recently been moved to Petauke from the Northern Rhodesia/Congo border and had some hair-raising stories to tell about the deteriorating situation in the Congo.

Her son had a bicycle and since Simon and Christopher had not yet learnt to ride one, this was their opportunity. Simon soon got the hang of it and then I helped Christopher, round and round the lawn until I was exhausted. I then gave the gardener 6d. to teach Christopher to ride and he did. Trevor and the DC returned to say that there was no trace of our ambush and no human being in sight. The vast maize fields were an obvious hiding place, but we had to get back to Lilongwe and Trevor could not stay and search all day. We were very grateful for their hospitality and for giving Simon and Christopher a chance to learn how to ride a bike. After lunch we drove to Fort Jameson, the last town in Northern Rhodesia, and on to Fort Manning in Nyasaland. It was good to pass into Nyasaland and see the leopard on the roadside board. We called at the police station in Fort Manning, where we drank a welcome cup of tea and caught up on gossip and news about postings, before our last lap to Lilongwe. Allowing for deviations and an ambush, the journey from Cape Town had been about 3000 miles, but our trials and tribulations were not yet over.

It was getting dark and we kept running in and out of heavy rain. When it was quite dark and about halfway to Lilongwe a federal customs barrier stopped us. Because the road to Fort Manning passes through Mozambique for a few miles, there is a customs post on its re-entry into Nyasaland. The African in charge decided to be awkward and not to let us through because we had not got our triptyque or any other document for our car because we had handed all these in at Beit Bridge on our re-entry to the Central African Federation from South Africa, which was the correct procedure and we had never had a problem before. The car still had a Paris number plate and that completely baffled the official. We showed him our passports stamped at Beit Bridge, but that made no difference. The barrier was finally lifted when Trevor followed him to his office and read the Riot Act, but then a Nyasaland Transport Company bus refusing to dip its lights or move from the middle of the road immediately blinded us. We were getting used to these challenging obstacles, so we set our teeth and crawled round the bus, just managing not to stick in the soft mud on the side of the road. We arrived at Lilongwe hotel at 7.30 p.m. with two little boys fast asleep in the back of the car.

We were warmly welcome at the hotel and met many friends. When we sat down to dinner, Dave (the hotel owner) sent us a complimentary bottle of very fine French wine. After more friends and chatter we eventually got to bed and turned out the lights at 1.00 a.m. What a day it had been and what a start to a new tour!

* * *

So began the tour that turned out to be our last in Nyasaland. Politics had crept into everything and had altered the atmosphere in the peaceful, beautiful backwater of Nyasaland. Dr Banda was vehemently opposed to the Central African Federation. He feared that Nyasaland would be swamped by Southern Rhodesia and would never attain independence in its own right: to this end he was infallible and constantly referred to the CAF as 'the stupid CAF'. Nyasaland had benefited enormously from the federation, which lasted from 1953 to 1963. Large sums of money were pumped into education, communications, health (Queen Elizabeth Hospital at Blantyre) and agriculture, and most services, including the police, had bigger budgets. There was a boom in the building industry as new personnel arrived to manage the steadily expanding services and small businesses. Lonhro bought up transport services and garages and needed local managers. One so-called whiz kid who came to Lilongwe was Ron Colley, a bachelor who invited us to share his 'enormous house' until ours was ready. We moved in with him the very next day and stayed for about a week along with Nanny, William and Alfonso the gardener.

Now that Trevor was Assistant Commissioner, Central Province, we were entitled to a nice old police house and an enormous garden with huge lawns, a productive vegetable garden, fruit trees and, best of all, a lovely citrus orchard with oranges, grapefruit and lemons. We channelled the water from the bathrooms (of which we now had two) into the citrus garden and by means of judicious planning directed it in such a way that we always had some trees in flower (lovely orange blossom flower next to our bedroom) and some bearing fruit. I made stacks of grapefruit marmalade and of course the more common three-fruit variety. We also had guavas (a fruit very high in vitamin C), avocados, mangoes and pawpaws. I made a few alterations to the flower garden and produced some quite respectable dahlias at the appropriate season. As always, we kept chickens, so had a good healthy supply of fruit, vegetables, eggs and the odd hen.

Most old houses in Nyasaland had the kitchen detached from the house, which was awkward in the rainy season when rain diluted your soup and in the cold season when it was difficult to keep anything hot between the kitchen and table. One friend used to give her cook an extra shilling if everyone sat down to hot soup at her dinner parties. Our house had the old kitchen attached to the back of the house; it was poky and equipped only with a Dover wood-burning stove and one deal table. As I did all the cooking, I rebelled and the PWD eventually agreed to install a stainless steel sink in one of the rear rooms, put up shelves and give me a brand new Belling electric cooker, which was a real joy. There was one sink on the back *khonde* exposed to the elements and I refused to use it, thus my insistence on a sink in my kitchen. I don't know how the dozens of previous *dona*s had managed. I had masses of shelves put up in the room alongside my new kitchen for all my china, crockery and glass, and used a third room as my storeroom, which was supposed to be kept locked, but now and then was left open.

While we were still with Ron we got news that some of the boxes and trunks we had sent on in advance from Cape Town had arrived in Blantyre and some in Salima. At least they were in the country, which was a relief.

By Easter we were more or less unpacked. It was nice to have Trevor home over the long weekend to help choose where to hang our much-loved pictures. Usually I had to do it and he did not always agree with my decisions. We also sometimes managed to slip down to the lake for a day with a case or two of beer from Salima police station.

Though this old house was very spacious and its rooms had high ceilings, which was nice in the hot weather, there were not all that many rooms. We had three big bedrooms with built-in cupboards, two bathrooms, a sitting room with French doors onto a large *khonde*, a hall and a dining room. We had brought a very nice Hornby train set back from the UK and were wondering where to put it. We eventually decided to set it up in Simon and Christopher's bedroom so it was laid out on a huge board resting on boxes. However, it took up rather more space than we had anticipated, so we asked the PWD for bunk beds. They were puzzled by our request because we had such large rooms, but they obliged and that made life more comfortable.

The PWD had whitewashed the inside of our house and the servants' quarters, which were quite spacious, but William complained about a problem with bugs and asked me to do something about it, which I immediately did by calling in a firm called Anti-Pest. The routine was that on Anti-Pest day you shut all the windows and doors and vacated the house for the day while they came and sprayed it with a powerful insecticide that destroyed all known and unknown bugs and kept the rooms bug free for about a year. On opening up in the evening there was only a slight smell that soon wore off. For months afterwards, any mosquito or fly that flew in and touched a wall dropped dead. It was a good system. The cockroaches and bugs were eliminated from Nanny's, William's and Alfonso's rooms and they were most grateful.

After the Easter holidays, Simon and Christopher seemed quite pleased to return to Bishop Mackenzie school and soon settled down. Although we had missed Merilyn badly over the Easter holiday, we knew she would be all right with Robert and Lorna and their children Anne and Sue. My friend Ann (Lady Riches), who lived in London, escorted Merilyn from Victoria to Paddington to catch the train to Cardiff where Lorna met her at the station. In those days there was a separate compartment for ladies next to the guard's van, in which we arranged for her to travel as a child.

My old governess Wy came to see us with a friend. They had booked into the Senga Bay Hotel on the lakeshore near Salima, so we went down to the lake for a weekend both to see them and to fetch Wy, who was to spend the rest of her holiday with us. It was fun having her to stay and our twins fascinated her. Several friends asked us out, which was nice for Wy who enjoyed our way of life. She flew back to Bulawayo on a Beaver aircraft via Salisbury.

The round of drinks parties, tennis and swimming continued at a decent pace. Trevor's life was less stressful than in Limbe during the emergency, but he had to keep on his toes, for a number of changes were afoot. The huge crowds Banda attracted were usually peaceful, though a few hotheads who thought Banda was not working for independence quickly enough made a lot of noise.

Lilongwe now had a big multi-purpose hall where the odd film was shown, with *El Cid* and *West Side Story* being among the early ones we saw there. Sir Roy Welensky also addressed a political meeting in the hall.

The commissioner of police came to stay with us for a few days during one of Banda's visits. The acting chief secretary Peter Youens came with him and they held talks at Peter Nicholson's house. Peter was the PC and a charming and experienced administrator. His wife was said to have kept a chameleon in each window of her house and because Africans were terrified of chameleons — some ancient belief in reincarnation — her house was never burgled.

There was a great drama one night while the commissioner was with us. Alfonso's wife was heavily pregnant but unsure of her dates. I had asked Alfonso if his wife would like to have her baby in hospital, but she did not seem keen, though I thought it would be better than in our modest servants' quarters. This evening he rushed in very agitated to say that his wife was having her baby in the lane on her way to hospital. She had thought that perhaps it would be a good idea to have her baby in hospital and when she recognized her labour pains she began to walk. Events overcame her in a rush and she gave birth to twins in the ditch. I telephoned for an ambulance, which eventually arrived and bundled her off to hospital with her two very small babies at 3.00 a.m. All was well and she soon returned. She claimed that because I had twins and because Alfonso worked for me she was bound to have twins.

For young police wives abroad for the first time, coping with life in central Africa can come as a shock. We were all very badly paid and some young wives took jobs serving in shops or as typists in offices, but they all found having domestic servants the most difficult adjustment of all. Having never had servants in the UK they had no idea how to cope. Some were dictatorial, which the Africans resented so promptly left, while others allowed untrained servants to flounder without supervision or guidance. Having gone through a stream of unsuitable servants, some of these women would seek my advice. I used to say that if an applicant has no experience, he or she must be shown how to do everything, how to sweep, dust and clean the bath. If you are hiring a cook/houseboy, first try him out and if he seems keen, teach him a few of your favourite dishes, simple ones at first, and progress from there. But, above all, only keep servants you like. There is no point in having people around if you dislike them. There is no rule that you have to have servants. Try doing it yourself, and eventually you will probably appreciate some help in the house.

Doing the ironing is bad enough on very hot days, but it is made worse by the fact that everything that is dried outdoors has to be ironed on both sides because of the dreaded mputzi fly, an insect that lays its eggs on damp washing in the sunshine. If the laundry is not properly ironed with a hot iron, the fly's eggs hatch and little maggots bury themselves in one's skin. They first appear as pimples but then become red and angry. The easiest way to get rid of them is to cover the pimple with Vaseline. This cuts off the air and when the maggot wriggles out through the Vaseline to breathe, one picks it off and dispatches it. A clear little hole is left in one's skin, but if dealt with early in the maggot's life it does not usually leave a scar. But if maggots are allowed to get too big, they leave a scar. Mputzi flies do not only lay their eggs on damp washing; they are attracted to anything damp, including a sweaty pillow or sheet. Simon had an mputzi scar on the side of his face that lasted for years. Christopher and Merilyn also had the odd one now and then. One careless mother had to have her baby's mputzis removed under anaesthetic in the hospital. She had not ironed both sides of his nappies and his poor little bottom was in a dreadful state. Mputzi flies are also liable to lay their eggs in hats that have carelessly been taken off and left in the sun, with disastrous consequences for the wearer's forehead. They sound horrendous, but one quickly learnt how to deal with them. This fly is easy to distinguish from an ordinary housefly, for it is much bigger and easier to swat.

From time to time I would have a group of young police wives in to morning coffee and we would discuss household problems like 'should I keep eggs in the fridge?' 'why is the meat so tough?' or 'how do I cook the local fish?'

I found one incident particularly hard to digest. A very junior officer had just arrived with his young wife and five children (an unusually large family for a new recruit) and they were having difficulty fitting into the very small two-bedroomed house they had been allocated. The baby was in a cot in their bedroom and the four other children were sharing two beds. I was furious and when I told Trevor he immediately asked the furniture clerk in the PWD to give the family more beds. The clerk was reluctant to oblige because the officer's salary scale did not entitle him to that many beds. Anyway, Trevor cut through the red tape and got him a bigger house with an adequate number of beds.

One of the best pieces of advice I was given on arriving in Nyasaland was to make all one's curtains two-and-a-half yards long (we all made our own or got a friend or Indian tailor to make them), as that was the length of the longest window in any government-owned house. It was good advice because it is better to have a curtain too long than too short and it saved the expense of buying new curtains each time we were moved around the country. I passed on this valuable advice to many an arrival.

In June 1963 the West German government decided to send a trade delegation, plus exhibition on wheels, to central Africa and this duly arrived in Lilongwe. Trevor and the PC had prepared a suitable area in which to park the articulated vehicles and to mount the exhibition of German manufactures, which included hospital and kitchen equipment, office furniture and lots besides. They gave me a lovely little travelling clock in a leather case, which I only recently discarded because it was a wind-up one and the spring had given up the ghost. I kept it for over 35 years. They also gave us five torches (one for each member of the family) and Trevor a 35-millimetre Zeiss Ikon camera and Agfa binoculars. He was thrilled to bits. Swarms of Africans looked on in amazement at all these vehicles and their contents. I do not know how much business the Germans picked up from this exercise, but they certainly gave us a lot of pleasure. Their visit coincided with Simon and Christopher's sports day. Trevor was the official starter complete with starter gun. Simon and Christopher took part in everything they could and have certificates to prove that they came second in the three-legged race and third and second respectively in the egg and spoon race. That evening we invited the German contingent to a party we had organized at the police mess. They arrived very late, but seemed to appreciate being asked.

We were often invited to Mbabzi to play social tennis. On this particular afternoon Simon and Christopher were playing with Liz and I do not quite know what happened but Liz fell awkwardly and broke her arm in rather an alarming way. Her mother very cleverly made a splint with tennis racquets and, with the vicar having come in a station wagon, we were able to lie Liz flat in this vehicle so as not to aggravate her broken arm any further. While Doreen nursed Liz, I drove the station wagon to the Lilongwe hospital and the vicar drove Nanny and my children home in my car. It was very traumatic. Liz had a serious break, but the doctor managed to ease her pain and put the limb in plaster after X-ray. Doreen slept the night with us to be nearer Liz. Like most healthy children Liz was running around in a few days with her arm in plaster, sometimes in and sometimes out of her sling. Fortunately, the arm healed well, but as Simon and Christopher were 'playing' with her at the time, they were about seven, I felt very guilty.

Because the Central Province is fairly extensive, Trevor was responsible for a huge territory and he insisted on keeping in touch with his men in the more remote areas. Also, given that he preferred to be outdoors doing things rather than stuck in an office, he was often away for the whole day, or even two days and a night, in places like Dedza, Dowa, Kasungu, Fort Manning, Kota Kota, Ncheu, Salima and Chipoka. He went to the latter either in the DC's launch or by railway trolley, the little platform on a bogie that is propelled by heaving a handle up and down.

The next excitement was having Merilyn fly out for her long summer holiday. Elaborate schemes were devised for various friends in England to fetch her from school and get her on a BOAC flight. She had to spend a night in Salisbury where Jean Mills collected her and put her on the Blantyre Dakota the next day. From Blantyre she had to transfer to a Beaver for Lilongwe. It was such fun all to be together again and for the first few days I just devoted myself to her needs. We managed to squeeze in a weekend at the lake, for we knew she enjoyed the swimming so much.

The show came round once again and we duly took our exhibits, but did not collect any prizes this time — competition was increasing. However, we thoroughly enjoyed the show ball in the company, among others, of Ken and Beryl who had left their small son Jo with our two and Nanny. The band was the only thing that spoilt this show ball, for it was the worst I have ever heard. It was awful and I think disbanded soon afterwards.

We had another week at the lake during Merilyn's holiday. I did a huge bake before the trip of cakes, biscuits, buns, bread and anything else that would withstand the journey and keep in the fridge for a day or two, for I wanted to spend all my time on the beach with the children.

Having invited four African and five European police officers to lunch, I felt concerned about William's reluctance to serve Africans. I explained that Africans would soon be running the country under Banda and that he had better get used to the new setup and he begrudgingly acquiesced. The lunch went off very well and William did not let me down, but Christopher nearly did. I had told him that we were having people to lunch but forgot to mention that four were African. When the front-door bell rang, William was nowhere to be found, so Christopher went to open the door and was on the point of taking the four Africans through to the kitchen to talk to William when Trevor arrived with the others and we had an enjoyable meal.

On hearing of a vacancy for five at the lion camp in the game reserve, we quickly collected all we needed and sped up to Luangwa game reserve for four days. It was a rush but well worth it, for we saw masses of animals — elephants, rhino, giraffe, antelope — and a lion kill half a mile from the camp. The children were intrigued.

Luangwa, which is one of the 18 national game parks in Africa set aside for the preservation of wild life, is about equal in size to the combined areas of east and west Sussex, Surrey and Kent, and is situated in northeast Zambia. Norman Carr first developed the idea of wilderness trails in his book *Return to the Wild* and these were still popular 20 years later. Though the five big animals — elephant, lion, buffalo, rhino and leopard — immediately spring to mind, there is much more to see. The bird life is outstanding. Apart from the beautiful fish eagle with its haunting cry, there are lilac-breasted rollers, malachite kingfishers, storks, cranes and many, many more. The diverse flora includes the famous baobab, sausage and marula tree. A delectable liqueur is now made from the marula fruit and elephants become quite drunk if they eat vast quantities of it. There is also an abundance of insects — dragonflies, praying mantises and stick insects (some of which are over a foot long), the antlion (which scoops out pits in the sand to trap other careless ants) and hundreds of different butterflies. There is some animal, tree or insect to look at whichever way you turn.

Doreen and Bruce were going on a long holiday and they asked me if I would look after their schipperke dog Susie. As a child, my mother had always had a schipperke, which was specially bred for Belgian barges, so I was delighted to try one out. Our Minnie took to Susie and we thoroughly enjoyed having her. She was a very friendly intelligent little dog. When we went on leave they had our Siamese cat. Everyone helped everyone else in those days.

Sadly, the time came to load Merilyn onto a plane for her return series of flights back to school in Sussex. And, once again, various friends *en route* led her to the next stage of her journey.

Life was now changing for us. With Simon and Christopher happily settled at their day school, I decided to open a kindergarten. Though unconvinced about the need for nursery education for all children, I did feel that for the term before children went to proper school they could benefit from some form of routine and discipline and from working and playing with other children. I had very few rules, but the child had to be at least four years old and toilet trained. The hours were from Monday to Friday from 7.30 a.m. to 12 noon and I would not take more than 12 children.

I ordered whatever equipment I could not get locally from Salisbury. They were a nice bunch of children, mainly English and American. They were allowed to bring one toy each to school and be responsible for it. I taught them how to write their names, numbers up to 100 (more if they were ready) and the alphabet. We started each day with prayers, and then went on to patterns, pencil control, colouring and painting (what a mess). I then read them stories. Sometimes they asked for special favourites and took it in turn so that everyone had a choice and sometimes I read from Eve Bingham's lovely Africa-oriented *Long Grass Whispers* or *Where the Leopard Passes*. We played games on the lawn and at break we had orange juice and homemade biscuits. A garage, which was attached to the house and had its own *khonde*, was converted into a schoolroom and it served the purpose well. We had two garages, but with the car mainly for my use and Trevor mostly using his Land Rover, we did not use both our garages for cars.

I am delighted to say that my 12 little charges all got on very well when they went to school. The majority were expatriates; two Americans whose parents were missionaries were beautifully behaved, whereas the two Jewish boys were quite a challenge. With the now inevitable disintegration of the Central African Federation, personnel from Southern Rhodesia began to filter back there as opportunities arose and we lost many doctors. This was serious, but Israel came to the rescue and we had two Israeli army doctors and their families arrive. One doctor and his wife spoke perfect English but their children only spoke Hebrew. Their son Tamir was five, so needed to go to school and needed to learn English. The doctor came to me with his dilemma and for once I broke my own rules and said I would accept Tamir on the strict understanding that I would not teach him English, but if he wanted to join in and I could cope with him, he would be welcome. This was quite a gamble because he was much bigger than the other children and I wondered what I had let myself in for. Tamir turned out to be the most exciting and intelligent child I had ever encountered. In no time he learnt to speak and write in English (with its different script from Hebrew) and every day he added many more words to his vocabulary. He constantly asked for the English names of everything and never seemed to forget. His progress was astonishing. He had picked up English and spoke well by the end of three months and was in fact correcting the other children's English. His name was Tamir Ben-Menachim and I thought I would read of him one day as prime minister of Israel or a professor, but sadly, we lost contact and I wonder what happened to him. It was quite an experience. His mother was alarmed at his command of English and gave him Hebrew lessons in the afternoons in case he forgot his mother tongue.

Events were moving apace. With independence round the corner and more and more Africans in government, the situation began to alter. Banda suddenly sacked Mike, a much-loved DC in Nyasaland since the war and now PC Northern Province. It was an ignominious end to an outstanding career, for Mike spoke Chinyanja fluently and was hard working, but Banda disliked him and told him to go. On their way south and to their exit, Dr Sword gave them a party in Lilongwe to which we all went to say our fond farewells and to express a wish to see them in England

197

where they were bound. The writing was on the wall and one wondered how many more people Banda would dismiss.

Our little police mess had filled quite a gap in our lives. For, apart from the occasional film, of which wild animal expert Norman Carr's *Return to the Wild* was a memorable example, we could do a limited amount of entertaining there. The next time the commissioner came to stay it was convenient to entertain him at the mess each evening, instead of going through all the palaver at home, and other police officers could meet him socially.

The next significant departure was that of Meg and Theo Bradshaw, who had been tobacco farmers in Nyasaland for many years. They had two sons, one in Europe and the other in Southern Rhodesia. Meg and Theo had been kind to us and to many others and we had spent innumerable happy days at their home with or without tennis. Theo had introduced Trevor to duck shooting on the Bua River, which he loved. When they came to Lilongwe they were never empty handed, but always brought honey, fruit or something special. But Theo had done something to upset Banda and it was fortunate that he was able to leave Nyasaland the way he did before Trevor had to arrest an old friend. They moved to Southern Rhodesia and he was told never to come back. There were several farewell parties for them, including one at Mbabzi.

Christmas was coming round again and we had managed to scrape up enough money to fly Merilyn out for the holidays. It seemed wrong not to have the family together for Christmas. She arrived safely and fell into a hectic round of children's parties. I loathe giving children's parties and this year we made full use of the children's Christmas party at the mess, which was very well done and everyone had a great time. In mid-January Merilyn had to fly back to Burgess Hill and the escorts' routine worked like clockwork. On a through flight from Lilongwe to London via Blantyre and Salisbury, passengers were entitled to a meal if they were between flights at the airport and were given vouchers for that purpose. Merilyn had a couple of hours' wait at Chileka airport in Blantyre and we had asked Beryl to see Merilyn onto the London plane and to make sure she got a meal. Beryl then phoned to say that her presence had been superfluous. This little girl who could hardly see over the counter had banged on the lid and said, 'My daddy says I am to have a free lunch. Can I have it please?'

She knew the ropes by then. The airhostesses were very good and she was well looked after. BOAC was outstanding in this respect and the hostesses with special responsibility for these children were known as aunties. With so many of us having to send our children to school in the UK, this was a valuable service.

* * *

In the 1950s and 1960s a strange movement was gaining a foothold in Northern Rhodesia, on the Southern Rhodesian border at Livingstone near the Victoria Falls and in the east of Nyasaland. An African woman from Zambia called Alice Lenshima, who claimed to have risen from the dead, declared she had died 11 years before and had woken up a few days later with a God-given mission to found a new Christian Church, the Lumpa Church. The doctrine she laid out was harsh for Africans to embrace: it forbade polygamy, drinking, smoking, primitive dancing, divination, witchcraft and politics. When followers of the movement tried to enforce its restrictive codes there were violent clashes and many deaths.

As the prospect of independence loomed, political temperatures rose throughout central Africa. Northern Rhodesia's United National Independent Party (UNIP) resented its followers not being allowed to participate in political events. One unfortunate youth, a member of the Lumpa Church, played truant from his school and was given a severe beating by a UNIP member. The Lumpa Church retaliated by burning down a neighbouring village. There were many incidents, feelings were running high and eventually the Northern Rhodesian government declared a state of emergency. The number of deaths was increasing and more serious incidents were getting nearer and nearer Malawi. As Trevor was in charge of Central Province and it borders Northern Rhodesia, he became concerned when 99 people were killed near Lundazi. The Lundazi police station was attacked and at Chipoma, ten miles from the Malawi border, there was a fierce battle and bitter fighting with at least 28 people killed and 50 more deaths in the same area.

Lumpa church services were similar to other Christian services and Alice herself composed most of the hymns. Her doctrine was a mixture of theology from the Holy Scriptures and African superstition and many referred to her as a prophetess.

199

With the outbreak at Chipoma a little too close for comfort, Trevor decided to reconnoitre the area, which was fairly remote with seasonal roads for part of the way and then only a track. Being the dry season, the roads were passable, so he took his Land Rover. Lundazi in Northern Rhodesia was about 120 miles from Lilongwe but only about 60 miles from Lake Nyasa, for this particular part of Nyasaland is very narrow. Trevor told Derick Tricker, his number two, and me where he was going. As luck would have it, headquarters and half of Zomba seemed to need him immediately and they could not find him. Before the invention of mobile phones and with a radio of only limited powers, he was incommunicado. I was not worried, but as soon as headquarters discovered that he was not in Lilongwe but had gone to the 'danger zone' on a 'recce', they were furious and ordered him back directly. As he never got the message from headquarters, he came back as planned. Zomba's attitude annoyed him; he had only gone to see what might be needed in a practical sense. As it happened the fighting did not overflow into Nyasaland.

The Revd Paul Mushindo had baptized Alice in 1953. She became a popular prayer leader and large numbers of people responded to her. With Christian life renewed in her village, a mission lorry transported her choir on tours round other villages. As Alice increased her following and became more popular (Africans could relate to her brand of Christianity), the established church missionaries, both Catholic and Protestant, began to distrust and dislike her, and they accused her of being a heretic. They felt uneasy because they saw the establishment of an African style church for Africans as a threat. The Lumpa Church did not only threaten the Christian churches; the rulers and chiefs felt that Alice's power undermined their authority also.

The Lumpa Church attracted people who thought the churches had done too little to resist the Central African Federation (1953–63). With non-party members being intimidated and subjected to violence, some Lumpa churchgoers defected to UNIP in order to take part in the political activities leading up to the 1962 general election. The Lumpa Church was declared the enemy of the nation and its members' houses were burnt, crops destroyed and many were beaten. Further battles raged when many then deserted UNIP for the Lumpa Church. Kaunda was now prime minister and he was asked to affect a solution. Alice was arrested in 1965 and a number of her followers fled to the Congo.

The killings continued until the mid-1970s and there was harassment by Kaunda's forces. Alice planned an escape to Angola, but it went wrong and she was arrested and imprisoned in Livingstone. She wrote to Kaunda asking for less harsh treatment and, five years later, in 1975, she was released and put under house arrest in Kaunda Square in Lusaka, where her supporters had built her a house. Alice died in her sleep on 7 December 1978. They kept her body for a week in case she rose from the dead again and 10,000 people attended her burial on 15 December.

Whether we like it or not, Alice left her mark and Christianity will never be the same in central Africa. Her success as a leader, at one stage she had 1.5 million members, forced the Roman Catholic and Scottish churches (which regarded pagan or traditional customs as sinful in the sight of God) to Africanize their attitudes and services. She turned thousands of people to God within her short life. By adapting long-held African customs and beliefs to Christian usage, Alice made it easier for Africans to be both Christians and members of their tribe. When the Lumpa Church was banned, many Africans did not drop Christianity but worshipped with the Catholics and Scots who had Africanized their services and, to the churches' delight, their numbers swelled.

Alice brought many good things to church life. Choirs hold competitions and wear uniforms, and women are now allowed to preach — Alice was the first, despite being illiterate. She also eradicated witchcraft and through her love she taught her members to share the little they had. I wonder what heights her power would have achieved had she not been arrested and incarcerated for 15 years. Much has been written about Alice and her Lumpa Church. I have only given a brief outline, for the 'troubles' did not actually spill over into Nyasaland, but killings did reach the border and Trevor was quite right to survey the situation.

* * *

In 1959 a strange large ape appeared in the Kandoli rainforests on the lakeshore near Nkata Bay — a lone female adult chimpanzee, which was a mystery because chimps are not indigenous to Nyasaland. One theory advanced to explain her arrival was that a female chimp had escaped from a travelling Brazilian circus near Lake Nyasa in Tanganyika. Experienced observers remarked that she had evidently spent much of her previous life in captivity because she was quite friendly and rapidly became a tourist attraction. Another indication that she had had contact with civilization was that she adopted a blue PWD tractor that was working on the roads in the area and sometimes refused to leave the vehicle. Many photographs were taken of her at the time and Sir Glyn Jones apparently spent many happy hours filming her. Her personality then changed. She became unpredictable and attacked several people, inflicting serious wounds. She developed a special dislike for photographers and bit one who was climbing a tree after her. She became increasingly short-tempered, attacked people without provocation and the villagers began to fear her. When a dog annoyed her, she grabbed it, took it up a tree and then dropped it — the dog died instantly.

It was decided that, as she did not belong in Nyasaland, she should be captured and sent to a zoo. So she was flown in a special cage to Chester. She died in April 1964 from an incurable lung disease caused by a severe infestation of hookworm. This is believed to have been the reason for her increasing bad temper — she must have been in some discomfort. She had been named Ufiti, which means witchcraft in the Nyanja language.

Banda's ambition to see the end of the Central African Federation came about at midnight on 31 December 1963 — an historic day for Nyasaland, now well on its way to full independence. Following a general election, Banda was appointed prime minister and, on 26 September 1963, the future pattern of events had been announced. The political scene was changing rapidly and African ministers were taking over the reins of government. Dr Hastings Kamuzu Banda went round the country making long speeches, some lasting two to three hours. He was a great orator with a grand sense of theatre and his audiences frequently numbered between 15,000 and 20,000. All this meant a lot of work for the police, but luckily the gatherings were peaceful and the crowds were good humoured, at least that is what I remember. But most of all I remember the very long hours Trevor was away from home whenever Banda was in the Central Province, for he never came home until the 'operation' was 'stood down'. The date set for Independence Day was 4 July 1964 and there was to be a week of celebrations. It was six years since Banda returned to promise his people that Nyasaland, now called Malawi, would gain its independence and become a sovereign state. It was a remarkable achievement. All his cabinet ministers were well educated and mostly university graduates from Uganda, Fort Hare, Rome, Delhi and Bombay.

Readers may feel that I have over-simplified the process of Africanization, but I prefer to leave the detail of how Nyasaland became Malawi to the historians and men who actually sat in government and undertook the negotiations between the federal government and HMG in London and locally.

* * *

In the meantime, the excitement surrounding independence had almost reached fever pitch among the Africans. The main events of course were to take place in the Southern Province and *the* cere-mony at midnight 5/6 July 1964 at the central stadium in Blantyre when, to symbolize the transfer of power, the new national flag would be raised and the Union Jack lowered. Similar ceremonies would take place at all district headquarters all over the country, including Lilongwe. The new flag would be flown from the top of the Mlanje mountain, the highest point in the country, and bon-fires lit from hilltops throughout the land. The Queen's and the KAR's regimental colours were to be handed over to the Malawi Rifles, the new army of the independent state.

HRH The Duke of Edinburgh had flown in to do the honours. He arrived on the afternoon of 5 July and left on 7 July. On 6 July Prince Philip handed over the investments of government to the prime minister, again symbolizing the transfer of power through the constitution granted by the Queen becoming the property of Malawi. That evening there was a state ball at the Colby Centre. At the state opening of Parliament in Zomba on Tuesday 7 July, Prince Philip, representing HM the Queen of Malawi, read the speech from the throne. There was then a lunch at Government House and Prince Philip departed in the afternoon.

A state ball was arranged in Lilongwe for Monday 6 July to

which we received a gilt-edged invitation with an RSVP and note saying: 'owing to pressing expense of Independence Committee, a cheque should accompany acceptance note, *not* cash.' We duly accepted and sent our cheque. We were told that a table would be reserved for us, so arranged for a few friends to make up a party and to meet at our house beforehand. When we arrived at the new town hall, we found two rows of chairs all round the perimeter of the room and not a table in sight. We were welcomed and graciously shown to our allotted place right under the powerful amplifiers, which successfully killed any attempt to have a conversation. We were handed a crate of beer, a bottle of whisky, a crate of Coca-Cola, two plates of tired sandwiches and a bottle opener, but *no* glasses. Here we all were in our best gowns and men in full evening dress and mess kit (complete with spurs) drinking beer and Coca-Cola from bottles. It was announced over the Tannoy that, since there were no glasses, we were to take a swig of beer and then top up the bottle with whisky. After some energetic dancing Trevor's cummerbund disintegrated, so he rushed home to change it and took the opportunity to return with a basket containing glasses, water, soda water and ice cubes. Now we could get on with the party. The band was terrific once we managed to move our seats away from the amplifiers and had got used to the volume. Only Africans could produce such rhythms; they just made you get up and dance. The room was packed and got very hot, so having seen Malawi launched we left soon after midnight.

Trevor was up early the next morning to drive down to Zomba to see his old friend Jimmy Orr. Jimmy and Trevor had been friends since their 1938 BSAP days in Southern Rhodesia and had been together on many escapades in Eritrea, Somaliland and Ethiopia during the war. After the war, Jimmy joined the Kenya police and while he was there Prince Philip visited Kenya on one of his tours and Jimmy Orr was chosen to present the Police Guard of Honour. Prince Philip knew Jimmy from their school days at Gordonstoun and they arranged to meet for a chat after the ceremony, during which Prince Philip offered Jimmy a job, which he accepted, at Buckingham Palace as his PA for occasions when he was not with the Queen. Since Trevor had known that Jimmy would be accompanying Prince Philip to Malawi for the independence celebrations, he had arranged to squeeze in a quick visit to

Zomba to see Jimmy before he and Prince Philip departed on Tuesday 7 July.

* * *

As Trevor gave 101 per cent of himself to his job, I saw it as my duty to provide a well-run and tranquil home. He needed peace and quiet at home, to switch off, enjoy his children and totally relax. He knew he could rely on me for the wellbeing of our family, friends and servants and that left him free to get on with his job, knowing I would support him and give him whatever assistance I could. I like to think that I achieved this goal. The heartbreak came with the inevitable partings — first Merilyn to school in England and now it was nearing the time for Simon and Christopher to be sent to a prep school. I was dreading it.

I go quite cold when I think of Pa being packed off to England from India at the age of seven, yet this was common practice in the late nineteenth and early twentieth centuries. We had done our research and almost decided on a school in Berkhamsted (where my father and brothers had been) when we received a brochure on a small PNEU prep school in Surrey. One criterion on our list was that the school should include children with parents serving overseas. Many boys at Desmoor in the village of Ewhurst had parents overseas (in the armed forces, colonial service and some BOAC pilots) and they flew to different parts of the world every holiday. Also, being near Heathrow, they would escort boys to and from the airport, which was just what we wanted.

So we decided on Desmoor School and all the preparations for getting two little boys to boarding school were set in motion. Desmoor had sent out a test to establish what standard Simon and Christopher had reached so that they could be placed in an appropriate class. A résumé of the sort of knowledge and skills expected of a boy of eight or nine accompanied the test. Simon and Christopher duly sat the test and to Mr Sanders's horror (he was headmaster of Bishop Mackenzie) neither boy came anywhere near the required standard. Trevor and I were asked to go and see Mr Sanders and we too were shocked. We knew it was a happy, albeit somewhat limited, school, but we also knew that if Simon and Christopher were ever going to get into a good public school they would need a few years at an English prep school to stand a chance. So we decided, probably immorally, to ask Mr Sanders to coach Simon and Christopher for a while and then let them take the test again in the hope that they would do better. With the honour of the school at stake, not to mention the future of our sons, he agreed and thankfully it worked.

Our next hurdle was the clothes list. Daniel Neale (a shop behind Selfridges) was the appointed supplier of the school uniform. (Ma used to get my best clothes sent out to South Africa from Daniel Neale and I have fond memories of a very smart chocolate brown checked winter coat with a velvet collar.) With very little time to get all the gear for Simon and Christopher, I sent the list (along with the boys' measurements) to Daniel Neale and asked them to supply everything on it, including the school trunk, which they should pack.

To the store's credit, it was all ready when we arrived about two days before Simon and Christopher were due to start school. Having spent most of their lives in shorts and T-shirts, the boys were absolutely delighted with their posh new clothes. What thrilled them most were the studded football boots. They tried them on there and then and rushed round the store with an imaginary ball. The shop assistants were tickled pink, for they said that most of the children they kitted out were sullen, blasé and uncooperative. I had to hand it to the shop; for a few extra pounds, nametapes were sewn on and everything was marked with a name and number, *and* they delivered the trunk to the school. I had not got around to hiring a car so I took the boys to school by train and the school met us at the nearest station.

I had flown over with the boys and left Merilyn (who was out for her long summer holidays) with Trevor because she was not terribly well after an attack of mumps. The gland on one side of her neck had developed an abscess that had failed to respond to antibiotics and had to be lanced, which the Israeli doctor did in an alarming and cruel manner. He whipped her away from me and took her into a rather primitive theatre at the cottage hospital in Lilongwe and all I heard were Merilyn's screams. I go cold thinking about it, for I can still hear the poor little girl screaming. For some reason the local anaesthetic had not taken and when I got her home she was still crying from the shock — the relief of not having a huge hard lump in her neck had not yet registered. I too was very upset because I could not comfort her. Eventually, Trevor went to the hospital and got something from the sister, which helped and she eventually slept — what a nightmare it was. One had to be tough to survive in some of those out of the way places. Anyway, because of all this Merilyn was unfit to fly and a close friend looked after her until she was better. I later met her at London airport and, after a day to recover and to bond again, I took her back to school.

So here I was in England on my own with Merilyn back at school, and Simon and Christopher busy exploring and apparently enjoying Desmoor. I was wondering how I was going to fill in the term. I could not fly back to Trevor until the next year because we had used up our allocation of flights and we could not afford an extra return flight for me. Luckily, I am blessed with very good friends and they took pity on me. I first went to stay with my school friend Jenny at her flat in Camden Town. While I was there I decided to rent a car for the children's exeats, for it was too awful without one. I hired a Morris Minor and asked Jenny if she would like to come with me to collect it from a firm in south London where I had struck a good deal. She said she would, so, having worked out a route back through London, we set out by tube and bus, collected the car and drove back to Jenny's flat without any trouble at all; she was an excellent navigator. When we got out of the car, I said to Jenny, 'Do you realize that this is the first time I have driven in London?' Her reply was that, had she known, she would not have come.

The little car was marvellous, for it meant I could be a 'proper' parent and attend the parents' days, Christmas plays and outings at both schools. Luckily, the schools were not far apart and exeat days tended to coincide, so we made the most of them. In between I visited various friends, including George and Margaret in Gloucester where I was able to be of some use. George's mother had recently died and his father (who belonged to the generation of men who were unable to look after themselves) was on his own in the house George had built for his parents on the farm. I became Uncle Frank's housekeeper for a while and it was nice being on the farm with George and Margaret only a few yards away.

I needed to rent a suitable house for the Christmas holidays, so decided to look in the Chichester area where I had two cousins — my mother's cousin in Birdham and my father's cousin in Itchenor. I found a centrally-heated little bungalow in Selsey.

Back in Malawi, Trevor was making plans for our future, for he did not want to remain in the police for long after independence. The idea of becoming a Queen's messenger attracted him so he applied and was asked to appear at an interview in London during the first week of December 1964. I met him at Heathrow and we had a few very happy days in London. He duly attended his interview where he discovered that the salary was a miserable £1175 per annum, rising to £1481 over nine years. This was not going to pay three school fees even if we had (which we did) a pension, so he put Queen's messenger out of his mind. It was once thought to be a glamorous job, but could be wearying with all the travel and flights on tourist class — there was no luxury there. Strangely, Queen's messengers travel first class on short European flights, but tourist for the long hauls. We were aware of all the travelling and fatigue drawbacks, but the salary slammed the door firmly shut. While Trevor was in the UK we managed to get the children out for a Sunday and had a nice family lunch. Trevor was also able to see Desmoor and to meet the headmaster and other staff. We hired a Hillman Imp for this weekend and could *not* get it into reverse, which was quite a handicap, though they gave us a discount when we took it back. Trevor then returned to Malawi and I remained on to have the children for the Christmas holidays.

Meanwhile, Dr Banda had got rid of some of his original cabinet and gathered men round him whom he liked and felt he could trust. Trevor had always got on well with him and now Banda insisted he move to the Southern Province to be near him, an order that could not be ignored. We had made up our minds to stay for one year after independence and then return to the UK, but Banda tried to persuade Trevor to change his mind and remain on. 'We need people like you whom I can trust,' he had said, which was very flattering, but the work of the police had altered so much that Trevor felt he could not both stay on and be true to himself. So, with William's help, Trevor packed up the house and they moved to the big police house in Sunnyside, Blantyre.

You may be wondering what happened to Nanny when all three children were in the UK. When we explained the situation to her, there were tears all round and we felt awful. Several families offered her jobs and made enticing salary offers, but she steadfastly turned down the lot. She said 'Simon and Christopher were my special babies and Merilyn, like my daughter, I have finished now with children. I am happy to return to my village and look after my mother who is now very old and needs help,' and nothing any other family suggested made her change her mind. We deposited a lump sum for her in her post office savings account and Trevor gave her a lorry to take herself and all her possessions back to her village near Mwanza in the Southern Province. Merilyn and Nanny kept up a correspondence for some years and then it suddenly stopped and we sadly heard no more. I owe a great debt to Nanny. She made my life so much easier and she adored my children. I shall always be grateful that she came to us.

Back in Selsey we had a very quiet Christmas. We visited our two cousins quite regularly, but it was not the same without Trevor. I took the children back to their schools and then flew to Malawi and Blantyre. What a welcome I got! It was lovely to be back with Trevor and to sort out the house and garden. Alfonso, I am glad to say, was still with us and between us we tackled the garden, for the previous occupant had not taken much interest in it. In no time we had lots of flowers, a productive vegetable garden and of course chickens — it was a big house on a large plot. Our social life was fairly hectic but the house never really seemed like home because the children had never been with us there.

Having taken the children back to school but before leaving Selsey in January, I arranged to rent another house in Selsey for Easter 1965. Instead of the children flying out for Easter we decided it would be better for me to go to England. Trevor had handed in his resignation to Dr Banda, who reluctantly accepted it, and we planned to leave Malawi in July. Of course we were still limited with air tickets.

The most notable and pleasant aspect of not having the children with me was being free to accompany Trevor on day trips round the Southern Province, which I thoroughly enjoyed. We would take a picnic lunch or at times be invited to lunch at some outpost. Trevor preferred to drive than be driven (although we always took his driver on these country trips) and most of the journeys were in the police Land Rover, which was very uncomfortable. All the

209

exhaust and heat from the engine seemed to be directed onto the front passenger's feet, so I was forced to sit with my feet up on the dashboard. It was not a pretty sight, but it was more comfortable than rattling about in the back and not seeing much. Trevor was eventually given a Ford Zephyr, which was comfortable on tarred roads, but there were few of those, and then a Humber Snipe, which was again not good off tarred roads.

I was really beginning to relax and enjoy life when the phone rang at 2.30 a.m. on 13 February 1965 and all hell broke loose.

* * *

A little background to this rebellion might be helpful. Soon after Nyasaland became Malawi in July 1964 Dr Banda had rid the government of several well-spoken, educated young cabinet ministers who had been growing impatient over his refusal to rush Africanization. At a stormy cabinet meeting, these ministers who included Chipembere, Chiume, Chirwa and Chisiza presented Banda with an ultimatum. He was to abandon his pro-Western policy and bring into line the accepted standards of left-wing pan-Africanism and give immediate recognition to communist China, thereby ensuring that Malawi join in the popular African game of playing the East against the West. However, they had over-estimated their strength and influence, for Banda was able to gain sufficient support to crush the revolt.

Had the rebel ministers succeeded, an anti-European regime influenced by Chinese communist agitators would have replaced the Banda government. Five of the deposed ministers went into exile in Tanzania. Chipembere chose to be restricted to his home in Malindi, but then escaped to organize his band of guerrillas in remote parts of the country. It was this that led to the attack on Fort Johnstone police station on 13 February 1965. Chipembere then escaped to Tanzania by the skin of his teeth in mid-May.

When this little war was at its height and Trevor was near the action in the Fort Johnstone district, it was not much fun for me to rattle about in the big police house on my own. William insisted on sleeping on a camp bed in the kitchen to guard me while the troubles, as he called them, were on. Then, when Ken and Beryl came to lunch one day from Mikalongwe (William reminding me to serve rice as this *bwana* loved rice) and invited me to stay with them for the duration of the crisis, I immediately accepted, packed my case and joined them. William still insisted on sleeping in the house. This time he was guarding the dog and the cat.

The police and army now had the use of a plane to fly commanding officers to and from Chileka and Fort Johnstone. This made life a lot easier, for it meant I could see more of Trevor when he flew down for the day. There were a lot of wild duck about in the swamps and the fishing was good, so I was detailed to get his shotgun and fishing rod to Chileka. The only problem was that we were unable to fit the fishing rod into such a small plane. It was not a collapsible telescopic rod and the only way it could be manoeuvred in was to remove a door. This they did and put it on again and then all three men piled in and set off to war. For the interest of plane enthusiasts, I think the plane was an Apache.

Trevor got home every three to four days for 24 hours or so, which was great, but as the plane was not always available and very often the weather was against flying, he did get very tired. At the end of March, I spent a few days with Lee Fuller and her husband Brian in Zomba and she and I drove up Zomba Mountain, where the Queen Mother had so loved to pick wild flowers, and had a lovely walk round the plateau with its magnificent views. Fortunately, Trevor managed to come home for a few days before I flew back to England for the children's Easter holidays. Before I left I gave Alfonso several packets of vegetable seeds, including butter head lettuce, for I knew he would be proud to show me how well he had done when I returned in a month's time.

Having rented the house in Selsey three months earlier, all I had to do was hire a car, collect the children from their schools, drive to Selsey and unpack. To accommodate all the school trunks, I hired a Cortina estate and then swapped it the next day in Chichester for a Vauxhall Viva, which was quite adequate for the four of us. The weather was nice, so we did not have a bad Easter holiday. We saw quite a lot of our cousins and Jenny came to stay. My children got on very well with her and she adored them. Robert and Lorna also came for Easter with Anne and Sue. Heaven knows how we all fitted in, but we all enjoyed ourselves. Then it was time to pack up and take the children back to their schools, clear up the house and fly out to Trevor again. Thank goodness this colonial torment of forever saying goodbye to my husband and/or children and leaving one or other on a different continent was coming to an end — at least the end was in sight. Trevor had had enough of working in independent Malawi.

I was due back in Blantyre for a wedding on the Saturday, but for some reason we were delayed 24 hours in Nairobi and I missed the wedding. But there was a bonus. When I eventually arrived at Chileka, Trevor was waiting at the foot of the steps by the plane.

On walking round the garden to see what Alfonso had done, I was puzzled. Everything looked fine, had grown well and was free of weeds. The lawn was cut and the flowers in bloom, but where were the lettuces? The ones growing in my garden were enormous, but they were not butter heads, so I asked Alfonso what had happened. He shamefaced said that the seeds I had given him had all germinated and were doing well when the chickens got in and demolished the lot. He knew I would be furious to come back to no lettuces, so he asked his friend up the road to give him some plants so that I would have some on my return. I laughed and congratulated him on his ingenuity.

I may have missed the wedding but I was in time to accompany Trevor to Dr Banda's dinner at the Shire Highlands Hotel in Limbe to meet African delegates from Togo, Upper Volta and Ivory Coast. The fizz had gone out of the little war when Chipembere escaped over the border to Tanzania, but Trevor wanted to go up there for a final check on the situation. I accompanied him (in the over-heated Land Rover) and we stayed at the Palm Beach Hotel near Fort Johnstone where I spent a very pleasant few days lazing on the lakeshore and enjoying a break. Our room was only a few yards from the water and lovely fresh chambo (telepa) fish was served at most meals.

On 22 May 1965 we learnt that Chipembere had turned up in New York. We understood he planned to further his graduate studies and receive medical attention for an insulin dependent diabetic condition that had not been improved by four or five months living rough on the run. About 400 of Chipembere's supporters were imprisoned, including able men the country (starved of skilled men) could have used in important positions.

With all opposition thoroughly cowed, Dr Banda now ruled in the autocratic style to which he aspired. He raised and armed private armies, the Young Pioneers and the Malawi Youth, to carry out his dirty work, thus undermining and demoralizing the conventional police and army (the Malawi Rifles). It was obvious now that we had made the right decision to leave Malawi, for we no longer felt comfortable in this country in which it had been so lovely to live and to bring up our children. We were sad to go, but Trevor could no longer be a proper policeman and he was not prepared to compromise his principles; and I wholeheartedly supported him.

While we were at the Palm Beach Hotel news came through of a ferry tragedy at Liwonde, with over 100 people believed drowned and about 50 able to get ashore. The ferry sank near the southern bank, otherwise even more would have drowned. The government announced that compensation would be paid to families who had lost relatives in the tragedy. In the absence of a passenger list or proof of who was travelling, the claims far exceeded any possible number of people on the ferry. Some applicants even dug up recently buried corpses to produce as evidence. After a very short while the compensation handouts were closed. There were plans in hand to build a river control barrage, over which a road would pass to replace the ferry at Liwonde, but that would take time and finance.

✳ ✳ ✳

Malawi was to pass from its present slow and often cumbersome but picturesque modes of crossing rivers to monuments in concrete and steel to bridge the wide, swiftly flowing and mostly crocodile infested rivers. Dr Banda had stressed the urgent need to erect bridges on all the main routes that still used ferries in the hope of preventing further ferry sinkings and tragic drownings.

Previously, only bridges that carried continual traffic were built. Now, with heavily increased traffic the length and breadth of Malawi as a result of development and economic expansion, and with modern, more efficient and quicker means of construction, bridges would become more and more commonplace.

The Liwonde ferry that floundered and sank in May 1965 was made of two strongly built pontoons with bulkheads, topped by a wooden deck with safety rails. It was slung on a cable and towed backwards and forwards by an attached diesel-powered launch. This 80-yard crossing took five minutes, but one usually allowed 10 to 15 minutes at the ferry for unloading, the maximum load being eight saloon cars or the equivalent of 20 tons.

Other ferries were much smaller with individual modifications to suit particular parts of various rivers. The two ferries at Chiromo and Chikwawa lower down the Shire River made use of the swift current to get across. The diesel launch and ferry were set at a certain angle in the river and the current carried the ferry across, much as one sets a sail in a wind to reach a certain buoy. These two were both fairly quick crossings, with the old hand-operated ferries, so much a part of the country, being the slowest. With labour cheap and plentiful, a team of men (usually wearing sturdy gloves to protect their hands from the steel cable and wide-brimmed hats plaited from palm leaves for protection from the sun) pull the ferry across the river on a system of pulleys. Because of the lower altitude, it was always hot at a ferry crossing and, having spent ten minutes in the sun hemmed in by breezeless banks, one could appreciate why the men wore beach hats.

On a slow crossing, it was always delightful to hear the team of Africans burst into song as they set the rhythm of their work. The song would almost certainly be about the river, food, crocodiles or women, the four subjects most closely related to their lives. They depend on the river for their work and their food. And without their women to toil in the fields, grow their crops, cook their food, carry their water and occasionally fall victim to a crocodile while fetching water, just where would they be?

Despite so many Africans living close to rivers and lakes — indeed they have to live near a natural water supply — very few can swim, which was one reason for the high death toll in the Liwonde ferry disaster. Of the 150 on board at the time of the sinking, 100 lost their lives when the ferry was only 12–15 yards from the southern bank. Though a strong current on the southern side did not help, 50 people did manage to struggle ashore.

One man who found himself in the river grabbed a piece of floating timber, only to have it knocked from him by a passing survivor. He then grabbed the next thing he could find, which was a lifebelt. At the same time he noticed a girl in difficulty and managed to pull her towards the lifebelt; together they were hurled

214

downstream, went whizzing through the sluice at the barrage and eventually came to a stop in reeds under an overhanging branch four miles downstream. They were still unable to get out of the water, but saw lights near the bank and shouted for help. They called and called and although the villagers heard them they were too superstitious to investigate; they merely thought the river spirits were being noisier than usual. When the waterlogged couple were still calling at daybreak, a more venturesome young villager came to investigate. When he saw there was no spirit, he raised the alarm and some men turned out to rescue the pair, who had by now had seven hours dangling in the water. They told of the sinking of the ferry and the villagers guided them back to Liwonde where they received appropriate medical attention.

Another tale of endurance from three miles downstream came from a woman who had been swept off the ferry, thrown into the river, hurled dizzily through the same sluice gates (but unattached to any timber or lifebelt) and found next morning all bundled and soggy in the bulrushes on the bank by the early water carriers. They at first thought she was dead, but something made one look more closely. The old woman sprang to life and, much to their astonishment, addressed them as angels; she thought her nice squishy bed was in heaven. The villagers managed to persuade her that they were merely humans and very much down to earth. After the old woman related her sketchy memories of the night before, she spurned any medical aid and said she must get home at once, for they would be wondering where she was. So off she stumped on her two bare feet to walk the ten miles to her village.

With six wet months followed by six dry ones, river levels are constantly rising or falling, so ferries often had to move to other places so that vehicles could be driven on board reasonably safely, with obvious consequences for the approach roads. Some ferries had a ramp that was let down for loading and pulled up during the crossing; for others, in more remote areas, there would be only two planks between the ferry and the shore, one for right wheels and one for left wheels, so accurate and careful driving was vital.

More hazardous than some of these ferries are the bridges made from tree trunks and branches of various shapes and girths precariously lashed together with strips of bark. I have seen such bridges (for want of a better name) sink under the weight of a

Land Rover. On reaching the far bank one heaves a sigh of relief and is amazed that the rickety structure has held up once more.

But with progress, modernization and the all important safety element, sturdy bridges, the creations of modern engineering, will make travel in Malawi seem very tame and ordinary by comparison. Indeed, to many it will hardly seem like central Africa.

* * *

For the Queen's Birthday in June, every colony put on a parade to which everyone would turn out in his or her best uniforms, bib or tucker, and Malawi was no exception. The parade was held at Zomba and the KAR (now Malawi Rifles) 1st Battalion presented the colours. With marching, counter marching and the band playing, it was in fact a mini trooping the colour.

HE the Governor General Sir Glyn Jones presented the New Year's honours and awards to their various proud recipients. We, along with many others, had been invited to Government House after the parade where many people congratulated Trevor for having been awarded the Queen's Police Medal.

We were given several farewell parties, some private, some official and all very touching. The African police officers gave us a party and presented us with the Malawi emblem of two leopards against a rising sun carved in wood and with a suitably engraved brass plate. This always stands on our hall table wherever we are. I was particularly touched at this party because an African gave me a special mention in his speech and presented me with a carved ivory brooch, which I often wear. He said, 'When we paid for the Malawi leopard wood carving we found we had some money left over, so instead of drinking some beer, we thought we would give Mrs Bevan a present to remember us.'

On leaving the district, the Southern Province police gave us a magnificent farewell dinner at the Shire Highlands Hotel and presented us with a copper tray and four-piece copper coffee set, which is much admired. Another goodbye party was at the police headquarters' mess in Zomba at which Trevor's brother officers presented him with a silver entrée dish.

That June was hectic. On packing up the house for the last time, I was sorting out, throwing away and deciding what to sell and what to take back to the UK. I decided not to take our old Queen's green dinner service, old glasses, bashed saucepans, the washing machine or lawn mower. I gave a lot to William and Nanny, who had turned up to pay her respects and to say her final tearful farewell. What they did not want William decided to sell for me, so he laid it all out on the kitchen *khonde* and had a thoroughly enjoyable time. Mrs Mwalo, our nextdoor neighbour and the wife of Banda's minister of information, came over one day to see what she would like. I overheard William tell her, 'Take care of anything you buy from my madam. You are very lucky to have anything from my madam and you cannot take it home until you have paid the full amount.' She said that her husband was away; she had no money and did not know when he would back. William's retort was 'bad luck, I repeat you do not take anything until you pay in full.' I was intrigued, so I peeped out and there was Mrs Mwalo down on her knees in a deep curtsey with her hands together as if she were talking to a chief. This was the old-fashioned African way in which women showed their respect for (subservience to) senior men. I was amused. A minister's wife had met her match in my authoritative William.

One of the saddest things was parting with Minnie the spaniel and Puss the Siamese cat. Luckily, they both went to loving families and were well looked after. We then dashed up to Lilongwe for a weekend, stayed at Mbabzi and said goodbye to our Central Province friends.

Trevor and I had always wanted to climb Mlanje, Malawi's highest and most majestic mountain, and now time was running out. The Forestry Department, which managed Mlanje Mountain, had planted cedars and other trees on the slopes and plateau for commercial use. Brian, the head forester, was used to climbing this mountain and in his younger days would think nothing of running up twice a day if necessary — and Mlanje peak is 9843 feet above sea level. Having organized the logistics for a two-night stay in the forestry chalet on the mountain, Brian and we set off. We took the Land Rover as far as possible and then began the Likabula ascent, wow. The two men soon left me behind but I slogged on, determined to keep going. There was a path to follow and the last few hundred feet were really hard work. Trevor and Brian were on top enticing me on with hot tea laced with whisky. I made it and

217

never had tea tasted so good. The chalet, build entirely of cedar wood, was delightful and the roaring cedar log fire smelt heavenly. Brian's faithful servant had lunch ready for us and we spent a quiet afternoon ambling round the plateau. The night was freezing (at that altitude there was a heavy frost), but the sun soon warmed us up and we had a super three-and-a-half-hour walk round Luchenze and a picnic lunch beside an icy trout stream.

In 1905 an attempt was made to bring English trout to Nyasaland's rivers. Fish eggs were dispatched, but as this type of fish was used to a cold climate the eggs died of heat during transport. The next year the fish eggs were packed in ice and they arrived safely in Zomba. They were put in the Mlungusi stream on Zomba Mountain, and later into various streams on Mlanje Mountain, and they are still there (I hope). There were magnificent views in the clear mountain air over to Zomba Mountain in one direction and down the Shire valley and across the plain to the southern end of Lake Malawi in the other. Next day we walked the other way on the plateau under Chambe peak, had lunch at the chalet and then began our descent. We arrived home at 6.00 p.m. thoroughly weary and triumphant (but both had very stiff legs the next day).

Between climbing Mlanje Mountain, farewell parties here, there and everywhere, packing and tennis parties, Malawi was about to celebrate its anniversary of a year's independence. Four days of jollification were organized and Trevor was of course involved each and every day in making sure that the police force and police band were all present and correct. There were football matches, a Malawi Young Pioneers' parade, a youth rally, a military display, more football, a state banquet at Ryalls Hotel, 21 traditional dancing displays, delegates from several countries to be escorted here and there and, on 7 July, the state opening of Parliament and finally the state ball, phew. Africans have a tremendous capacity for enjoyment and over these days of celebration they certainly showed it. Luckily, though a few programmes overran, all the arrangements went according to plan and everybody had a jolly good, if exhausting, time.

We only had a very few days left and what a rush it was. Everyone was so kind and generous that we felt we were being torn apart emotionally. It was now mid-July and we had made arrangements with long-suffering friends to have our children for

218

the first part of their summer holidays. We could have flown straight back to London there and then to be in England for the beginning of their school holidays, but there was too much against us. First, it was part of the golden handshake to be given first-class tickets on a final sea voyage back to the UK and we did not want to miss that. Also, we wanted to take our car with us and we needed to see my parents in South Africa to say goodbye to them. So when we had packed up everything we spent the last two nights in Malawi at Mikalongwe with Ken and Beryl. Then, on 20 July 1965, we drove out of an important era in our lives, leaving mostly happy memories of Nyasaland and wishing Malawi well.

We followed the Tete–Mozambique route. Our last stop in Nyasaland was Mwanza and we made good time to Salisbury where we met my brother and his family for a meal at Meikles Hotel — the old Meikles Hotel where in his bachelor days in the BSAP Trevor had once held the record for getting from one side of the ballroom to the other without touching the floor. Petrol was blissfully cheap in those days and I see we put in seven gallons for £1.10s.0d. Having no children with us we travelled further and faster each day and reached Bonza Bay in record time.

We had previously arranged with the Union Castle Line that it was in order for us to put a trunk or two on the *Pretoria Castle*, berthed in East London docks, and for us to join the liner a week later, with our car, in Cape Town. This gave us a few more days with Ma and Pa and lightened our load. We rushed about with last minute shopping and Ma and Pa gave us a lovely farewell party, which was nice as everyone (or so it seemed) we knew in East London and further afield was invited, so we saw many of our friends. I had an uncanny feeling that this visit was a very important one. Pa was nearly 85 and, though fit as a fiddle and still swimming and riding, I had a premonition that I would not see him again, so I felt I must make every minute count. (I did see him two years later.) After painful goodbyes, we left early on 28 July for Cape Town via the Garden Route, spending one night *en route* at Knysna with cousin Meredith and Ena. We crept out of the house very early — hopefully not disturbing anyone — and drove straight to the *Pretoria Castle* in the Duncan dock at Cape Town harbour. At the top of Sir Lowry's Pass overlooking the Cape Peninsula we stopped and got out of the car to take a long last look at Africa. We had travelled 2566 miles from Blantyre on our last African journey — we just stood in silence deep in companionable and emotional thoughts. We reported on board to the purser and, although the ship did not sail until the next day, he allowed us to go straight to our very fine first-class cabin. The car was hauled up in a 'cradle' and stored in a hold.

On the dot of 4.00 p.m. the *Pretoria Castle* sailed out of Cape Town harbour, as every Union Castle liner had done for years, with the band playing, streamers flying and everyone on board at the rails waving, laughing, crying or just saying goodbye.

The *Pretoria Castle* was the flagship of the Union Castle Line. Commodore Byles was at the helm and we found ourselves at his table — an honour as it turned out and great fun. As we hit the Atlantic rollers the first night, it was very rough and an elderly lady fell and broke her leg. In view of the sea conditions, the lady's age and our proximity to Cape Town, we turned round and returned to the Duncan dock to get the patient to Groote Schuur Hospital. As soon as the old lady was safely in an ambulance, we set off again and, this time very quietly, steamed out to face the fierce Atlantic once more.

The 14-day voyage passed all too quickly. We both needed the rest and relaxation and enjoyed the social life it offered. As we both love ship travel, we joined in all the various deck games in the mornings and, after superb lunches, slept every afternoon ready for the evening's entertainment.

Four or five days out of Cape Town we stopped at the remote Atlantic island of St Helena. It is the second remotest island on earth, with only Tristan da Cunha 1000 miles south being more remote. We had an important passenger on board bound for St Helena, the new governor, a charming man we had got to know at the commodore's table. St Helena is a quaint little island ten miles by five and full of old buildings, very old cars and old values. The streets are safe at night and the gaol is seldom occupied. It is a volcanic island and the terrain is steep, with narrow valleys, some sheltered and tropical others windswept and bare. It has one bird, the wirebird, that is not found anywhere else in the world, but we failed to see one; and 33 plants and 20 fish are endemic to the island, which is not bad going for such a small place. The people are fiercely royalist and every shop displays pictures of the Queen and other members of the royal family. The island's greatest claim to fame is that Napoleon Bonaparte spent his last days there as a prisoner of the British at Longwood House. There is little work on the island and sadly the flax industry had recently collapsed, so St Helenians seek work wherever they can find it. England is the most favoured destination, but many go to South Africa (my mother's laundry maid was a St Helenian who had married and was living in Cradock). Some go to Ascension and even the Falkland Islands, but there was no regular ship calling, so these sojourns abroad were indeterminate in duration. (Now there is a regular service. A little ship, the *St Helena*, plies between Cardiff–St Helena, Ascension–St Helena and Cape Town–St Helena six times a year.) There is no quay at Jamestown Bay where the ships anchor; to get ashore one takes a motorboat ferry to some very slippery and slimy steps. You are lucky if you arrive on shore with dry shoes. We hailed a taxi, an ancient Chevrolet, and were hurtled round the hairpin bends and steep inclines at breakneck speed, but as there were only about six other cars on the road, the journey was less hazardous than it sounded. We went to Longwood House and saw Napoleon's frugal dwelling. Leading from Jamestown at sea level to the top of one of the mountains are 699 steps. We alighted from the taxi at the top of these steps and took our time descending. Local children were running up and down as if they were on a beach. (There is no beach at St Helena, for the volcanic peaks rise straight up out of the water.) We were told that some daredevils slide down the steps lying horizontal with their neck on one rail and their ankles on the other and just whiz down in no time at all. The other highlight was to meet Jonathan, an enormous tortoise aged more than 100 living in the Government House grounds with several other tortoises said to be half his age.

It was then back to the *Pretoria Castle* via the same slippery steps and ferry and we set sail for Ascension Island, where we dropped anchor. With a tremendous swell, and landing a tortuous experience by launch, we were not allowed ashore. In those days the USA had a huge base there for satellite tracking and the BBC a transfer station. It too is a volcanic island and, from what we could see, it is harsh and bleak, with no evidence of the lush tropical plantations we saw in some of St Helena's valleys.

The next stop would be Southampton, but until then there was all the traditional shipboard entertainment, including the fancy headdress evening. Trevor and I again went as the heavenly twins, for we now knew how to construct the two constellations and it was unlikely there would be anyone on board who remembered us doing the same thing on a different ship of a different line several years before. Anyway, we had a fabulous evening.

At Southampton the AA had very efficiently got our car unloaded and filled with petrol, and had organized the UK number plates and road tax disc. We drove straight to Karen and Derick Tricker who were looking after Simon and Christopher for us. We spent the night with them and the next day drove up to London to meet Merilyn off the 'ladies' compartment of the Pullman train from Cardiff to Paddington. At last the family was together again and, once the slight guilt tension had worn off, we were all so happy.

We stayed at the Overseas Club in Earls Court while Trevor went to the Commonwealth and Foreign Office for his debriefing and valediction. We then 'did' London with the children — the changing of the guard at Buckingham Palace, the Science Museum, and the river launch from Westminster Pier to the Tower of London. In the evening we went to Leicester Square to see *My Fair Lady*, which we all loved. We had so enjoyed the river trip that we decided to do it again and see the *Cutty Sark* and later the Natural History Museum. We must have been exhausted mentally and physically, but I do not recall hearing any complaints.

Before I left England at the end of the Easter holidays, I had arranged to rent another house in Selsey. This was not going to be ready for us for another few days, so we accepted an invitation to spend those days with George and Margaret Hubert at Bredon's Norton. It was good to be on the farm again and, as it was harvest time, Trevor was able to give George a hand. George was worried that, being unused to heavy physical farm work, Trevor would hurt his back, but he was all right and thoroughly enjoyed himself. It was very hot and the children had a play pool in the garden. We also took them swimming at a friend's house once or twice in Eckington, where I was delighted to see how much Simon and Christopher's swimming had improved.

As Gloucestershire was not far from Wales, we decided to drive over to thank Robert and Lorna for having Merilyn for the first part of the summer holidays. A four-berth caravan parked in the garden served as their spare room. We were very comfortable and it was good to see our old friends. Trevor was convinced we should buy a caravan as an economic form of holiday for the five of us, so Robert took him off to a caravan show and they came back full of enthusiasm for this and that make, and the next day Lorna and I went with the men. I was confused about the various details of the various makes and said that I would leave it to him to make up his mind, but then went on to say that I thought we should hold our horses and see what the immediate future held, for we still had to buy a house and may not have anywhere to keep a caravan. Reluctantly he agreed with me.

At this time there was great excitement in South Wales with the opening of the Severn Road Bridge, so the next day we drove over it on our way back into England. We had to queue for two hours to get onto it, for it seemed that everyone in South Wales had chosen that day to sample the magnificent engineering feat. It was certainly impressive and cut the journey time down considerably.

We spent the rest of the holiday in Selsey. The summer remained nice and hot and the children were on the beach a lot. We saw quite a lot of my two sets of cousins again, which was nice.

Then it was time to kit the children out for school once again. It was still very warm and I remember Merilyn complaining bitterly that they had to go back in September in their winter clothes and boil. Our tenancy came to an end in Selsey and we went up to London for a few days before moving into a delightful large house my cousin Reg Rice had set up for us in Itchenor. There we spent the winter trying to work out the rest of our lives.

With the whole family in the same country, the partings were now less stressful and we were of course able to have the children for all their holidays, half terms and exeats. For once I did not feel torn between husband and children, which was a great joy.

Old House Farm was splendid, comfortable and warm and we were able to have various friends on their way to and from Nyasaland to stay. The villagers were kind and friendly and, being Reg's cousin, helped. I also found an ex-DSG girl living just down the road. She had been as the school some years after I had left, but had the same fond feelings about it. Old House Farm had productive fruit trees so I made about 20 pounds of different jams and pickles. I hated to see the fruit wasted.

Being near Chichester we were able to see several superb shows at the Festival Theatre, which was a privilege and something we had missed in Nyasaland. Though with Trevor's future undecided we had not yet bought a house, I nevertheless frequented various auctions and house sales and made some fantastic purchases. We had to start from scratch, so we needed most household goods. I bought some excellent rugs for a song and lots else.

Soon after the children went back to school in January, Trevor accepted a job with an old established and respected firm of lawyers in Gray's Inn. Thus began a year or so of commuting, leaving home in the dark in the winter months and returning in the dark. Commuting was one of the reasons he had left England 36 years before. He was not very happy, but, as he said, bills had to be paid. As our tenancy drew to an end I began to house hunt. While we were homeless, my school friend Jenny took us in again in London, so at least Trevor did not have too far to travel to Gray's Inn. My remit now was to find a suitable house within an hour's travelling time to Gray's Inn, preferably on the southern or western side of London. After endless days of viewing and almost in despair, we settled on a new house in Sonning Common, between Reading and Henley. As we were not totally sure of our future we decided to leave Merilyn at her school and the boys at their prep school in Surrey. There were many good independent schools for boys and girls in the area and when the time came for them to be moved we would have a wide choice.

We remained with Jenny for the rigmarole of the house purchase and, getting excited about owning our very first house, I decided to go to the Ideal Home Exhibition. I bought a decent sized Hoover fridge and a Hoover floor polisher and scrubber were thrown in. I still have the floor polisher. What is more, when I said we had not moved into our house yet, Hoover offered to store the two items and deliver them free to Sonning Common. (Would that happen in 2001? I think not.)

After much cajoling we managed to get the keys to the house on Maundy Thursday 7 April 1966 and collect the children for the Easter holidays on the same day. John Lewis came up trumps and delivered the beds as arranged. And, hey presto, there we were, family complete in our first owned home. It snowed and snowed.

We settled into English village life and Trevor commuted. We did DIY at the weekends, sampled and enjoyed dozens of country pubs, especially on the Thames, and went to Twickenham and Wimbledon whenever possible. I played lots of bridge and tennis, joined the local church, went to floral arranging classes and attended the meetings of the Women's Corona Club (run for the wives of colonial officers) at its headquarters in London.

I was selfishly wallowing in the pleasure of having my whole family in one country, of being able to attend the children's various sports' days, prize givings and concerts, and of not having to endure painful departures at the beginning of each term. But I could see that Trevor was unhappy. Although the partners and associates at the legal practice in Gray's Inn were all pleasant people, he found the work insufficiently challenging and hated the daily commute from Reading to Gray's Inn and back.

* * *

Trevor came home one winter's evening with a big smile on his face. 'How would you like to live in Ras al-Khaima?' 'Where?' Out came the atlas and there it was, one of the seven Trucial States at the eastern end of the Arabian Sea near the Straits of Hormuz. It transpired that the independent sovereign Trucial States that had scratched a living from fishing and piracy had close links with HMG. In return for giving up piracy, HMG had undertaken responsibility for their defence and foreign affairs, and had a political agent accountable to the Foreign Office in permanent residence. With the discovery of oil and prospect of great wealth, the ruling sheikhs of the Trucial States had asked HMG to send them men who could set up a police force along British lines.

When a dusty file among the colonial records in the Foreign and Commonwealth Office (FCO) revealed that Trevor had retired from Nyasaland and, more importantly, could speak Arabic, he was approached and offered a posting. In discussions at the FCO Trevor went to great pains to point out that the Arabic he had learnt back in the 1940s was different from the Arabic spoken in the Gulf. 'Never mind,' they said. After much discussion, Trevor accepted the posting on a contract and on the understanding he be sent on a refresher course. This was arranged and about six ex-colonial policemen from various countries and one other from

Malawi all gathered at Heathrow on 2 February 1967 to fly out to Aden to the Military School of Arabic Studies. Once again it was a difficult parting for me as it was into the great unknown, yet it was curiously like seeing a bunch of 'big boys' off to school.

This was 1967, the year when Aden was 'handed over' and its shops were full of merchandise being sold off at ridiculously low prices. (Among other things, Trevor bought me a new Kenwood food mixer with all the attachments for £25.) There had been a decline in shipping and the large expatriate community sustained by the coal and oil-bunkering depot was leaving. Also, with air travel having replaced the ocean going liners that used to call in there, Aden had ceased to be a shopping Mecca. All in all, it was a tricky time for Aden. Britain was pulling out, there was much unrest, and there were serious floods. It does not usually rain in Aden, but it did that year. The Commissioner of Police, Aden was an ex-BSAP pal of Trevor's, so it was nice for him to have a home to escape to every now and then, for the course lasted six months and he grew tired of the Crescent Hotel. He was glad to return home to Sonning Common for the summer holidays.

So the parting years were not over. Here we were, at it again, but somehow it did not seem quite so horrible. With the children being that much older and beginning to take partings more calmly and the fact that we had an established base in England, our own home, made a difference. But our emotions were still being torn.

Just before Trevor flew out to Aden I received the devastating news that my mother was terminally ill with cancer. I was in a dilemma. I felt I should fly out immediately to Bonza Bay to be with her, but who would cope with my children? I then received a lovely letter from Ma's greatest friend Helen, the doctor with whom I had grown up. She said, 'I know you'd like to fly out to be with your mother, but she has asked me to tell you on no account are you to abandon your children just to be with her. There is nothing you can do for her. She is being well looked after in her own home with her beloved Roy and you are not to worry.' Small comfort, but I was still very worried. Helen kept me informed almost weekly. Also, I knew that Ma was surrounded by good friends who would pop in to help in whatever way they could.

With Trevor back, we had a happy summer holidays with the children. We hired a motor cruiser for a week on the Thames, and had great fun cruising from Reading to Lechlade near the source of the Thames. The weather was not too bad and at lunchtime we called at some lovely riverside pubs. The Barley Mow at Sutton Courtney stands out in my memory as one of the best. Ours was an ordinary cruiser, very comfortable and adequate for our needs, but there were some very posh motorboats and their passengers dressed to kill. When we went into some of these riverside pubs for our main meal of the day we were reasonably well dressed, but alongside the 'toffs' we looked like their crews.

Trevor was due to fly out to his new job at the end of September, so he and I spent the rest of the holiday viewing schools for Simon and Christopher for the next September. We decided on the Blue Coat School at Sonning on Thames in Reading. We met and liked the headmaster, were shown round and were suitably impressed. A school founded in 1646 with proud traditions and connections was just right for our boys. It had moved three times in 350 years, each time to larger premises. Being situated on the Thames, rowing was one of the many sports it offered.

With my mother's illness uppermost in my mind, we agreed that once Trevor had flown to Ras al-Khaima and the children had returned to school, I would fly to East London to spend time with Ma and then fly on to the Middle East to join Trevor in Ras al-Khaima to prepare for the children's arrival for the Christmas holidays. As we were going to live in a rather primitive area, I had to get the children inoculated for cholera and ensure that their other injections were up to date to cover the Christmas period.

When I took the children back I informed their respective schools of our new address and contact number in the Trucial States, and told them I was going out there via South Africa.

Trek Airways offered reasonably priced fares to South Africa and at the end of September I flew Dan Air from Gatwick to Luxembourg. Though my ticket from Luxembourg to Johannesburg was with Trek Airways, we stayed on the same plane, a Constellation with bunks for sleeping at the tail end. We had a 24-hour stop in Barcelona (a crew rest period), which we spent in a lovely old-fashioned well-appointed marble and mahogany hotel, then reboarded for an overnight flight. The aircraft was full of healthy South African's returning home. After dinner had been served, four of us started playing bridge and, as it was a bumpy flight, the cards slid all over the place and there was quite a lot of laughter. The passengers were then asked not to make so much noise because the stewardesses occupying the bunks at the rear of the plane wished to sleep. Since we had just had a rest stop in Barcelona for the crew, we were flabbergasted and sent a message back to say that this was the first flight we had been on that was run for the benefit of the crew, and carried on with our bridge. At Johannesburg I caught a local plane to East London where, to my delight, Ma met me. She had lost weight but outwardly seemed fine. She warned me on the drive back to her house that I would notice a big deterioration in Pa in the two years since I had seen him. I was puzzled by this remark, for I thought I had come to see Ma, who was ill. She also told me that for the last two years she had been praying every day that Pa would die before her, for she knew he would be unable to cope on his own; he was now 87.

Pa certainly had aged and I am glad Ma had warned me, but we had no idea what was in store the next week. One evening Pa said he did not want any supper and was going to bed, which was very unusual. He then had a massive seizure, a stroke, and never got out of bed again. He died ten days later. Ma and I tried to cope on our own nursing him day and night, but I could see it was too much for her, although she was determined to do it. I engaged a night nurse and, with the doctor making daily calls and the nurse at night, we felt we could cope. I wired Trevor in case I would have to alter my plans and extend my stay in South Africa. Ma and I took it in turns to sit by Pa's bed, keeping his mouth moist and making him as comfortable as possible, for he was in a deep coma. The doctor said anyone else would have been dead by then, but that Pa had such a strong constitution his body was refusing to die. I sent a telegram to my brother Dick in Southern Rhodesia, who flew down to arrive the day after Pa died (Ma's birthday on 17 October). Pa died in the afternoon while Ma was on her bed having a rest and I was sitting with him. I had just rinsed his mouth and he ceased to breathe: it was peaceful and undramatic. I had been with animals when they had died, but all I can say, with honesty, is that it was a beautiful, calm, dignified ending to an eventful life — and a final parting for my dear old dad.

After the funeral and cremation, a simple service conducted by a well-loved vicar, Dick and I did what we could to help Ma who took the whole episode in a stoical and dignified manner; her prayers had been answered. Although she had lost the one and only man she had ever loved, she could now let go and give in to her illness, for she really did not want to be without him. In a strange way during those first few days of widowhood you could see her relax. She said Pa would never have wished to live unless he were able physically to do what he wanted to do and now mercifully he was at peace. She did not struggle any more.

Ma was adamant that I should not delay my return to Trevor any longer. Dick and I were concerned about her living on her own and not being well. As luck would have it, one of her great friends, Connie Bell, was at a loose end, so I asked her if she would like to come and live with Ma as a companion. Bonza Bay was full of people who wanted to help, but I felt Ma needed someone living in the house. Connie jumped at the idea and it was a very happy solution. Ma's great friend Helen, the doctor, popped in at least once a day and Dick and I felt comforted by these arrangements. Before Connie actually moved in, Ma flew to Southern Rhodesia to be with Dick and his family. This was a mistake, however kindly meant, for it exhausted her, so she returned home to Connie's care and as much rest as she needed.

I felt uneasy about saying goodbye to Ma, for I knew I was unlikely ever to see her again, but she was very brave. She and Helen took me to the airport and it really was a horrid parting. Apart from the wrench of leaving Ma, there was the added feeling of leaving South Africa and all that I had known there. I wept all the way to Johannesburg.

Friends met me at Jan Smuts airport and we spent a few hours chatting before I caught the VC10 flight to Nairobi. I spent a weary night at the overflow New Stanley Hotel, about which I was not very happy. The next stage was on a Comet, the beautiful ill-fated plane soon to be grounded after too many disasters and crashes. I was lucky. It was an interesting flight from a passenger point of view. Apart from the British pilot and flight crew, everybody else on board was Indian, Pakistani or Chinese. The latter, all quoting from the *Little Red Book* (it was the Mao Tse-tung period), seemed delighted to be going home from Tanzania (via Karachi) after having trained a few converts. A scruffy and very bewildered-looking African among them was presumably being taken for further communist indoctrination and teaching. At 30,000 feet we were served *the* most excellent curry.

At Karachi, there was another overnight stop. I did not get much sleep because the airport runway seemed to be outside my bedroom window and under my pillow. A smartly dressed hotel steward of the 'old school' brought me tea at 5.15 a.m., which was most welcome, and I climbed aboard another VC10 on the last lap to Dubai. I departed at 6.45 a.m. and landed at Dubai at 6.45 a.m. and Trevor was at the steps of the gangway to greet me. It was such a relief to be with him again, to relax and to gear myself up to meet the new challenges of life in an Arab state.

5

Introduction to Ras al-Khaima: Trucial States (UAE)

By 1967, Ras al-Khaima, one of the seven Trucial States, had been bypassed in the march of civilization. Its history can be traced back to biblical times and the reign of the Queen of Sheba. Though she is said to have principally lived and kept her main palace at Marib in North Yemen, traces of a vast city with gatehouses wide enough to drive a pair of chariots through abreast can be seen and walked over on the slopes of the Jebel Russ. Its walls cover an area that could have housed thousands of people and I visited the ruins several times. However, in the thousands of years that have passed, wind and erosion have obliterated all immediate detail other than a sunken vaulted room that could have been either a dungeon or a water storage tank. There are no ceramics to give a clue. Locals strongly believe that it was one of the Queen of Sheba's palaces from where she ruled the land and controlled the Gulf. Though nobody seems to know what could have supported a city — the mysterious ruin keeps its secret — with its panoramic view over the land to the sea and to the town and natural harbour, the site was well chosen.

Ships are said to have been plying the Gulf since 2500 BC. Assyrians and Babylonians with cargoes of frankincense, spices, pearls, metals (copper) and timber (mostly teak from the Indian subcontinent for building dhows) passed this way. Ships are still being built by hand in Ras al-Khaima without plans or specifications, age-old traditions handed from one generation to another.

* * *

In 1967 Ras al-Khaima was a fairly primitive state and there was no proper road to Dubai. Trevor had a Land Rover and we used to drive most of the way along the beach at low tide. The tide dominated these journeys — one either timed them carefully or clambered up sand dunes. It is now a sport, but we did it for real.

Trevor had been allocated a flat until the house being built for us was ready. He had acquired only a minimum of furniture and had borrowed the cutlery and crockery because he wanted to wait for me to choose it. So, on my arrival I was taken to a huge warehouse stacked from floor to ceiling with Noritaki, Wedgwood and masses else. 'By the way,' Trevor said as we went in, 'we must leave in 20 minutes because of the tide. Choose a dinner service in 20 minutes.' I dashed round and made a good choice under the circumstances, for it is still my best. I went for a Noritaki, which had a similar pattern to Wedgwood, which I had always liked.

The drive up the coast was quite exciting the first time and I was very tired by the time we had made it home intact. The flat was on the first floor with empty shops underneath that were being used as storehouses. An Italian doing survey work occupied the flat across the landing from us; he had a beautiful tenor voice and we were frequently serenaded through the walls to strains of Verdi and various Neapolitan arias. This made a pleasant change from the Indian teashop across the road that played Indian pop songs all day long on three cracked records. An open-air cinema that showed Indian films with a very loud sound track provided us with night noise. The cinema was only a few yards from our flat and if we sat out on our balcony we could watch the film for free.

My earliest impressions are of continuous *noise*. You would not believe that such a small place could be so noisy, what with loud pop music, the hooting of car horns, pi-dogs scrapping over morsels of food, donkeys roaming around and constantly braying. One had to become immune to it or go back to the UK (and I have not even mentioned the helicopter arriving and leaving).

A few days after my arrival we were invited to a cocktail party in Dubai where I was to meet most of the people we would be seeing for the next five years, and ten days after this party was the TOS (Trucial Oman Scouts) ball, *the* social occasion of the year. The TOS, the local army, was founded in 1952 with mostly Arabs in the other ranks and British army officers on secondment. They were an energetic bunch of men who patrolled the desert sorting out feuds, water-well disputes and boundary raids, and giving help where needed. It was an adventurous and far from dull life for a young British army officer who could speak Arabic. Their headquarters were in Sharjah and squadrons were scattered over the Trucial States in such places as Mnama, Msefu and Ham-Ham.

Having received this formal invitation to the TOS ball, I was in a bit of a state because I had no ball gown with me, for I had packed all my long dresses in a suitcase for Merilyn to bring out at Christmas time. There was nowhere in Ras al-Khaima to buy a ball gown, so I asked Ruth Willis (our nursing sister) if I could borrow her sewing machine to make a suitable garment. I dashed down to Dubai and bought a rather nice green silk sari length with a silver thread border. I designed and managed to make a rather nice gown — even if I say it myself. As men far outnumbered women, some army wives flew out just for a few days to be at the ball (it was not a married posting) and to see their husbands. Also, a planeload of young women was flown in from Bahrain to partner the unattached young TOS lads.

It was a grand evening. The TOS band piped us in on arrival (the bandsmen were mostly Baluchis or Pakistanis and one of their native musical instruments is similar to the Scots' bagpipes) and we joined about 300 people all milling around. The room was beautifully decorated and a superb buffet supper was provided along with unlimited drinks. At 5.00 a.m. a breakfast of mulligatawny soup and fried eggs (an old Indian Army custom) was served; we enjoyed the feast, then collapsed into the Land Rover to be driven home along the beach

* * *

Ras al-Khaima is a small sovereign state and mostly desert, but the high mountains of the Jebel Russ range gave us an unlimited supply of beautiful clean water. Dubai is equally blessed. And you can grow anything in a desert provided you have water. At an agricultural experimental and research station at Dig Dagga about 12 miles out of town, the director Ted and his Jordanian assistant Mohammed, a graduate in agriculture from the American University in Beirut, had instigated a marvellous scheme. This involved

233

choosing a local man in a district, giving him a basic training in agriculture and then setting him up with the necessary tools and seeds to become an adviser to his own people. This worked very well and Ras al-Khaima was soon exporting fruit and vegetables to Dubai and other places in the Trucial States.

At first the availability of fresh vegetables was erratic, but once the new road was built regular supplies could be guaranteed. We felt very lucky being able to buy melons, citrus and all kinds of vegetables in a desert country. The introduction of lucerne and other fodder crops made the expansion in domestic animals possible and there was great excitement when an aeroplane arrived with 29 in-calf heifers and a bull. The aim was twofold: to provide a milk supply to enhance the diet of Arab children and to increase the existing milk supply by crossbreeding these Friesians with the scrawny low-yielding local cows. Comfortable paddocks were built and lots of shade provided, but the cattle had to be hand fed because there was no grazing as such. The first calves were born and we had fresh milk, then fresh cream. It was such a luxury; I made butter from time to time when there was a surplus of cream. The Arabs were not very keen on drinking milk and it took them time to establish the habit. Up until then their milk had been from camels and goats. Of course not all the calves were heifers, so the bull calves were slaughtered for veal. Unfortunately, these beasts were too young for beef, so the flavour of the meat was disappointing, but it was marvellous to have fresh meat.

Once a year the Trucial Oman Scouts (TOS) organized a shooting party, a sort of Bisley, at Manama. Squadrons competed against each other and against the various police forces. Ras al-Khaima had two teams, which did well, and one event for the expatriates, a kind of *Dad's Army*, which the Arabs loved. The Arabs were all *au fait* with guns and laughed their heads off at some of the expatriates, mostly bankers and businessmen, who seldom, if ever, had handled a gun. This was a huge occasion and Arabs appeared from everywhere, on foot, by camel, by Land Rover. Tents were pitched to provide shade for the spectators and there was a drinks tent, but no cloakrooms; you just walked into the desert and, if you were lucky, you found a bush big enough to squat behind. In the early days I was sometimes the only woman among 3000 men, but later on some more women came from the

British agency. It was always very hot and I sometimes found it cooler to use a parasol than wear a big shady hat and trouser suit. I had rather a nice parasol one year when a battalion of the Coldstream Guards was out learning desert warfare. The commanding officer Colonel Watson asked me if I thought I were at Ascot. I hasten to add I wore a dress to match my parasol.

Trevor had been allocated to Ras al-Khaima, Bob Burns to Sharjah and Jack Humphreys to Dubai and these men and a few others met every Monday afternoon (Friday was our day off as we were in the world of Islam) at the British agency (the same as an embassy but not given that status because of the nature of the treaty). I used to joke about them all sitting there swapping secrets, but it was serious stuff and vital for each to know what the other was doing.

Depending on the tide, we either went straight home or were invited to someone's house for supper and then went home by moonlight, navigating our way through the desert by keeping the Orion constellation on our right-hand side. When Trevor was at his weekly meetings, I joined the few people who played tennis. There was no court in Ras al-Khaima, but good ones at the agency and at the RAF station at Sharjah. My regular partner was the RAF doctor; the station dentist Simon, whom I later saw umpiring at Wimbledon, was another regular. My doctor partner and I entered the 1969 open Dubai tennis tournament and reached the finals before being beaten; they gave us each a beer mug. Now the Dubai tournament is on the world circuit with all the top names.

There was a nice pool at the agency and we often swam there. The ruler's son Sheikh Khalid let us use his pool, which was shaded and secluded because Arab women sometimes swam there. In very hot weather you needed the shade if you were to stay in the water long (with a drink in your hand) because the reflection from the sun on the water made it hotter than ever. In the cooler months (December, January, February and March) we swam in the sea, but even then we had a *barusti* on the beach (a shelter made of palm fronds and branches through which the breeze could pass). Because of sharks, we seldom swam in the open sea, but several creeks behind the main coastline were sheltered and too shallow for sharks, so this was our playground. After storms the shape of the creeks would alter and we would have to make new tracks over the sand dunes to find the best bathing beach. Nearly every Arab family had two houses, one in brick for the cooler months, and a *barusti* in which they slept in the hot weather and which they usually replaced each year.

With no sign of our house being ready for the children's Christmas holidays, the ruler had to order the builder (who had disappeared after having run out of tiles and pipes but was later found on another building project in Abu Dhabi) to come back and complete the job. In some ways this enabled me to have more say in how things were done. For example, I insisted on having the Venetian blinds put on the outside to keep the sun off the glass (in my opinion this was one reason why the houses were so hot) and then the very necessary fly-proof gauze put on the outside of the Venetian blinds. We had some angry arguments here. I also insisted on the kitchen layout, which the builder found very odd, but as I was the one to be using the kitchen, by being stubborn I more or less got what I wanted and what was practical.

The house was near the edge of a creek and at high tide the water sometimes reached our boundary garden wall. With the water table so near the surface and without a proper damp course, fluffy stuff, which looked like snow, appeared on the ceramic tiled floors each morning. Meanwhile, the damp got into the walls and the emulsion paint began to peel off. Oh dear, I got so fed up with no one doing anything about it that I slopped some transparent thick varnish all over the inside of the walls up to window level in the hope that by sealing the lower part of the walls we would not have any more damp seeping through. It was quite unorthodox, but it worked and, after a while, I had the whole interior painted with emulsion and it began to look quite nice.

We needed accommodation for the Christmas holidays while all this was going on, so the ruler lent us a huge flat (it took up the whole second-floor) in the old town. It had a deep veranda on which there was nearly always a breeze and that afforded fine views of the creek to one side and the old town and sea to the other. We were very comfortable there. There were no curtains, so I had to sit down and make some. I cut them for the windows of our unfinished house in the hope that they would do for the flat. It was not a perfect fit, but it saved me making two sets of curtains and bedspreads to match.

Ras al-Khaima's expatriate community in 1967/8 stretched to 25, which included the various children and grandparents who flew out to be with their families for the Christmas holidays. We felt that, as it was Christmas and there was no priest to hold a service, we would like to have a carol service. Since Ted and Enid Tucker had the largest sitting room (Ted ran the power station and was a very important person) we decided to hold our carol service and nine lessons there. Music from the King's College chapel choir was provided on tape. Word got around and the odd TOS in the district joined us and sang lustily, as did the Egyptian doctor, who claimed that he liked singing carols, and some Lebanese.

Trevor and the others were given Christmas Day off (though not a holiday in Islam, Jesus Christ is recognized as a prophet). The ruler was a great family man and he knew it was a family occasion for Christians. To our delight, he and his two sons joined us on Christmas night. We had all met at Ted and Enid's for a party and were playing traditional silly games. The ruler thought it hilarious to see the head of his police lying blindfolded on the floor with a rolled up newspaper in his hand trying to bash the other chap, also blindfolded and lying on the floor, both yelling out 'where are you Moriarty?' Our small community felt very privileged to have the ruler come and wish us happy Christmas and join in the fun — it was all very relaxed and friendly. I am sure this does not happen in many Arab states.

Our quiet little backwater was about to change with the discovery of oil in the Gulf. Bahrain had oil and Kuwait was one of the first and certainly the most productive of the producers. Further east in the Gulf, Abu Dhabi had struck oil. Dubai was drilling for it and fast becoming a successful import/export-free port. Its ruler Sheikh Rashid Al Maktum, who knew a thing or two about commerce and successful trading, was known as the Merchant Prince. He was a good ruler and the country was stable, so it attracted many businesses and the town boomed. Dubai had an international airport and good port facilities, all well run.

Not wanting to be left behind, Ras al-Khaima's ruler Sheikh Saqr gave concessions to an American oil company. Then everything began to expand. With British, American, Austrian, German and Italians now among the many expatriates working there, there was an increased need for law and order, which was where Trevor came into the equation. Whatever anyone else says, Arabs have a great respect and admiration for the British, so they asked the FCO to help them organize their police force along British lines.

Of the seven Trucial States, Ras al-Khaima is the most spectacular scenically. It has the waters of the Gulf on the west, a huge range of high mountains, the Jebel Russ, to the east, and patches of greenery created by date palm and vegetable gardens on the flat plain in between, lending interest to an otherwise ordinary desert scene. Towers dotted along the seashore serve as reminders of the days of piracy, for it was from these lookout posts that the pirates spotted the ships they considered worth plundering. The towers are 20 feet high and curious to look at, for they have no door. The only means of access was via a rope to a door some 12 to 14 feet above ground level; the rope was then pulled in behind and the tower was secure from intruders. Descent was down the rope. There were openings high up to let the breeze in and one odd-looking aperture, the loo, high above the ground like the medieval loos in some British castles.

When Trevor accepted this job in Ras al-Khaima, the terms were different from the former colonial ones. To start with, it was a contract job and Trevor had the security of being paid by HMG. Ras al-Khaima and the other Trucial States did not of course have any colonial links, but when they asked Britain for help, ex-colonial policemen were the only men with the right experience and ability to meet the criteria.

Trevor and I made a pact that we would all be together as a family for every school holiday wherever we were, and, whether the children flew out to the Gulf or Trevor flew to the UK, this was a condition of him accepting the post. We kept to the pact, bar one exception when I flew back to England on my own in late March 1968. With the new house not ready and the temperature very hot (85–90°F) we decided that it would be more sensible for me to be with the children for their Easter holidays in our house in Sonning Common. Also, I was concerned about my mother's health and communications were better between South Africa and the UK than they were between South Africa and Ras al-Khaima.

Sadly, I received a telegram on 24 April to say that my mother had died in the Mater Dei nursing home in East London. Death, whichever way it comes, is a shock and I was upset that, at 70, cancer had shortened her life. My brother coped with the funeral and with selling the house, so there was no real need for me to go to South Africa. Warm tributes were paid to Ma. Everyone loved her and she never bore anyone a grudge. She was an inspiration to those who knew her. I still miss her more than 30 years later.

The Gulf States get unbearably hot in June, July, August and September. Humidity is about 95 per cent and the air temperature 100° to 120° in the shade, most uncomfortable. I am not very good in extreme temperatures and, as these were usually the best weather months in the UK, we arranged for our year to comply.

The children flew out for the Christmas and Easter holidays; kind friends took them for half term; I flew back in time for the summer half term; and Trevor would arrive for the summer school holidays. After the autumn half term (around Guy Fawkes time) I would return to Ras al-Khaima and the pattern would be repeated. The children loved coming out and had wonderful holidays. Nearly all the expatriate families kept to this schedule and we all felt very happy with BOAC (pre-BA), which flew school specials at holiday times with aunties to look after unaccompanied children. This was a great relief should a child feel sick or whatever. BOAC was good about communicating with parents and we would get confirmations of bookings or alterations of flight times sent automatically and, what is more, we were allowed to be at the foot of the gangway to welcome our offspring at Dubai airport. There were only two London–Dubai flights a week, so the children sometimes left before the official end of term. A strike of BOAC pilots two consecutive Decembers caused much consternation among the parents who imagined their offspring marooned at Heathrow and getting the wrong flight. But, despite the strike, the local BOAC manager, who also had children coming out, kept us informed with a daily bulletin on the situation and possible alternate flights. They really were very good to us. In the early days, BOAC invited all parents of children flying out to a cocktail party and supper prior to meeting the flight from London. Imagine that happening now? On the flight each child was given a tin of sweets and had their Junior Jet Club logs filled in. Happy days.

To all intents and purposes Ras al-Khaima was a feudal state. The population was about 30,000 and if anyone, however lowly, had a complaint, he or she could go directly to the ruler and get a

239

ruling there and then. Thus, there was no bureaucratic red tape and everybody seemed content with this ancient custom.

Though referred to as the palace, the ruler's house is in fact quite modest with fans and air conditioning. His office and rooms for public entertaining are in a block known as the Majles in the same square as his home. Sheikh Saqr and his two wives had previously lived in the fort in the old town that housed Trevor's office, the police headquarters, the barracks, courtroom and gaol. It is by far the best-looking building of any age and character in Ras al-Khaima. The Ras al-Khaima flag flies from a tall square tower at one corner. The flag, a simple red rectangle with a white surround, dates back to pirate days and the 1820 Treaty.

Just before moving to our new house I had the frightening experience of being on the edge of a hurricane. It had been raining and, with the saltwater table only a couple of inches below the surface, a lot of water had nowhere to go and it was becoming difficult to distinguish roads or tracks from desert and soft salt marshes. The ruler had invited Trevor to an all male dinner at the Majles on the other side of the creek, but I was not concerned about being on my own. However, during the course of the evening the rain got heavier and heavier and the wind reached gale force; with no door or window properly fitted, there were a lot of banging noises and much wind whistling about. I decided to have a bath and go to bed, but when I was in the bath all the lights went out and the rain started to come through the roof. The noise of the wind howling really became quite menacing. Floundering about for matches and a candle, I found myself walking through inches of water; with the verandas flooded, the water had run back under the ill-fitting doors into the sitting room and my Persian rugs were afloat. I almost panicked. I was the only person in the building, so I telephoned Trevor at the Majles. But the phone was out of order, so I had to pull myself together and wait. The howling of the wind was getting louder and louder and the building shook once or twice. I thought, it this it? Eventually, what seemed like hours later, Trevor returned soaked to the skin. He swore that the Land Rover had floated some of the way back. He had strayed off the road into feet of water and sunk into deeper water, but this particular Land Rover had an exhaust pipe going up the side of the cab into the air. How lucky can you get?

By a quirk of fortune, it was *not* a Land Rover for desert work; not uncommonly, it had got mixed up in a consignment destined for a wet climate. In the early hours of the morning the wind abated and when we looked out we saw that we were on an island surrounded by sheets of water. We then heard over the radio that we had been on the edge of a nasty hurricane. Thank goodness it was no closer, for it was an experience I do not wish to repeat; the drains were flooded and the smell was unbelievable.

In early 1968 we moved to our designated house and settled down to the challenges of life in Ras al-Khaima. It was never dull and we did not know from one day to the next what would happen or who we would meet or entertain. On the whole, apart from camel racing, the locals in Ras al-Khaima were not very keen on sport as we know it, though we did get Sheikh Khalid (the ruler's eldest son) to play men-only tennis. But one sport they loved and excelled in was hawking (falconry). This ancient seasonal sport with the bustard as the main quarry is still much in evidence in the Gulf States and Iran. A good peregrine falcon is worth a lot of money. Even in England as much as £1000 was paid for a pair during James II's reign in the seventeenth century.

Early one morning I came across a whole row of falcons sitting on blocks (outdoor perches) in the sun outside a hotel in Dubai, all wearing hoods and attached to their perches by jesses (leather straps round their legs). Being highly trained, they were quiet and seemed happy. They belonged to a sheik who was about to fly them by VC10 to hunting grounds in Iran. John Whitelaw, a TOS officer and Scotsman, had several peregrines and it was fascinating to watch him demonstrate those beautiful birds. For this reason, he was popular with the Arab falcon fraternity and they often went out hunting together.

Manama, the TOS camp that held a rifle meeting each year, was on the other side of a wide gravel plain and some of its officers were well set up with comfortable messes. A Squadron, which Major John Whitelaw and his second in command ex-marine Tim Courtenay (now deputy Lord Lieutenant, Devon) commanded, stood out as a haven of civilization right down to the silver pheasants decorating the mess-room table. When the children were out on holiday Simon and Christopher were invited to join these TOS officers for shooting parties and exercises, which was very exciting for two teenage boys. Merilyn was asked to help make curtains for Msafi camp, once.

In Oman, located on the Indian Ocean east of Ras al-Khaima and the other states, Sheikh Quabus was also benefiting from oil revenues, but had a communist rebellion on his hands both in the Dhofar in the south and on the Masandam Peninsula at the northernmost tip of Arabia. Communist infiltrators were thus stirring up trouble in two parts of the Oman and this was spilling over into the Trucial States, where British forces under the command of General Watson were helping General Graham in Oman cope with the infiltration. A joint intelligence service was built up over the years with district intelligence officers (DIOs), who all spoke fluent Arabic, taking up residence in scattered and remote areas to organize networks of informers. This was an effective system because strangers are soon spotted and reported in these small communities and villages. The TOS (with headquarters in Sharjah) patrolled the area between the Rub al-Khali (Empty Quarter) to the south, the Masandam Peninsula to the north and Abu Dhabi to the west. Sheikh Zaid of Abu Dhabi had his own defence force of 2000 (also run by British officers on contract) and, not content with that, he invited the TOS to patrol his state too.

DIOs would turn up from time to time to enjoy a family meal with us. Their work was lonely, but only men cut out for that kind of life were sent. The north Gulf coast is rugged and huge mountains rise sheer from the sea, so there are no roads, not even a beach road at low tide. One DIO used to turn up quite frequently by boat to stock up on food and drink for a month at a time — shades of Trevor's experiences on the Red Sea in the 1940s.

Our lives in the Western world are filled with umpteen excitements and happenings. In the UK we have annual sports fixtures like the Triple Crown for rugby, the FA Cup for soccer and the boat race, but for Arab tribes living in the mountains of Ras al-Khaima, life is very different. The Shi-hu tribe is divided into two groups, the Wali of Dibba and their opponents who cast off the allegiance. The highlight of their year is an armed battle using muzzle-loaders fed from brass-studded bandoliers crisscrossing their shoulders. Six or more are actually wounded in the battle and when the fight is over they merely return to their mountain villages to talk about this year's battle and to prepare for the next.

Trevor did not put a stop to this annual event as the borders were ill defined and the battle could have been in Oman or Ras al-Khaima and he had no wish to court an international incident. But he put a couple of squads of men along what was roughly recognized at the border in case things got out of hand. He also arranged for any wounded to be taken to Ras al-Khaima hospital, for the Shi-hu had no transport. This mountainous region with an unmarked border where only the Shi-hu live is no place for an innocent walk or climb, for the Shi-hu often shoot at intruders. Trevor was shot at and had holes in his Land Rover to prove it. Thank goodness he was not hurt. We sometimes took visitors up the Jebel of Shimmel Sheba, where the Queen of Sheba allegedly had her palace, and the Shi-hu sometimes took pot shots at cars there, luckily missing each time. This was never taken seriously, for even the Shi-hu realized there was no intent to occupy or take possession, but it added greatly to the visitor's excitement.

Arab weddings in this part of the world were dull for the women incarcerated indoors while the men danced, sang and had a great time. When an American couple working for the oil company got married and were given a party in Ras al-Khaima, we women (Arabs, expatriates and the bride) were herded into a house and fed chicken, rice and soft drinks while the men outside danced and sang. The ruler had arranged for a group of Shi-hu to bring their drums to lead the all-male dancing. Having escaped from the women's house, I was intrigued to see the drummers light a fire to dry out and shrink their drum skins, which had slackened because of the high humidity. When during the course of the humid evening the skins stretched in the damp air, once again the fire was stoked up and the drums were warmed, the men bent over the fire holding the drums and revolving them slowly to acquire an even heat. The dancing and singing went on late into the night.

I had not been in Ras al-Khaima long when a young man appeared at the house one evening, introduced himself as from the British Council in Ras al-Khaima and, in the next breath, asked if I would help him teach English. 'I'm not a teacher,' I said. 'Doesn't matter,' he replied. The country's sudden new oil wealth had engendered an ever-increasing demand to learn English and he said he could not cope. I was not keen, especially when he said he would like me to take evening classes for adult males. I discussed it with Trevor and he said, 'Go ahead if you want to.' I can never dismiss a challenge, so I agreed and after a brief introductory course in teaching English as a foreign language, I took my first class of a mixture of Jordanian, Palestinian, Syrian and local men. The Jordanians and Syrians were extremely difficult, for they had a smattering of English and liked to show off and argue about split infinitives. As Arab males, they resented being taught by a woman and made me feel as though I were not there. Only when I managed to burrow through this wall of resentment, could we get on with the lesson. The locals, who were mostly Trevor's young policemen, were eager, hard working and no trouble at all.

My nextdoor neighbour Elizabeth Nahas not only spoke and wrote her native Armenian, with its own script, but she was also fluent in written and spoken Arabic and in written and spoken English, which made me feel totally inadequate. Her Lebanese husband Tewfik was a secretary at the American Oil Company. When Elizabeth invited me to accompany her on one of her frequent visits to the ruler's wives and other women in the harem, I jumped at the opportunity and was duly introduced to Sheikher M'ahara, the ruler's second wife who had six children, three boys and three girls, his old wife Noora, and his son Khalid's wife, also called M'ahara. When these women heard that I had twin sons, they were intrigued and Sheikher M'ahara demanded to see them. It is quite something for 12-year-old boys to be summoned to a harem, but they duly appeared, sat down very demurely and at the earliest opportunity asked if they might leave as they had just heard the helicopter land, which was far more interesting to them. The women pinched and pulled me to make sure I was real and not wearing a wig. I have red hair and the only red hair they had seen was dyed with henna, so they wanted to ensure it was my own. They also rummaged in my handbag, just through curiosity for nothing was ever removed. Arabs always ask you how many *living* children you have, not just how many children, for with dirt, disease and ignorance infant mortality is very high. Though most of the conversation took place through Elizabeth as interpreter, I have always found that, language apart, women all over the world find ways to communicate. I went on these visits quite often, for they could never visit me in my house in case a *man* saw them. These women did not wear a veil in the house, only when

244

they went out. Sheikher M'ahara had her own driver and Land Rover with black curtains draped round the windows so no one could see her. An intelligent and astute woman, she kept her finger on the pulse of Ras al-Khaima life. She would park her Land Rover beside the parade ground and tell me afterwards how she had rated the parade. 'Tell Bevan,' she would say. Trevor was amused, but he never met or even saw her. When we visited the sheikhers, they offered tea, which was usually black and sweet, as was the coffee, fruit and sticky sweet cakes.

One day Elizabeth and I were in the harem (the word means the women's quarter) and I was admonished for giving English lessons to the men. Would I come to the harem and teach them? This group of women, who were all related to or connected with the ruling family, were illiterate in Arabic, never mind anything else. But they were mature, highly intelligent people who resented being unable to help their children with their homework, follow some of the television programmes or understand the expatriates. I conveyed their request to the British Council, which condescendingly suggested the women join the classes held on British Council premises. I explained that these mature women could never leave the harem and would not be allowed to attend such classes. The teenage girls were lucky because Ras al-Khaima was one of the few places with a girls' secondary school and they would be allowed to attend classes, but not their mothers, aunts and grandmothers. Eventually, the British Council agreed to let me hold two lessons a week for the sheikhers and to hand over my male class to someone else, which was a relief. One morning a week I took the older women by themselves, and on the second day I took a group aged between 12 and 60. The younger ones had a sprinkling of English from school, but no conversation as such. They were very shy at first, but after a while would talk in English quite freely with me, but dried up in front of strangers. The British Council's Alexander method, based largely on cartoons, repetition and conversation, worked well, but would not have suited high-flying technologists, which was not its aim. I thoroughly enjoyed the lessons and the illiterate women learnt at an alarming rate. With masses of servants, they had little to do all day, so spent hours on their English. I was not teaching stumbling five-year-olds, these were astute, mature, intelligent women and I soon learnt that

245

illiterate intelligent people *never* forget anything. This was good for me, for I could not be half right or dither about anything; I had to be spot on and 100 per cent correct *always*. I drove my own short-wheelbase Land Rover all over Ras al-Khaima, much to the envy of these women, and eventually even the men guarding the sheikhers' home ceased to take any notice of me going in or out.

I was lucky to have the use of a Land Rover. I would have felt marooned and miserable without independent transport, for there was no other way of getting around. Land Rover had an assembly plant in Iran and the Shah of Iran saw fit to give Sheikh Saqr a fleet of them. The police were given a generous number and mine was on the strict understanding that it would be returned if the police ever needed it. That occasion never arose and when the children were out on holiday I was forever taking them swimming or visiting; what is more, they learnt to drive in it. Merilyn had got her English licence in 1970 and sometimes pinched it for parties, but the boys learnt to drive in it from scratch. Trevor said they could drive anywhere *but* on the roads, so they would go into the desert to make their mistakes once I had taught them the rudiments. At low tide they spent many hours practising reversing, parking and various imaginary assault courses beside the creek near our house. One day Chris ran into the house panic stricken because the tide was rapidly coming in and one of them had got the Land Rover stuck in the heavy wet sand and could not get it out. I went back with him and gave the boys a lesson in four-wheel extra low gear driving and, much to their relief, we pulled out of the quagmire without difficulty.

These Iranian assembled Land Rovers had part plastic bodies, and this particular vehicle's bonnet had a habit of coming undone, flying up and obliterating one's view through the windscreen, which was a trifle disconcerting. Eventually, one of Trevor's mechanics made a reliable catch and it felt a lot safer. Whatever country we were in, Trevor always made sure that one of the mechanics in charge of the police vehicles was an Indian. They are master craftsmen when it comes to improvisation and very often we were hundreds of miles from any spare parts or conventional garage.

Our life in Ras al-Khaima was very sea oriented, whether for recreation and pleasure, or for the various activities connected with the oilrig, fishing boats or naval patrols. Every Friday, being our non-working day, we used to go out on a dhow for a day's fishing, weather permitting, and catch an enormous number of fish, including 20-pound groupers; even I caught some without too much trouble. We fished with line wound round a wooden block. A few people used conventional rods but the wooden block was as effective and when there were lots of people on the dhow, rods could get in the way. The dhow crew were helpful and kind and the *nkuda* (captain) was a real expert. He knew exactly where to drop anchor to catch the most fish under different weather conditions. At the end of the day we would have far too much fish for our own use, so the crew could take what they wanted after we had set some aside for ourselves, which usually went straight into the freezer. Some fish tasted better than others and we learned dozens of ways of serving Gulf fish. We would take the surplus to the hospital and give some to friends. No fish was wasted.

Dhows had been sailing in and out of Ras al-Khaima for thousands of years, but bigger ships were needed for the oil explorations, which meant developing the harbour and excavating the channel to take the deep-keeled workboats that feed the rig. A survey was carried out and suitable stone located, quarried and brought to Ras al-Khaima from Khor Khowai in huge lorries to build the arms of the harbour out into the Gulf to define a deep, sheltered channel to the quayside. Quays were extended and warehouses built; indeed a bustling enterprise developed where there had been nothing more than a few steps down to the *abbra* (ferry) that took you across the water to the fish and vegetable market in old Ras al-Khaima. I often took this ferry with my shopping basket to stock up on fresh fish and vegetables. There were nearly always sharks lined up alongside the other fish on the jetty. Some of these were hammerhead sharks, or rather hammerless because the fishermen would cut off the hammer bit, which caused untold damage thrashing about and tearing the fisherman's net. The sharks' bodies were not eaten, but dragged up to the date gardens to be put on their compost heaps. Nothing was wasted. The tails and fins were cut off and dried in the sun and sold to the Asian market, where shark's fin soup is a great delicacy. (It was often served at the Chinese dinners we attended in Singapore. I wonder if we ever consumed a Ras al-Khaima export?) The main fish catch is salted and dried and sold to India, Pakistan and some to Iran.

We had a small outboard engine on a dingy, which gave the children enormous pleasure and it was quite safe in the inlet creeks where we bathed and had our picnics. They learnt elementary boat craft, which would always be useful. One of the Arabs had a powerful motorboat that towed water-skiers, which was a favourite pastime for those who could stand up on water-skis.

Those of us who lent towards less energetic forms of exercise found a rich reward in collecting shells. Merilyn and I collected a whole tea chest of various shapes and sizes and Trevor was horrified when we insisted on bringing it back to England. The best time to find undamaged shells is at low tide, especially during spring tides when there is either a full or new moon. I have a lovely collection of shining cowrie shells — they shine because they are alive and contain a slug-like creature. Gomez (the house-boy) would disembowel the shells for us by soaking them in a bucket of fresh water. We found very beautiful queen conch shells, a delicate shade of pink and about eight to ten inches long. Scallops, limpets, clams up to 12 inches long, fan shells, sand dollars and, if we were lucky, a nautilus, which is the exterior skeleton of a cephalopod (octopus). Its bag-like body has no internal shell and an external shell is rarely present; there are no fins but eight arms with suckers. These nautilus shells were beautiful, but paper thin, very delicate and difficult to pack. Oysters were there for the taking, hundreds on the rocks. We would collect them in a bucket when the tide was on the ebb. Trevor adored oysters and often made his supper of them. No one else had bothered to gather the harvest. Arabs would not touch oysters (they do not eat shellfish, at least not in Ras al-Khaima). We often served them as a first course and Trevor was a living example of how good they were to eat. When we first discovered them we bent and broke many knives and kitchen utensils trying to open them. In desperation I wrote to Harrods for a proper oyster knife and one arrived by airmail the next week. After that it was easy.

We collected coral in all shapes, some quite lovely. I once found a coral encrusted pipe on the beach, about two foot long and two inches wide. We made it into an unusual table lamp. One often saw lumps of coral used as stones in the walls of houses, or sometimes they would turn up as paperweights or doorstops. After a particular fierce storm we were walking along the beach and the children picked up a lot of coins, mostly copper, covered in verdigris. They cleaned them up as best they could and, realizing they were very old, sent them to the British Museum for identification. In a very nice instructive letter encouraging them to be observant and wishing them well, they were identified as sixteenth century and of Persian origin. It was exciting to find ammonites, the fossil remains of a number of types of extinct shellfish, for some date back as many as 100 million years; we have one still. Merilyn and I made several shell pictures, which look very attractive hanging on our bathroom wall. A few have faded, but they bring back happy memories. Among the other oddities Trevor found in his old fort-cum-police station were canon balls of various weights, which must date back to the nineteenth-century clashes with British troops. We use them as doorstops.

We had a *barusti* shelter built of palm fronds to provide shade on the beach, which was essential, for it was far too hot to sit in the sun. Sunshades were fine but on holidays when everyone was on the beach there were not enough to provide adequate shade. Sometimes we would just sit in the water wearing a large shady hat with a cold drink and masses of Nivea cream. There was no sun block then, but we got terribly burnt if we did not use something and Nivea was readily available and certainly helped us.

* * *

Britain carried out its fundamental treaty obligations towards the Trucial States by speaking for them in the international arena and by defending them against external pressure and aggression. To fulfil this defence role, Britain maintains a Royal Navy squadron in the Gulf and has been granted military, naval and air base facilities in Bahrain and other parts of the Trucial States, with the RAF's main base at Sharjah. (This has now all changed.) Royal Navy patrols were carried out all the time, plying up and down the Gulf and several calling at Ras al-Khaima. Some were frigates and some were minesweepers. I recall HMS *Zulu*, HMS *Leander* and HMS *Beachampton* to name a few. Lieutenant Jeremy Blackham, who is now an admiral, commanded HMS *Beachampton*.

One of Jeremy's calls at Ras al-Khaima was most opportune, for it was during the Christmas holidays and Simon and Christopher, now at the Reading Blue Coat School, had a holiday quiz to complete. In the absence of any local reference library, we did what we could as a family and anyone who called at the house was tested for various answers, but being a classics scholar, Jeremy could answer all the questions in that category. So, with his help, the quiz was completed, much to Simon and Christopher's relief.

When we went aboard the minesweeper HMS *Beachampton*, I was amazed at how cramped everything was; the wardroom was tiny. I could understand why the crew welcomed going ashore.

A steel ship in the blazing sun on the Gulf can be quite hot anyway, but as we went up the gangway to lunch aboard the frigate HMS *Leander*, the heat seemed to intensify and we were welcomed on board with the news that the fridge, freezer and air conditioning had all broken down. On this day there was not even a breeze and people holding warm gin and tonics were visibly melting under the awning that had been put up on the deck to give shade. We had been invited into the wardroom for lunch and, of all meals, it was spaghetti bolognaise. Understandably, with the fridges out of order they had to serve something well cooked, or we would all have had food poisoning, but I do not remember eating much. When the captain asked me what I would like to do after lunch and I said I would like to see round the ship, he showed consternation, for on the flight deck (the frigate carried a helicopter) naked and semi-naked matelots were soaking up the sun to get as dark an all-over tan as possible (though I shall never know how they could stand being in the sun in that temperature). I was courteously shown round the ship, including the flight deck, and found the radar and all the various hi-tech instruments very interesting. (Now all that is old hat, for since the Falklands War Royal Navy ships have just become floating computers of one kind or another.) When it was time to leave, we lined up to descend the gangway and climb aboard a naval cutter to take us ashore. Needless to say, we immediately made for the nearest cold drink.

While patrolling the Gulf, Royal Navy vessels quite often came across the corpses of illegal immigrants floating among the debris in the water. With the economic boom in the Gulf States and with Ras al-Khaima fairly close to high unemployment areas like Pakistan and Baluchistan (in the southeast corner of Iran), illegal immigrants, attracted by the easy money to be earned on the building sites, would be sold passages to the Gulf States in unsuitable craft. The boats, usually flimsy river craft with the free board built up with reeds, would be packed with people, often with only standing room, who were desperate for work. None of these immigrants was legal, there was no documentation of any kind, but the boat owner made money from these poor souls who had scrimped and saved to pay for a passage to what they thought would be the Promised Land. Storms were not infrequent, and violent when they occurred, smashing the craft to pieces and drowning the passengers — such is man's inhumanity to man. At night, when the lights on shore were in sight, the captain would often ground his laden boat crammed to the gunwales on a sand bar near the Ras al-Khaima coast and the men, having stood shoulder to shoulder for many hours, would be plunged into the water and left to get to the beach as best they could. What they did not know was that there was a deep channel between the sandbar and the shore. It was exceptional for anyone to be able to swim and many drowned. The boat, now lightened by shedding its human load, would float off the sandbar and back to the other side of the Gulf.

I remember a Royal Navy patrol vessel once stopping just such a boat, which was bobbing about on the water with engine failure. Heaven knows how long the people had been marooned at sea jam-packed in the fierce heat with no shade! The patrol vessel secured a towrope to the boat, but it fell apart when the patrol vessel began to pull. A ghastly scene ensued of dead bodies falling out of the wreck from a lower deck and emaciated men drowning in the water. No one knew how many people were on the illegal boat, but the navy picked up all the dead and alive bodies it could see, transferred the men from the wreck to the its own vessel and, towing what was left of the wreck, steamed slowly back to the nearest harbour, which happened to be Ras al-Khaima.

Trevor was alerted and everything was done to help the living and bury the dead. Trevor was going down to the harbour for a final check of the wreck, which was tied up alongside the quay, and I asked if I could accompany him. He warned me that it would not be a pretty sight and he was right. While walking along the quay looking at the flimsy wreck, I saw a leg sticking out through a hole in the side of the boat. I called Trevor over and he then discovered several more bodies in the bowels of the ship, being used as ballast, or so it seemed; they had been stuffed in like sardines in a tin. It was a nasty episode and after it patrols were stepped up, but the illegal immigrants still arrived and were employed. Arabs are not keen on manual work, so were only too pleased to see someone else do it for them.

The gold smugglers' boats were totally different. In the 1960s Dubai was of little importance, but in the 1970s when it became a free port it developed into one of the world's most important gold trading centres and smugglers shipped many thousands of pounds worth of gold bullion to India, where the appetite for gold is insatiable. This trade in the early 1970s was said to be worth £150 million. In India gold is venerated as a sacred symbol of the goddess of wealth and is an essential ingredient in almost every social ritual. The humblest and poorest Indian woman will have some gold, a nose ring, earring or bangle. Better off women often buy more gold in preference to a modern washing machine. Gold is used in some medical cases and even in food; some Indian dishes were sprinkled with gold leaf until the practice was banned. Gold is especially valued as an insurance against inflation, thus making it an essential possession for every family. India has no gold of its own and when the government banned all gold imports in 1947 because they were eating into the country's foreign reserves, the gold smugglers took over. With the ruler of Dubai encouraging all forms of commerce, the gold trade flourished. Boxes each containing 200 bars of gold, each stamped 999 to indicate 99.9 per cent purity and each weighing about four ounces, are sent by air freight from the vaults of London bullion dealers (or Zurich bankers) to dealers and banks in Dubai. I remember seeing what looked like rather odd bricks on an open handcart being dragged along a street in Dubai one morning and could hardly believe my eyes when I realized I was looking at gold ingots. So far the transaction is above board and legal, and at least in the early days very little attention seemed to be given to security. Dubai city straddles a winding creek with boats of all shapes and sizes moored along both sides of the quays; the gold transporters' dhows, equipped with Rolls Royce (or Kelvin) engines, are among them. The dealer buys his gold from a bank and takes it unceremoniously in his car to the dhow and no one turns a hair. These boats take about five days to reach Indian territorial waters; they travel alone and rarely encounter an Indian security vessel. With a long open coastline it is easy to land the gold, which is then taken to Bombay, the main distribution centre. The gold bars are usually carried in specially made waistcoats (each holding 100 bars with a sewn-up pocket for each bar) that are worn under ordinary loose-fitting clothes. Once the laden waistcoat has been passed to the Indians, the gold smuggler's dhow turns round and innocently sails back to Dubai. Like any other, the gold trade has its ups and downs, but I believe it was at its height in the 1960s and 1970s when it was not uncommon to have someone introduced at a reception or party as a gold smuggler. It made life in the shires seem dull.

Vessels plying the Gulf ranged from enormous crude oil tankers called VLCCs (very large crude carriers) to small fishing boats. Dhows were the most typical and if Trevor's police captured one in an illegal transaction the boat would normally be sold to cover legal expenses or pay compensation. However, Trevor thought it would be good idea for the police to have their own patrol boat to watch the Ras al-Khaima coastline for illegal immigrants and to carry victuals and police to the Tumb islands (which belonged to Ras al-Khaima) in the Straits of Hormuz. Policemen stationed for a month at a time on these very small but strategically important islands needed revictualling. About 350 people live on the two main islands and a lighthouse on Tumb protects the narrow entrance to the Gulf. The ruler wholeheartedly endorsed Trevor's proposal, so the police acquired their first boat, a well build dhow with an enormous Rolls Royce engine. Apart from its police work, this boat gave us many happy hours of fishing and the pleasure of being able to take visitors out into the Gulf.

On one holiday when the children were with us, Trevor organized a cruise (patrol) up the coast to the Masandam Peninsula, the top end of Arabia and supposedly the hottest place on earth. The Masandam overlooks the Straits of Hormuz, which are narrow and there is always a boat or tanker coming in or going out. One day while dreamily looking across the straits, the whole landscape seemed to move and I realized that one of the largest tankers in the world, heavily laden, was passing into the Indian Ocean. Later, we were invited on board British Petroleum's flagship, which was quite something. They used a bicycle to get from stern to bow, had plastic grass round the swimming pool and luxurious living accommodation. They spent weeks at sea because the Suez Canal was closed and these huge ships had to sail round the Cape of Good Hope. They drew so much water that they could not sail up the English Channel without scraping when fully laden, so they anchored in deep water in Torbay where another tanker came alongside to lighten their load; they then carried on to Rotterdam. When the Suez Canal reopened, these VLCC became obsolete because they were too big to pass through the canal.

The now deserted Masandam Peninsula once housed a bustling cable station and coal-bunkering service, with the cable from Arabia to the Indian continent being laid from there across the shortest expanse of water. The buildings, with wide shady verandas and sited high up to catch the breeze, were in ruins. It must have been ghastly to have had to live day in day out for long periods in that heat. There was a crumbling jetty to which we managed to make fast and the children immediately went swimming in beautiful clear water with millions of little colourful fish in the coral. Luckily, the boys had brought their snorkels, so they had a fascinating time. We did not sail at night, but camped on the open deck. It was far too hot to go below deck in the hold and anyway it stank of dead fish. We were fine on deck under the stars, the crew at the stern end and we at the bow. The loo was a primitive contraption overhanging the stern transom with just enough room for your feet on two strats of wood and the sea below you, where you performed squatting (quite a feat in rough weather). During the night poor Merilyn developed a tummy bug and had to run the gauntlet of the sleeping Arab crew to get to the loo. Then during the night a storm blew up; at a safe anchorage and attached to the crumbling jetty, we did not worry, but were amazed next morning to see that several boats, including a Royal Navy frigate, had slipped into the safe anchorage during the night. We had been so busy rigging up shelter from the rain by pulling a very smelly sail over the boom and lying huggermugger under it, that we had not noticed the other ships. (It is not supposed to rain ever in the Straits of Hormuz.) Merilyn was now very miserable, so Trevor decided to launch our dinghy to go and ask the RN frigate's medical officer for some medicine for her. They were astounded to see us in such a place and immediately supplied the correct remedy. Merilyn was cured in hours and was able to enjoy the rest of the cruise-cum-patrol. On our way back to Ras al-Khaima, Trevor asked the *nkuda* to take us into the Elphinstone inlet, a fjord-like bay in Oman territory, which the Royal Navy used as a safe haven during the war because aeroplanes could not attack shipping in such an enclosed space with sheer cliff faces rising hundreds of feet on three sides. But was it *hot*? Phew! The air was totally still and the reflected heat from the rock walls on three sides was unbearable. British matelots from days of yore had left graffiti (some of them quite amusing) in huge white letters on the rock faces. We did not stay long in this inferno, but it was worth putting up with the heat for the experience. With the entrance well concealed and at an angle, the inlet was easy to miss, so it was a good hiding place for allied shipping in wartime.

A well-established shipping and mercantile company in Dubai had a branch in Ras al-Khaima for the purpose of supplying fresh crew to the VLCCs. These large tankers did not stop to change crew. A Gray MacKenzie boat would take the new crew and victuals into the Gulf, tie up to a VLCC and make the change as the ships were in passage; the supply boat would then cast off and the tanker would pick up speed and not stop until in the English Channel. The exchanged crew would be taken to the airport and flown to their homes until their next voyage was arranged.

Sheikh Khalid and his wife M'ahara invited us as a family to dinner on several occasions. These were pleasant evenings, for the sexes were not segregated and we all sat round a table. An Arab *fadil* (feast) is an all-male affair in which the guests help themselves from huge trays of roasted sheep or goat stuffed with chickens on a bed of spiced rice. (With plates but no cutlery, one soon learnt how to tear off a piece of meat, roll it into a ball with the rice and pop it into your mouth.) Salad and fruit is also served. At such feasts the sheikhs and VIPs eat first; when they have had enough they retire and the next lot down the hierarchy sits down; and when they have finished the drivers and hangers on finish what is left. Our ruler and Sheikh Rashid of Dubai moved with the times, so they sometimes included wives in the invitation. I used to enjoy these meals very much.

Sheikh Khalid visited London with his wife and mother while I was in England one summer, so I invited them to our house near Henley for the day. They arrived in a chauffeur-driven limousine and, after lunch (I served chicken and rice), I suggested we visit Mapledurham, a beautiful and historic English house on the Thames. However, as we were about to get into the cars, we noticed that his mother was missing. She had gone back into the house and we found her on her knees saying her belated midday prayers to Allah. Good Muslims pray five times a day and nothing was going to stop Noora from discharging her duty. Another time we had Khalid's younger brother to stay; he was at Mons Military School and later we went to his passing out parade.

Sheikh Khalid and M'ahara were generous to our family. Once when we were dining with them they gave me four gold bangles and Merilyn a magnificent gold necklace, which we call her mayoral chain as it was no ordinary necklace. The boys and Trevor were given watches. Later, Khalid arrived at one of our parties with an old Arab sea chest for me. I was thrilled. Merilyn and I were also given pearl chests made of solid wood and patterned with brass inlay. They are about a foot high, two feet long and a foot deep with little compartments inside for different sized pearls and a flat surface covered in felt on which to sort them. These chests make excellent sewing boxes and I treasure mine.

The day after our dinner with Khalid and his family, it began to rain cats and dogs. It is not supposed to rain in Ras al-Khaima more than once in five years and this was the second year running in which heavy rain had fallen. It was so heavy that it washed away a new bridge on the new road to Dubai. The storm at sea was so fierce that the waves had washed away the tracks to the beach, so if one could get onto the beach at low tide in the Land Rover there was no way of finding out if you could get off again at the other end. As Merilyn was supposed to fly back to school that day and we were unable to get to Dubai, we had a problem. We managed to radio someone in Dubai to cable her school that she would be late because of floods. The school thought we had gone mad and there was a mix up with the telegram. The boys were not due to fly back yet, so after quite an upheaval and cables going to and fro we eventually got all three children on the same plane and Merilyn was nearly a week late for the start of term.

The floods not only mystified the school but they also turned the desert green overnight. It was an amazing sight. Masses of flowers appeared within days and one could not believe it was the same landscape. Seeds that had lain dormant for years sprung into life within hours. The desert really did bloom, as the Bible says. The grass grew about a foot tall; the wandering sheep, goats and cattle that came to graze must have thought they were in paradise.

In addition to the military and naval VIPs to whom we were honoured to offer hospitality, archaeologists and anthropologists arrived from time to time and one took up residence next door to us. Professor and Mrs Walter Dostal were charming people from the Institute of Anthropology, University of Berne. Finding different shaped pots seemed to give momentum to his expeditions out into the deserts and up the mountains (with an escort). On one occasion he was thrilled to find a particularly ancient pot that was being used to jack up the roof of a Shi-hu house. The Shi-hu could not imagine why he should want such an old thing.

Then we had Miss Beatrice de Cardi, president of the Council for British Archaeology, who was very charming and patient with those of us who were archaeologically illiterate. I went with her to the alleged Shimmel Sheba and, through her eyes, was able to put a totally different interpretation on the landscape. She pointed out probable watercourses and gardens from ancient times; she read the landscape. The only trouble was that Trevor kept calling her Miss Bacardi (like the rum). She kindly said she was used to that. I got the impression that Shimmel Sheba was not really in the millennium in which she preferred to work — it was not old enough. But her thoughts on it were interesting and it is a great privilege to meet people of such standing, intellect and knowledge.

Living in Ras al-Khaima, of which most people had never heard, we met some very interesting people from all walks of life and meeting some such people led to other fascinating experiences.

A handsome, charming bachelor colleague called David Neild had many interesting friends visit him from the UK. One of the most exciting of these was Royal Ballet prima ballerina Doreen Wells. With her beautiful figure and enormous energy, she put us all to shame by the way she rushed around wanting to see and do everything in the short time she had. She very kindly arranged for Merilyn and me to be sent tickets for Covent Garden when we got back to England in May. After seeing her dance in *Giselle* and *The Two Pigeons*, which was a treat, she invited us backstage to her dressing room, which was through a rabbit warren of narrow winding passages up and down stairs. There was nothing glamorous about that side of the stage, but we had a wonderful evening and thoroughly enjoyed the ballet.

With all the political talk about the possibility of setting up a federation of Arab states, ITN became interested in the region and we had the fun of having Peter Snow for dinner. The evening began with a cocktail party in his honour on Ras al-Khaima's brand new tennis court. He is very tall and was literally head and shoulders above everyone cramped into this limited space. Then David brought him, Chris Faulds and Hugh Thomson, who were also from ITN, over to our house for dinner. While engaged in animated conversation, I said to Peter, 'There can't be many countries you have not been to in the course of your TV work,' and he said, 'I would love to go to South Africa.' I egged him on about South Africa with David giggling in the chair next to me because Peter was going overboard about the good things in South Africa (there were not many in 1970). David knew I was South African and he knew that Peter did not. I made some remark and when David said, 'Sheila is of course South African,' Peter put down his glass, pulled his jacket over his head and crawled out of the room. We had a good laugh and the rest of the evening was hilarious. The ITN crew were delightful and great fun.

The stone used to build the arms of Ras al-Khaima harbour came from Khor Khowai, a settlement on the coast about ten miles north of Ras al-Khaima town. There, a German firm had built a camp for its staff, developed a quarry and constructed a jetty. The stone, which was sent to other parts of the Gulf including Abu Dhabi, was much in demand because, being granite and sulphur free, it was high quality. The workers' small houses had been shipped over in prefabricated flat packs, put together on sight and, complete with air conditioning, were better than some in Ras al-Khaima. But, despite a little shop of their own that stocked German sausage and rye bread, it was not all plain sailing. The Shi-hus in the mountains took exception to *their* stone being excavated, so began to shoot at the German workers. So, with the Shi-hus holding them to ransom, something had to be done.

Eventually, after lengthy negotiations with the ruler, the German boss and Trevor, and the presence of British troops brought up from Sharjah to guard the camp and its equipment, the Shi-hu agreed to accept cash plus a piped water supply constructed by the German engineers as compensation. They immediately exchanged the money for goats and camels, their kind of wealth. The German company, Helden & Franck, had brought in a lot of capital and jobs where none had been available previously and were of real benefit to the Trucial States.

Some of the Germans and Austrians who spoke English joined the Ras al-Khaima expatriate community. We became particularly friendly with an Austrian couple called George and Dagmar Spica. George was an energetic and hard-working engineer and Dagmar, who was strikingly beautiful, was a hairdresser and, as such, was very popular. With no hairdresser in Ras al-Khaima, if I had needed my hair setting for a particularly smart occasion I used to go to a Persian lady in Dubai who only took on a few clients and worked from her own apartment. She was meticulous and I felt that every hair on my head had been individually dressed, but she was very slow; a visit to her lasted at least three hours, though it was well worth it. Dagmar's arrival was heaven sent; she lived nearby, was an excellent hairdresser and could cut hair properly. She had all the equipment at her house so I would regularly go up to Khor Khowai to have my hair done, which was bliss in such a remote part of the world. I had often struggled to do my hair myself and had sometimes made an awful mess of it. Dagmar was also a strong swimmer, an accomplished water-skier (she had represented her country) and, needless to say, a great snow-skier as well. She and George joined our weekly beach parties and we always enjoyed their company; they made a great contribution to our little community. The Shi-hu war had prevented us from going to Khor Khowai to get Dagmar to do our hair, but once British troops were sent up from Shajah, Trevor said it was safe for us to visit her. Merilyn was with me and we got caught up in a convoy of soldiers driving to Khor Khowai. They were in the standard order for convoy — lights on, so many feet between vehicles and travelling at the regulation speed, which seemed very slow, so I put my foot down to get out of the dust the convoy was making. We, two European women in a Land Rover going the same way, received whoops, whistles, and yells as we weaved through the army trucks. We had a lot of fun waving back and hooting at them. Were we mad? Or was it just an effect of the desert?

The American Oil Company put on a cinema show once a week and we, including the Germans and Austrians, all turned out for that. Piet Matiess, the chairman of the American Oil Company, was German by birth, as was his wife; their families had emigrated to America when they were babies. One memorable occasion was the showing of *Those Magnificent Men in Their Flying Machines*. Piet thought that this was the funniest film he had ever seen. He laughed so much that he could hardly stand at the end of the performance; and he insisted it be shown again the following evening because he wanted to make sure that he had not missed any of the funny bits; he could not remember any entertainment to match it; he just loved it. When *Lawrence of Arabia* was shown dozens of Arabs came and one said he had not realized that colour films had been available in 1917.

We were all very grateful for this weekly show. The films were organized for the oil company people, but we were given a standing invitation to attend, which was a generous and much appreciated gesture. It was open cinema — we brought our own chairs and sat round the huge screen. Some nights we were grateful to have a woolly cardigan and rug round one's knees. The desert can be very hot and very cold.

In this part of the world the shepherd leads his flock; he does not drive them, as in the UK. Sheep have more hair than wool and often have their ears cut off to make them hear well. Their hooves are never trimmed and because of the soft sand they never wear down, so they wobble around on what look like winkle-pickers; they look as though they are wearing Turkish slippers at least four sizes too big and many indigenous cattle are the same. Some guard dogs also have their ears cut off to improve their hearing.

Goats roam around the town eating whatever they can find, cement bags or any other paper lying around; if they are lucky the sheep, goats and cattle are given a handful of green grass or lucerne from Dig Dagga in the evening. They are not cared for, but each animal belongs to somebody. The Arab reserves his real love of animals for his camels, then horses. If they are too poor to own camels the poor man's beast of burden is the donkey. You see them carrying massive loads on untrimmed hooves like the sheep. I believe a donkey can carry four times its own weight.

Ticks are quite a problem and camels go into the sea to wash them off; though I never saw a red desert fox, they are particularly molested by ticks and they too sit in the seawater, with just their noses sticking out, to drive off the ticks.

We never knew what we would see next in Ras al-Khaima. Walking along a beach one evening, Trevor and I came across a Heath Robinson contraption and several turtle shells. Apparently, a young man of European extraction had decided to make his fortune selling turtle oil to the European cosmetics market. Ras al-Khaima fishermen brought turtles in from time to time in their nets, but would tip them back into the water. This young man then offered to pay for each turtle brought to him. His methods were primitive: he rendered the turtle flesh down into oil in old oil drums, poured it into ten-litre containers, sold it to the cosmetics market and received reasonable recompense. But his supply was erratic, as was his payment to the fishermen, so they lost interest and the enterprise fizzled out. I was not sorry. There must be better ways of producing horrendously expensive turtle oil.

On another occasion we were called to the beach because a whale shark had been washed up. This is the largest fish in the world, 65 feet long with a mouth that can be six feet in length. It is harmless and only eats plankton. Somehow it had got itself beached and was dead by the time we saw it; shortly afterwards it started to deflate (like letting air out of a large barrage balloon) and began to smell terribly. Not many people have seen a whale shark (only called whale because of its huge size), for it is a cold-blooded fish with no need to surface. It mostly lives in very deep waters; Jacques Cousteau called it a 'peaceful giant'.

At the other end of the scale we often caught small sharks and dogfish while out fishing. Once when we were out on the dhow, someone caught a very fat dogfish and Issa (one of the crew) told Chris that it was about to have babies. Chris was curious, so Issa performed a caesarean section and out popped several alive and perfect little sharks. Chris kept them in a bucket of seawater for the rest of the day, then tipped them back into the Gulf where I have no doubt they survived. A shark can give birth to as many as 20 young and they are all capable of looking after themselves from the minute of birth. During the five years we spent in Ras al-Khaima, I do not recall one case of a man being taken by a shark. The fishermen knew them well, treated them with great respect, did not try any heroics and were themselves seldom in the water, thus avoiding the danger of an attack. The sharks caught in their fishing nets were expertly dealt with.

The greatest joy was dolphin watching. These beautiful agile creatures used to play in the water at the prow of the boat and race along at a tremendous speed. We seldom went out without seeing them and sometimes a large shoal would dive, whirl, turn, roll and jump round the boat so gracefully. Dolphins are peaceful creatures normally, but will attack sharks if the mothers are about to give birth and the shark is showing too much interest. They ram the shark's underbelly with the point of their nozzle, thus producing an internal rupture to the organs that eventually kills it.

As everybody knows, 4 July is Independence Day in the USA. With round the clock work on the oil rig, the American community in Ras al-Khaima had grown by leaps and bounds and had chosen to celebrate Independence Day by inviting everybody to an enormous barbecue on the beach. Ras al-Khaima was not known for being the entertainment capital of the Middle East, so Trevor and a few friends decided that they too would mark the auspicious occasion and not let the Americans have it all their own way. So, with of course the friendliest intent, the British mounted a canon on a Land Rover truck (old canons are found abandoned all over the place). They lashed it to the bed of the truck and fixed it to be able to fire blanks. Trevor then kitted himself out as Britannia in an old slightly frayed Union Jack with a hole cut out of the middle for his head, on which he wore a gold cardboard crown. He held a golden triton and, to complete the scene, strung a small tape recorder round his neck with which to play *Rule Britannia*. David, John Whitelaw, Tim Ash and several others were in on the act and enjoying the joke. On arriving at the beach barbecue, with music playing loudly and blanks being fired from the canon (firecrackers really), they made straight for the small mound the American's had built on which flew the stars and stripes. There was mild consternation among some Americans, who thought for a minute that the Brits had gone mad, but we had a lot of fun and everyone enjoyed the joke. The British were all asked to wear something patriotic and the Union Jack appeared in all sorts of guises. The party went with a bang after this mock invasion.

Making one's own entertainment is a vital part of life in remote overseas territories and the British are particularly good at it. The next event after the Independence Day party was a Roman evening at which no one was given a drink unless they had made an effort to produce a Roman toga or centurion outfit. The Arabs thoroughly enjoyed the spectacle, but seldom wore fancy dress.

* * *

A well-dressed Arab man always carries a gun and wears a bandolier full of cartridges or bullets, depending on his firearm. He also wears a *kunja* (dagger) in front with great pride. The *kunja* is curved, so he can sit down without injuring himself, and its handle is either richly embedded with semi-precious stones or encrusted with silver or gold.

Women wear brightly coloured dresses under the black *abba*s that cover them from head to foot when they are out of the house, and most women wear a mask (*birja*) that shows only their eyes. These masks are very unbecoming and the ruler's family do not wear them; instead, they carry lightweight shawls with which to hide their faces should they encounter a male. Females may only converse with male relations, but with the arrival of the telephone, their lives were revolutionized, for they could talk to men without being seen, which was a great advance.

I was slightly taken aback when a woman clasped me to her bosom and then spat over my shoulder (a sign of affection, the equivalent of a kiss), for it was a custom about which I had not been warned. Some Arab men rub noses as a greeting, but despite such cultural contrasts, we all got on well. But there is an awful lot of spitting, either to show contempt or because they need to spit when they chew tobacco or take snuff. There is also a lot of spitting during Ramadan, when good Muslims fast between sunrise and sunset for a month, for strictly speaking they are not supposed to swallow their spittle. Old people, small children and pregnant women are exempted from fasting during Ramadan.

Merchants' wives and the women in the ruling family were setting an example by having their babies in the small hospital where Ruth, a British nurse, was doing a wonderful job educating women. She ran antenatal clinics, encouraged hospital deliveries and postnatal checkups, and advised on feeding babies, general hygiene and diet. There was an Egyptian doctor, but being male he was not allowed to examine the women, so a great deal fell on Ruth's shoulders. Ruth had nursed in Aden prior to coming to Ras al-Khaima, so was used to primitive conditions, not to mention riots, gunfire and grenades being thrown without warning. In her work with mothers and babies she did much to counteract ignorance and wean women away from some of their more archaic customs. Because girls marry and have their first child very young, some births were quite tricky. In the villages, the local midwife, for want of a better word, would help with the birth and then pack the vagina with salt in the belief that it helped the uterus contract and stopped bleeding. Instead, it created scar tissue and painful complications with the next baby. Because scar tissue does not stretch, it usually has to be cut to prevent the uterus rupturing. Childbirth is traumatic enough without this complication. Some of the pregnant women Ruth took in had been in labour for days and had walked miles to get to the hospital. The Bedu (peasant) women had very strong constitutions, for they did all the work of tending the goats and sheep, fetching water, hoeing the vegetable garden, milking the animals and collecting firewood. Some were lucky enough to be brought in on a camel, some came by boat, and some even had the luxury of a taxi from the quayside to the hospital. At first, patients only came to Ruth when things had begun to go wrong. Even so, she performed wonders and mother and child were well cared for and given a proper diet. Unfortunately, they tended to discharge themselves too soon, only to find that the baby stopped thriving when they returned to their primitive homes and customs. They would come back to Ruth for another miracle, but sometimes it was too late. Infantile mortality was very high for a number of reasons, including very young first-time mothers, diet, dirt, disease and very often suffocation. Many tribes (but not the Bedu) believed that babies must not be exposed to the sun, so the baby would be smothered under blankets in the terrific heat. If a mother's milk supply failed and she had to bottle feed, in the early days this nearly always ended in disaster — the water to mix with the milk powder would be contaminated, the bottle would not be sterilized and flies would settle on the teat between feeds. Ruth had an uphill battle here because babies kept in these conditions invariably contracted gastro-enteritis. When the mother was doing her chores, she put the baby in a special cradle suspended on a tripod off the ground, which protected the baby from the scorpions, snakes, chickens and goats that tend to crawl or wander in and out of their houses. This cradle, which was really a box, had a thick layer of sand covered by paper on which the baby lay without a nappy. The sand was frequently changed (no shortage) and Ruth said she never came across any nappy rash. The baby in the cradle would have been even better off without a blanket, for many suffered from prickly heat, but some of these countrywomen thought that 75°F was cold.

Ruth had another nursing sister join her, Dierdre Fuller, who was just as hard working. At first Ruth had a fairly basic house and her hospital consisted of three single-storeyed concrete rooms with very little equipment, but it was fenced against wandering sheep, goats and camels. A guard on the gate ensured that only vehicles and patients entered. The two nurses were having nice new houses built for them and I was envious because they each had a staircase with access to the roof; it was lovely to sit out of an evening and watch the magnificent sunsets.

Though clinics were set up in other parts of Ras al-Khaima, Ruth still used to venture far up into the mountains and deserts to vaccinate the wandering tribes, Bedu and mountain dwellers against TB, smallpox and polio, to check up on mothers and babies and to give advice. Sometimes she would be warned off by rifle shot, but they soon got to know and accepted her.

On one such trip she found a severely retarded three-year-old girl weighing eight pounds whom, with her parents' permission, she brought to the hospital for treatment and proper feeding. Sheikha stayed for four months and we all got to know her. The ruler and M'ahara were interested in Ruth's work and gave her a great deal of support. They paid for certain special treatments and medicines, for the hospital's resources were, to say the least, inadequate. The ruler also paid for one-off operations that needed the skill of a Great Ormond Street surgeon. Sheikha's illness, TB of the spine, was made far worse by her undernourishment. Her parents had not starved her; they were just ignorant. With good food, fresh milk from Dig Dagga and lots of rest Sheikha responded magnificently and began to walk. Her father appeared one day and, considering her cured, took her back to their primitive life. Within about six weeks he brought Sheikha back again in a bad way and Ruth was horrified to see her tummy dyed blue (an ancient cure that never works) and, worse still, burn marks on her torso where she had been branded to drive out the devil they believed was causing Sheikha's problems.

Some would say these people have an advanced philosophical attitude towards a child's death. When a child dies, and it is not uncommon, the parents are not overcome with grief. It is fate as far as they are concerned and there are plenty more where that one came from. 'Praise be to Allah.'

Two Iranian-born young women of 18 and 20 were learning to nurse under Ruth's expert tuition. They were a great help and became very responsible. Their aim, which they achieved, was to get to England to train as nurses at an English hospital. I gave them some coaching in English in the hope that they would not find the language too much of a barrier.

There was great excitement in Ras al-Khaima when the go-ahead was given for Ruth's new well-equipped hospital. When the building was complete it was thrilling to open the boxes of equipment, mostly acquired through a Swiss hospital supplier that sent it as a package based on the number of beds. Most of the cases contained exactly what Ruth needed and expected, but two were quite unexpected — a case of champagne glasses and a pile of silk dressing gowns. Merilyn, who had now left school and had flown out to Ras al-Khaima to be with us for a while, was also helping out at the hospital and learning a lot. We all shared Ruth's pleasure in her new hospital, for with her high reputation, pioneering work and devotion to duty she had deserved a better workplace. A team from *Woman's Own* magazine came out in 1968 to see Ruth at work. They were gob smacked when they saw her having to carry out minor operations and procedures that only doctors do in the UK. Ruth had no alternative and knew exactly what she was doing. She always had the total trust of the patient and it was appropriate she be known as the 'Angel of the Desert'.

One reason for establishing a dairy herd at Dig Dagga had been the need to improve the children's diet and Ruth's pioneering work included getting mothers to give their children lots of milk, which was now pasteurized so quite safe. One of Ruth's many ambitions was to find a suitable woman in each village or district to teach basic antenatal care, childbirth procedures, baby feeding, hygiene and health. This person would be able to raise standards of health generally and refer serious cases to the hospital. With the new hospital, Ruth had the room and facilities to treat many more patients. The health-worker scheme was designed to operate along similar lines as the agricultural advisers sent out from Dig Dagga.

By 1971, the road to Dubai was tarmacked and almost complete, the new hospital had been built, a Lebanese firm was building a swanky new hotel with a casino and swimming pool and we had acquired a 404 Peugeot estate car. Our journeys were now not only comfortable but also twice as fast.

During 1971 it was my fortieth birthday and within a few days Merilyn's eighteenth, so we decided to give a really big party. There was no hall to hire and we did not want it at either the old or new hotel, so we borrowed a large mess tent from the TOS, which we put up in the garden, and cleared the sitting room for dancing. The music was on tape with one exception, *The Court of King Caractacus* sung by Rolf Harris, which was on a record. It is impossible to stay sitting down when you hear the beat of this crazy piece of music. In fact Trevor, who was organizing the music, became hooked on this record and played it every other tune until everyone was on their knees and exhausted, but thoroughly enjoying themselves. Gomez and I had spent days cooking and, as I always erred on the side of having too much, I thought we had a big enough spread for about 80 people. I was therefore horrified when Gomez came to me and said that the food was all finished and we had not yet fed everyone. Wow, what a disgrace! Out came all the tins of meat, vegetables and fruit from the store cupboard and no one went hungry. Then, at about 5.00 a.m. we ran out of beer, which was unheard of in the Bevan family. However, given our great community, Ted soon appeared at the door carrying a full case of beer, and cold too, straight from his fridge. So the party continued, in fact it never stopped, and we all went down to the beach and carried on for most of the morning. By midday I had had it and crept home to sleep, as I think most of us did. It had been a memorable evening.

* * *

With the Tumb islands strategically placed to observe oil tankers taking oil from the Gulf and freight coming in, Trevor had two policemen posted there on monthly stints. Though Iran already had two big busy ports at Bushire and Branda Abbas, about mid-way between the Straits of Hormuz oil port and Abadan at the western end of the Gulf, it appeared to want to control the whole Gulf. It may have seen the growth and prosperity in the Trucial States as some sort of threat, but this was quite unfounded because the Arab states only wanted to live in peace and make money.

The telephone rang at 4.30 a.m. (not unusual in a police house) with a garbled message that two policemen had been shot and Iran now held the Tumb islands. They had landed an invasion party and as our two policemen were heavily outnumbered they did not put up any resistance, but one got shot in his behind, poor fellow, and the other was taken prisoner. The entire population of 350 had been put into three dhows that were making for Ras al-Khaima.

The locals naturally got very excited and started burning and attacking anything Iranian. Iranians owned several businesses and the Bank of Iran was a target. To enable the police force to maintain control a curfew was imposed and for the next few days we were confined to our houses. Merilyn and I were confined to the house like everyone else, so we sewed and played tapes. Our favourite was the 1812 overture, which we played loudly without giving a thought to what was happening in the street. A British soldier (TOS) appeared at our door to ask if we were all right. 'Fine,' we said, 'why do you ask?' He then told us that the rioters had blown up the Bank of Iran only a few doors away, but we had only heard the canons on the tape.

Trevor always planned for all eventualities, including a possible attack on our house; buildings close by had been targets and once a mob of rioters gets the bit between its teeth, there is no knowing what will happen next. So, as a safeguard, Merilyn and I were detailed to go and hide in one of the American Oil Company flats. Trevor gave me a wad of cash, passports, air tickets and the new car, which we hid. These precautions were frightening, but if events got out of hand we stood a chance of escape by having had a little forethought. I was told that if we had to drive out and we found roadblocks I was to drive through and risk being shot at, and if they shot at the tyres I should just drive on regardless. 'What about you?' I asked. 'I shall be all right. It's best you don't know where I shall be. You can then honestly say you don't know if asked. Good luck and we'll meet either at home tonight, God willing, or at the airport.' He gave me a kiss and disappeared.

I knew enough to realize that Trevor knew far more than he was letting on and we all knew there were communist agitators around. There were also Palestinians around who bore the British a grudge for having allowed Israel to happen. During riots, all sorts of old scores are settled that have nothing to do with the cause of the particular riot; opportunists take advantage of a turbulent situation to settle their private grievances. Anyway, all was well and we returned home, Trevor having phoned the 'all clear'. It was a relief to see him and to be safely together again.

The next day we were still confined to our house, so Merilyn and I got on with our dressmaking under the intrigued eye of John Newman who had been deployed as our bodyguard. Our time in Ras al-Khaima was coming to an end and John was to replace Trevor. An able man (ex-Palestine police and Cayman Islands) he arrived the day the Tumb islands were invaded, so Trevor put him to guarding us because, being new to the country, he did not know the layout. He had never seen anyone make a dress before and was fascinated by the procedure and impressed with the final result.

It did not take many days for things to settle down and life to get back to normal weekly trips to Dubai, beach parties, fishing trips, bridge, visitors and visiting. It would soon be Christmas. The boys were due to fly out for their school holidays and we had the normal carol service and New Year's Eve party at Dig Dagga.

* * *

Sheikh Saqr and his family lived in modest comfort. Unlike some of the rich merchants, he was never ostentatious. He was a wise man with the good of his people at heart and he initiated or encouraged many schemes and ideas to aid development. He was particularly interested in the work at Dig Dagga and in the scheme to give land to agricultural training school graduates. He believed strongly that everyone should have land to farm.

269

A Scotsman, Jimmy Mitchell, was responsible for trades and technical education and he did a good job turning out carpenters, plumbers, plasterers and electricians. If demands could be met locally, there was less need to recruit foreigners. To encourage children to stay on at school, nobody was allowed to employ anyone under the age of 18. Pupils received free transport to school, though some had to walk many miles to get to the transport. These children walked barefoot by preference, only slipping their shoes on as they entered the classroom, for they *had* to wear shoes at school. The state school children received free school meals and were given two free sets of uniform a year. Kuwait also funded some schools, as well as a small hospital in the old part of town.

Though Shari'a law, as in the Koran, was the norm, there was a political agent in Dubai to preside over non-Muslim court cases.

* * *

Our five years in Ras al-Khaima had been most enjoyable, despite dust storms, floods and other minor frustrations. We learnt a lot, met wonderful people, lived well and experienced a way of life not available to many. We watched Ras al-Khaima grow from a dusty little village to a fair sized bustling town and felt fortunate to have lived in what was scenically the most majestic part of the Arabian peninsula. Many rich merchants from Dubai were buying weekend properties at Ras al-Khaima, for its distinctive mountain background was a great attraction after flat desert and sand dunes.

The Arabs in general and Sheikh Saqr in particular treated Trevor with respect and affection. Having left his mark and contributed greatly to the wellbeing and running of the country, he was paid many tributes on leaving. By incorporating the image of the ancient watchtowers, Trevor had combined old and new in the police badge and the locals loved it. He had jewellers in the gold souk make up police force brooches in gold for Merilyn and me as apt mementoes of Ras al-Khaima. From no roads to dual carriageways to four-star hotels and a casino, a cosmopolitan population had worked hard for its own good and for the good of Ras al-Khaima. When I went to say goodbye to Sheikher M'ahara, there were many Arab women present who had come to wish me well. I was very touched and most of us ended up in tears.

270

Introduction to Ras al-Khaima: Trucial States (UAE)

So there we were amid a warehouse of packing cases all ready and labelled for the sea voyage to the UK. When I went to the British Bank of the Middle East to collect our traveller's cheques and to say goodbye, I noticed that the stranger at the next cashier point had an unmistakable South African accent, so in Afrikaans I asked him what he was doing here so far from home. He looked at me in astonishment and said he was just looking around. We got talking and he turned out to be the South African ambassador to Iran and living in Tehran. He had always been interested in the Arab world, so had crossed the Gulf to visit Ras al-Khaima. I invited him home and we had our pre-lunch drinks and lunch sitting on packing cases. He was such a nice man and he gave us a card to contact his wife in Tehran. It was a pity we could not entertain him and show him round and a pity he would not be in Tehran when we planned to be there.

As a family we had all been flying at least twice a year over most of Europe and other enticing parts of the world. On our final flight back to the UK we decided to have a look at some of the countries we had been over flying. BOAC allowed us to break our journey between Dubai and London as often as we liked as long as we kept going westwards. So, with great excitement and anticipation, having been given a terrific sendoff by dozens of friends, we flew out of Dubai's brand new international airport.

* * *

Our destination was Shiraz in Iran. This ancient city has several very beautiful mosques, but the main attraction for us was Persepolis to which we took a taxi. Merilyn was with us and we spent the day wandering round this vast and impressive ruin Alexander the Great had ravaged in 330 BC. We took the same taxi to Pasargadae and saw Cyrus's tomb (Cyrus the Great founded the Persian Empire) and also had a look at Xerxes' tomb. All these wonderful romantic sounding names from ancient history gave us quite a thrill. This was March 1972 and the previous October the Shah of Iran had invited the world's dignitaries, princes and rulers to his coronation at Persepolis to celebrate the 2500th anniversary of the Persian Empire. A mass of exquisite tents on the plains had accommodated his thousands of guests. After the coronation, the tents,

271

beautifully coloured in pastel shades and looking magnificent, were used as a hotel for tourists. We spent the next few days marvelling at glorious mosques with colourful tiled or gold domes, which were quite breathtaking. There are many lovely gardens in Shiraz and we were impressed by how well kept and free from litter they were, with sweepers everywhere. In most of these gardens there is a mausoleum to some famous Persian poet. Shiraz, a lovely city surrounded by imposing mountains, is the old capital of Persia and is said to be the city of poetry, wine, roses and nightingales. We visited the *souk* and saw some wonderful rugs and inlay work. The silver work is famous in Iran.

We then flew on to Isfahan, the most beautiful city I have ever seen. We arrived at our hotel in the dark, but the view from our bedroom the next morning was breathtaking. Against a huge mountain backdrop are many beautiful shimmering gold and blue domes, minarets, palaces and the Khajir Bridge with 33 arches, each with a sluice gate to control the flow of water when open or to form a lake when closed. The bridge was built as a centre for peace and recreation with terraces on which to sit and dream.

Hundreds of years ago, Shah Abbas planned and constructed the Maidan as an arena for shooting and riding. Polo was invented here and the stone goals can still be seen. The Maidan is one of the most beautiful squares in the world both in its dimensions and because of the buildings surrounding it like the Palace of Ali Oamn and the magnificent Masjed-e Shah Mosque with its dominating dome. Of all the highly skilled craftsmen, my favourite are the miniaturists, an Isfahan tradition. I have a miniature painted on ivory hanging over my bureau and never fail to wonder at its beauty. It nearly broke the bank, but it was worth it.

As a clever transformation from an historical caravanserai to a modern hotel the Shah Abbas is a must, with its decorations a living tribute to Isfahan's present-day artists. And of course there is the *souk*, with its carpet weavers, miniaturists, textile decorators, engravers of silver and brass, workers in enamel, gold and silver, embroiderers, tile makers, potters and, last but not least, the coppersmiths, whom I found particularly intriguing. We then went on to the capital of Iran, Tehran, which is a modern city and not nearly as attractive as the two old cities we had just visited.

The plan now was for Merilyn to fly to Beirut to spend a few days with some Lebanese friends she had met in Ras al-Khaima, and then to fly on to England to open up our house near Henley ready for our arrival and to collect Simon and Christopher from school. Trevor and I were to fly on to Istanbul, Athens, Rome and Paris, spending three to four days in each place doing our own thing. We were constantly being rounded up at hotels to join a group. 'No thanks,' we would say, 'we are on our own.' Tehran is a bustling noisy modern city with snow-covered mountains that cool the air considerably. We had a spot of bother getting Merilyn onto a plane to Beirut, for it was a time when planes were being hijacked and feelings were running high in the Middle East. Some airlines were less security minded than others and eventually we secured her a flight by Swiss Air, but it was not leaving until the day after our flight to Istanbul. So we contacted the South African embassy and I introduced myself; luckily our friend of brief acquaintance in Ras al-Khaima had telephoned his wife to tell her of our imminent arrival in Tehran. She was so kind; she invited us round for lunch and offered to have Merilyn spend the night there and be taken to her plane the next day. This was marvellous, for Tehran was not a place in which to leave a young girl on her own.

We were lucky to have another contact in Tehran who provided us with a car, driver and guide, which was splendid and we whizzed round all the sights worth seeing. The crown jewels of Persia were a sight I shall never forget. Security was very strict and we had to get a permit from the bank where the jewels were kept in the vault. We saw emeralds and rubies as big as eggs and uncut in heaps; we saw hundreds of set stones in every colour and shape — pearls, sapphires, diamonds set in silver and gold, tiaras, crowns, belts, swords, brooches, bracelets, necklaces — you had to rub your eyes to make sure you were not dreaming. The coronation robes recently worn by the Shah and Sharina Nona, beautiful green velvet train trimmed with ermine and pearls and the Shah's impressive encrusted crown, were also displayed. The few days we spent in Tehran at the end of March and beginning of April coincided with their new year and people were celebrating everywhere. Had it not been for our friends, we would have had great difficulty finding accommodation. We had not realized it was their new year. We then flew on to Istanbul.

The thing one dreads most when flying is losing one's luggage. Well, we arrived at funny little scruffy Istanbul airport and my suitcase was missing. Trevor had his and only a very few of us had got off the plane. Trevor made a few enquiries and everyone was very friendly and smiled a lot but did not do anything. So Trevor offered to look in the baggage hold, for we had definitely seen the cases being loaded on at Tehran. They thought they would pacify this mad Englishman and let him look in the hold. He climbed up the steps and no, my case was not in the transit hold. Then the captain came down from the cockpit to see what was going on and Trevor explained that my case was missing. The captain ordered the London bound hold to be opened and there was my case, clearly marked Istanbul. What a relief that was, so there is something to be said for little old scruffy airports. Can you imagine this happening at Heathrow or any other modern airport?

On our way into the city from the airport in a battered old taxi, we asked to be taken to a hotel in the old quarter (the taxi driver could not understand why we did not want to go to the Hilton). Anyway, he had a cousin who ran just such a hotel. We were delighted; it was *old* and that is what we wanted, to soak up the atmosphere. The sheets were clean, the water was hot and the food was local and very tasty, all for £7 a night for two of us. One afternoon we heard a frightful commotion and dogs barking. We went out onto our balcony and there was a bear dancing. Wow! Gypsies are not allowed to bring their bears into town but they do and we watched this poor moth-eaten bear dance. He had had his claws and most of his teeth removed; no wonder bear dancing was banned. Still, it was a sight we never thought we would witness.

Our taxi driver appeared the next morning and insisted on being our guide. He drove us to whatever we wanted to look at, parked on the pavement and said 'I wait, you look,' which we did. Because Istanbul is situated on the confluence of three seas — the Bosporus, the Sea of Marmara and the Golden Horn — there were ever-changing scenes of ocean-going liners, naval vessels and freighters from all over the world, not to mention numerous local boats of different shapes and sizes, constantly passing by. We even saw several Russian freighters and a warship passing through from the Caspian Sea to the Mediterranean.

Many eulogies have been written in praise of the sixth-century

Byzantine edifice St Sophia, first a Christian church for 916 years, then a mosque (1453 to 1935) and now a museum. Remarkable and very beautiful mosaics dating back to Christian times had been plastered over for many years, but in 1931 the plaster was removed to show them in their full glory. The sixteenth-century Blue Mosque is another gem. One cannot visit Istanbul without seeing these two wonderful buildings. We went to the Topkapi museum and, though magnificent items were on display, most contained a generous coating of dust. Again, there were jewels galore, but badly displayed. We had a wonderful day sailing up and down the Bosporus, the banks lined with palatial houses and some made of wood had survived. We took the Uskada ferry to Asia Minor and Florence Nightingale's hospital at Squatari (1856) was pointed out to us. We saw the beginnings of the construction of the huge bridge that now links Europe and Asia, with the gigantic towers on either side from which it was to be suspended. The Galata Tower, dating back to Roman times, is another must. It was modernized in 1967 with an excellent restaurant at the top and coffee shops on the seven or eight floors below. We spent a lovely evening there — good food, good atmosphere and *wonderful* views.

The next stop was Athens, so we really were doing the grand tour with yet more ancient and classic history in Greece. The only snag was that it was the Greek Orthodox Easter and all the shops were firmly shut. 'Thank goodness,' said Trevor, so I never did get the leather coat I had promised myself. We treated ourselves to a room at the Grande Bretagne Hotel in Athens, which advertises itself as 'the meeting place for the world's leading figures' and it certainly was very nice and central. The service was excellent. In the evening when the maid came in to turn down the bed and collect the laundry, we were intrigued because she laid out a little towel embroidered with the words 'GOOD MORNING' in many languages on each side of the bed. Were we supposed to wipe our feet on it before getting into bed? The hotel produced a charming guide who showed us round the Parthenon and everything else on the Acropolis. We took a day trip to Corinth and I was struck by the small size of the Corinth Canal. We went to Poseidon, where Byron had 'wept and loved', very romantic with his name cut in the rock. As it was Easter, we were out in the country as much as possible and, wherever we went the Paschal Lamb was being bar-becued and the smell of rosemary being burnt on the coals was heavenly. On several occasions we were asked to join a party, usually in the garden of a tavern. We went to the Roman theatre at Epidavrus, which is quite magnificent — there is nothing we can teach those old Romans about acoustics. We enjoyed our trip to Piraeus with a walk along the seaside past boats, posh cruisers and all kinds of pleasure craft and found a superb fish restaurant for a tasty lunch. On the way back we passed vineyards, olive groves, some barley and a few sheep. An Easter procession marched right past our hotel that evening. It was a lovely sight with three bands, the boy scouts and girl guides, the army, navy and air force, the police and church dignitaries in glorious coloured robes waving incense about all along the route and everyone holding a lit candle. Our next stop was a Greek nightclub with belly dancers and, to round off, we went to Mycenae the home of Homer's *Iliad*.

We arrived in Rome and went straight to St Peter's and the Sistine Chapel. One of the best meals of our whole trip was in a little restaurant at the foot of the Spanish Steps with *the* most exotic display of fruit and vegetables arranged round a fountain. We walked off our dinner to the Trevi Fountain and just sat in wonder, soaking up the atmosphere and beauty. We were amazed to see dozens of tourist coaches arrive, stop for three to five minutes, and then drive on with hardly anyone getting out of the coaches but all snapping their cameras through the coach win-dows. We decided they were Americans 'doing' Europe in seven days. Trevor spoke Italian so we did very well wherever we went. We walked miles in Rome. It really is the best way to see the Coliseum, the Roman Forum and the endless fountains playing in the squares — so calming the sound of water cascading down. I loved seeing Michelangelo's Moses in St Peter in Chain's Church and the pietà in St Peter's exquisite carving — I was thrilled. I had fulfilled one of my ambitions by seeing them.

We then, for the last leg of our wonderful tour, took our first flight on the new exciting Jumbo Jet (747), which was very com-fortable because there were not many passengers going to Paris. Before we left Ras al-Khaima, we had ordered a new Peugeot to be picked up in Paris and we would fly it over the Channel and drive home. When we were selling our Peugeot estate in Ras al-Khaima, about 15 taxi drivers were fighting to buy it; estate cars make lucrative taxis because they can pack in as many as 10 or 12 people, though sometimes the springs are flat.

We checked out with the Peugeot people to ensure that everything was in order and that we could collect the car the following day. We did this after having spent a lovely evening dining on a *bateau-mouche* and cruising down the Seine. To end on a high note we went to the Moulin Rouge to be properly entertained and were not disappointed — the scene with the dolphins in their tank on stage delicately undoing a beautiful girl's bra was quite special.

Our beautiful Peugeot 504 in a golden sand colour was really upmarket, or so we thought. We drove to Le Touquet to fly to Southend. (We had done this several times before and had always flown to Lydd in Kent.) We checked in with British Air Ferries at about 5.00 p.m. to find that we were the only people flying with a car. We landed at Southend to find that the customs officer's only wish was to get rid of us as soon as he could so that he could get back to his favourite TV programme, so it was all very painless and informal. We had to drive through London to get to the M4 and reached home at 1.15 a.m. to find the children all well. We were tired, but thrilled to be in our own home and thankful for a trip of a lifetime.

And so ended a memorable, exciting, challenging and largely enjoyable five years in the Middle East. Now we would retire and enjoy life at our own pace, or at least that is what we thought.

6

Sana'a: Yemen Arab Republic

Some 2000 years ago, the country we now know as Yemen consisted of many small fierce kingdoms, including Saba, Qateban, Marib, Ansen and Hadhramaut. Sabau, the Queen of Sheba who visited Solomon in Jerusalem showering him with gifts of gold, spices and precious stones and in return 'Solomon gave unto the Queen of Sheba all her desire and whatsoever she asked' (Kings I v. 1–13), is believed to have come from these parts.

It is now nearly a quarter of a century since we left the Yemen where my late husband spent four years at the request of the FCO. The Yemen had recently undergone a revolution in which the Imam was deposed and the medieval state declared a republic. To survive in the modern world, the Yemeni government realized it needed help from the Western world and so asked the British government to send an adviser to help build a structured police force to maintain a secular law and order. Hitherto, all legal authority had been vested solely in the Koran. Trevor had just retired after 35 years with the colonial police and, since he spoke fluent Arabic, the FCO offered him a post in the Yemen.

Trevor had worked on the Red Sea opposite Yemen in the 1940s and had always been fascinated by this closed and secret country. An invitation to go there legitimately and in an official capacity was too good an opportunity to turn down, so on 2 November 1972 he flew to Sana'a where advisers in agriculture, veterinary and medical services, engineering and communications were already installed. Cable & Wireless employed a large team that was kept very busy.

We were breaking our family rule by not being together for Christmas, but circumstances made it unavoidable. Trevor arrived

278

safely and from his letters we began to realize that it was not easy for expatriates to meet their needs in the Yemen. To make him feel a little nearer home over Christmas, I made and iced him a Christmas cake for the FCO to deliver. I then drove up to London and into the FCO courtyard, which one could do in those days, and, having satisfied my urge to see the famous staircase, went in search of the baggage and postal room; fortunately I bumped into an ex-Ras al-Khaima friend who pointed me in the right direction. When I asked a worker in the post room if he would be kind enough to put the parcel I was carrying into the diplomatic bag for Sana'a, he replied 'Certainly. What is it?' I told him it was a Christmas cake and without batting an eyelid he took it from me and popped it into a bag marked Sana'a saying, 'We can't let our people go without Christmas cake, can we?' I thanked him profusely and left. Nobody asked for any identity and I was not challenged anywhere, which of course would never happen today. Anyway, much to the amusement of the Sana'a FCO contingent, Trevor received his cake.

* * *

The Yemenis fascinated Trevor, but trying to get them to agree to a penal code or the simplest traffic scheme frustrated him beyond belief. Only parts of the penal code he produced were adopted, for the rest was incompatible with the Koran; sharia courts covered everything else. He had more success with traffic ordinance.

Ordinary Yemenis are pleasant people and one farmer gave me 100 lbs of green mocha coffee beans. Though relatively little coffee is grown in the Yemen now, it was the Yemenis of yore who invented the beverage, which reached Europe in the seventeenth century, and the Arabica strain is still grown wherever coffee is grown. In fact, the word coffee comes from the Arabic 'qah-wah'.

Socially, there was very little integration because the cultures were so far apart. We encountered many different nationalities in the Yemen working on the United Nations' World Health Organization and World Food Programme projects, as well as numerous Chinese and Russian advisers. The Russians had been helping the armies and air forces of both sides in the war between North Yemen and South Yemen. In 1961, the Chinese, who had also aided and abetted both sides in the war, transformed the country by building a road, only *one* road, from Sana'a to Hodeida on the Red Sea — a distance of 144 miles, climbing to a pass of 10,000 feet above sea level. Not to be outdone, the Russians built a road from the port of Mocha to Taiz, but the Yemenis seemed to prefer Chinese behaviour and work methods to those of the Russians. The Russians taught by precept, not example, and at the end of a day's work would disappear to their segregated air-conditioned bungalows and vodka. The Chinese, on the other hand, slept in old army tents with their labourers on the side of the road they were building. They produced a textile mill in Sana'a, which gave employment to women — a radical move. Their technical school, however, suffered from an elementary drawback; the students had to learn Chinese before they could start their course on engineering or whatever. This did not go down very well, but even so they turned out about 80 graduates a year.

There is a lovely story about the Chinese ambassador who, wishing to give the president and people of Yemen a special gift, arranged to have Chairman Mao's *Little Red Book* translated into Arabic and suitably bound. The president said he could not possibly receive such a gift until he had an equally suitable one to show the Yemeni people's gratitude for all the work China had done for them. He said he would like to have the Holy Koran translated into Chinese and suitably bound. When the Chinese ambassador said, 'We have no need of the Koran,' President Iryani gave a wry smile and said, 'And we ...,' his voice trailed away.

It is Yemeni government policy to accept aid from wherever it is offered provided there are no strings attached; so West Germany built a new airport, Britain continued to send aid and Japanese merchandise was available in all the shops. The Chinese community (consisting of 50 lecturers) never mixed with us Westerners. There were some Russians living next door to us and, though their house was as small as ours, there were four families living in it; apparently, Moscow apartments are just as crowded.

With Yemen being a 'dry' country, we, along with the Russians and all other expatriates, had to get special permission to consume alcohol. We received our supply through the British embassy. We had to make a list of what we would like for the *year*. When the 'booze' ship docked at Hadeida, special care was taken to get all the British supplies up to Sana'a (on the Chinese built road). We had to have rather a large storeroom to accommodate all the cases of beer, wine and spirits. Trevor was a beer drinker so there were always more beer crates than anything else. He used to get some bottles of whisky for visitors. The Russians next door were crazy about whisky so we would swap bottles of it for true Russian vodka. When these Russians had alcohol in the house, they solemnly drank the lot. For a period of one or two weeks, there would be much noise and merriment every day and all day, then complete silence for a day or two while they all slept it off.

North Yemen (Yemen as we knew it) must be one of the most spectacular countries in the world. Its huge steep-sided mountains are cultivated from the top to the very bottom of the deep valleys in hundreds of narrow terraces. The soil is highly fertile and coffee, most vegetables, apricots, apples and many other fruits can be grown. The terraces were built thousands of years ago to aid irrigation, but sadly vast acres of fruit and vegetables have now been rooted out to make way for the ubiquitous *qat* crop; *qat* is a narcotic leaf. When Yemenis get twitchy around midday they rush off to their markets to buy bundles of freshly gathered *qat*, which they take home to chew until mid-afternoon. After a snooze they perhaps then return to work. I was invited once or twice to join *qat*-chewing gatherings, but managed to decline, politely I hope.

The most striking thing about Sana'a and other towns in Yemen is the architecture, which predominantly consists of huge multi-storeyed mud-brick houses with whitewashed surrounds to the windows. Yemeni builders must be highly skilled, for if a European tried to build such a house it would surely collapse after the first rains. In the countryside at Wadi Dahr, a particularly magnificent palace in the Yemeni architectural style looks as though it is growing out of the rock crag on which it is built. It must be the most photographed spot in Yemen, not only for the building, which is several storeys high, but also for its setting in a lush valley; the Romans called these fertile terraced valleys and mountainsides *felix Arabia* (blessed or happy Arabia). Yemen has remained undisturbed for many centuries and some even claim it was the cradle of Arab civilization.

The first couple of floors of these highly stylized Yemeni houses are made of huge slabs of cut stone, with the next four or five floors built in brick. The ornate windows are not at ground level but higher up, and the whitewash decorations round each window make the building look as if it is draped in lace. The narrow alleyways that twist this way and that between the houses were meant only for pedestrians, but now motorbikes and scooters hurtle about. These machines, like the lorries, are decorated with brilliant paintwork and festooned with strips of fur and ribbon. At the very top of each mansion is the men's room. This is not a cloakroom but a room reserved for men because it is considered to be the best room in the house. It is the highest, the coolest and holds the best view, and is where the men get together to smoke hubble-bubble pipes and chew *qat*. Some tribal sheiks from out-lying areas keep an old town house in Sana'a and many white-collar workers who own a modern breezeblock house still cling to the traditional Yemeni family house in town.

Sana'a is also a city of gardens, but one has to seek them out. All these gardens once belonged to the 50 mosques in the old city, but they are now run by a ministry and are safe from being built on. The soil is ultra fertile and each garden has its own well, produces fruit and vegetables and lies behind a high wall. (We planted a vine and in no time it had covered the whole of our, albeit small, garden and produced luscious grapes.) Like all ancient cities, Sana'a is walled and most of the wall still stands. A wadi outside the wall becomes a river when it rains, but for most of the year it is dry and used as a sort of ring road. The wall is damaged in parts and should be repaired before it is too late and, sadly, in several places it has been breached. There is one impressive old gateway, Bebel Yemen, where heads of people who had been executed were put up on spikes as a lesson to the population.

Most women in the street wear the veil and cover themselves in huge cloaks that are colourful and flow out like ships in full sail as they walk about. The men wear skirts (*lungi*s) and round their waists an embroidered wide belt to which the famous *djambia*s (curved daggers) are attached. The handles of the most highly valued daggers are made of rhinoceros horn and the demand has practically annihilated Africa's rhino population. The prices paid far outweigh the risks of being caught poaching and the relatively small fines imposed. Africans have woken up just in time to rescue and protect rhinoceroses before they become extinct. An ancient fertility/virility legend also feeds the demand.

Merilyn flew out for her Christmas holidays ahead of the boys and as Trevor's Land Rover only had comfortable seating for three he decided to take her and me on a grand tour of Yemen before Christmas and then take the boys round later in the holidays. We set off for the ancient city of Tiaz, Yemen's second city, and travelled on a dust road for 256 kilometres through magnificent scenery. Tiaz lies sprawled at the foot of the Sabir Mountain and mosques and minarets add beauty to the scene. We lunched with the manager of the British Bank of the Middle East and his wife who used to be in Ras al-Khaima. The highlight of our visit to Tiaz was a visit to the museum in the old Imam's palace. I am not sure if museum is the right word, for everything and anything the old boy had used or owned was stacked high in higgledy-piggledy heaps covered in dust and cobwebs. He had died in 1960 and nothing had been touched since. There were uniforms, dresses, cooking pots, soaps, jewellery, even furniture, but no order or labels; it reminded me of the attic of a stately home in which nothing had ever been discarded. The market was vibrant with piles of nice looking vegetables and, it is said, the best *qat*.

Before reaching Tiaz we passed through Ibb, which has a particularly beautiful mosque and, adjacent to Ibb at Jiblah, we saw Queen Arwa's mausoleum and the exquisite silverwork on her tomb. On a dusty gravel road about 140 kilometres from Tiaz a peculiar edifice on a roundabout in the middle of nowhere marks the spot where the Russian-built road from Mocha (Al-Mukha) port joins the main Tiaz–Hodeida highway, which was at least tarred. Our next stop was Zabed, a famous medieval university city where algebra was invented. It is an attractive town of white buildings in the hot Tahama desert plain that stretches for many miles between the Red Sea and the range of huge mountains on top of which Sana'a lies. As with most old Arab towns, it is entered through an impressive arched gateway and has a mosque in the middle from which little alleys go off this way and that. The architecture here, which is different (unlike Sana'a there are no tall buildings), is highly stylized with lots of latticework and the baked bricks with which the houses are built are hand made, very small and apparently kneaded like bread before being fired. If the

Yemenis can resist Western influences and pressures to modernize everything, they will continue to build with materials that blend with the natural environment. The design of the houses in Zabed intrigued me and I would have liked to spend more time there. The town of Zabed has now been declared a world heritage site.

But we had to move on to the Al-Ikhwa Hotel in Hodeida where Trevor had stayed on previous routine visits. We were shown our rooms, which were barely adequate. Luckily, I had brought my sewing box and was able to repair the holes in our mosquito nets, which are needed at sea level. The shower in the *en suite* bathroom did not work and the bath had no plug. (I should have known better, as it was always advisable to travel with a bath plug in remote parts of Africa.) However, we managed to wash and change after our hot, dusty journey and went down to dinner where it took some ingenuity to decipher the menu. When the Yemenis' English teachers are either Russian or Chinese, their spelling is bound to go a little haywire. We eventually decided that *latic* was lettuce, *beas* beans, *kari* curry, *hurts* heart, *mukroni* macaroni, *coloured sandwish* sandwiches with various fillings, *ice and tea* iced tea, *stick* steak and *sweat boding* sweet pudding, but we never worked out the meaning of *dry meat shab*. While engrossed in deciding what to order, a fat young Yemeni policeman rushed up to Trevor uttering endearments, clasped him to his bosom and kissed him firmly on both cheeks (Merilyn's face was a study). The young man then politely left us to our meal and joined us for coffee afterwards.

After a look round Hodeida, which was very hot, we set off on the 226-kilometre drive back to Sana'a. It was sweltering driving through the flat Tahama plain where a lot of cotton is grown to feed the Chinese-built textile mill in Sana'a that provides work for veiled Yemeni women. The terrain here is like parts of Africa, with sparse acacia-type trees and women wearing wide-brimmed hats woven from millet (sorghum) or maize leaves. I tried one and found it heavy compared with my light Panama-type sun shield.

Eventually, we reached the foot of the mountains and, snaking endlessly round hairpin bends, began to climb up towards the pass. The many heavily laden and decorated lorries grinding up or tearing down were our greatest hazard. With the gradient steep and the corners tight, one had to drive with great care; we frequently met lorries on the wrong side of the road and saw evidence of overturned trucks here and there. The driver has no time to look at the stunning scenery, at the green terraces from skyline to valley bottoms, and at villages perched on promontories as if from a children's fairy story. Some villages built on rocky outcrops are impregnable; they needed to be in the days of tribal warfare. Trevor skilfully got us to the top of the pass where we found a throng of Land Rovers and lorries resting in a car park after the climb, many with steam escaping from having become overheated. There was a coffee shop and post office in the car park where we stopped for a little while to stretch our legs and appreciate the cool mountain air after the hot Tahama plain. We arrived back in Sana'a safe and well and delighted to have seen more of this strange country.

I was next engaged in preparing for Christmas. With limited grocery shops we were very restricted and there was no chance of a turkey, but we could get frozen chickens. However, I was never sure for how long they been left in the sun on Hodeida quayside before being loaded on a lorry or how often they may have thawed because of the frequent power cuts. As a special treat for us infidels, one shop grandly calling itself a supermarket said it had brought in hams for Christmas. Excitedly, we went to town to claim our ham. I helped myself to a fairly large hunk from among the odd shaped pieces of grey meat in the freezer and paid for it (it was very expensive I remember thinking), but when thawed, it turned out to be a leg of pork. I had no idea where it had come from or how long it had been frozen, but as we had nothing else I cooked it thoroughly — probably overcooked it to be on the safe side; no one was ill.

We had invited two British nurses from the Save the Children Fund hospital to join us for our Christmas meal. I felt very sorry for these nurses and angry at the way they were treated. The Save the Children Fund recruited highly trained nurses to send to Sana'a, where there was a great need for their expertise, then put them in a house without doors to any of the rooms, an Asian loo (namely a hole in the floor), no bath, no means of heating water and a kitchen with nothing in it but one cold water tap. Having begged and borrowed items from other expatriates, their house gradually became vaguely habitable, but since it still had no bath, we invited them to bath at our house whenever they wanted to, which they regularly did. I think the Save the Children Fund was badly organized until Princess Anne took over and sorted it out.

Simon and Christopher flew out for the Christmas holidays in mid-December, so we were a complete family once again. In many ways it was a rather frustrating holiday, for there was no beach to go to and less freedom than in the Ras al-Khaima days. By booking well ahead we were allowed on certain days to use the British embassy tennis court for limited periods, which we did and had to have special balls for high altitude play. The British ambassador's three children were also out for their holidays and his wife arranged a donkey picnic for all the expatriate children. The plan was that we would arrive with our children at the agreed place at the appointed hour and the children would each be given a donkey to ride. A member of the embassy staff who knew about such things had arranged to get hold of the donkeys. There was not much guidance or supervision and the children aged from between eight or nine to seventeen all set off. A rendezvous had been arranged for a picnic tea. Some of the donkeys were in season and, as bad luck would have it, several of the youngest girls were given these particular ones to ride. When the jack donkeys tried to mount the jenny donkeys, the little girls were alarmed. 'What's your donkey doing to my donkey? Go away.' Since only Yemeni men had ever handled these donkeys, they were unused to the smell and manner of Europeans and, being stubborn creatures of habit, decided to take advantage of the situation and make for home. Such was the intent of the donkey Merilyn was on. She could not control the beast, became separated from the others and we became rather alarmed when she was found not to be with the crowd. Trevor quickly arranged a search party and luckily she was found and brought home safe and sound. (In my anguish, thoughts of captured concubines and white slaves came to mind.) I suspect the ambassador's wife had been reading *Peking Picnic* by Ann Bridge to feel inspired to organize such an event, which was as unsuccessful as its predecessor in China many years before.

There was a large contingent of Cable & Wireless staff in Sana'a and the young unmarried men, who lived in a mess, were forever holding parties, some of which were great fun. Once some of them asked us to go potholing with them. The very thought turned me

286

cold, but I agreed to go with the family just to have a look. At the entrance they all, including Trevor and Merilyn, disappeared into a large cavern and I was told where to wait to see them emerge from their underground experience. I took a photo of Merilyn as she came out covered in layers of dust and sneezing her head off. They had been particularly intrigued by one large underground chamber, which was quite dry and had no stalactites or stalagmites. They wondered if it had ever been used for anything.

When it was our turn to invite a few people in for drinks we included the ambassador and his wife. We got on very well with His Excellency, but his wife was another story. While looking at the photographs of the family Trevor had arranged round our little sitting room, she picked up a particular nice one of Merilyn and, pointing at me, said, 'This is not a very good one of you.' In my most dispassionate manner, I replied, 'that is not surprising because it's a photo of my daughter. I am kept in the bedroom.'

Unfortunately, there was very little for the children to do. We did not feel able to go for walks because, although we were unlikely to be molested, it was not considered the thing to do and the roads were dusty and without pavements. One could take the Land Rover out to some wadi and have a stroll and picnic tea in the countryside, which we sometimes did, but in no time at all we invariably found ourselves surrounded by curious locals gazing at the crazy Europeans.

One Cable & Wireless employee, who was a keen amateur astrologer, had a telescope and would spend hours on his roof studying the heavens. The clear skies of Sana'a were ideal for this purpose and he could see millions of stars. He invited us onto his roof one night to witness a comet whizzing through the sky and it was exciting viewing it through a telescope. He said he saw more in one month in Sana'a than one could in a lifetime in the UK.

Booking airline tickets was a bit of a lottery in Sana'a. There was a travel agent and we went along to get confirmation of the children's return flights to school in January. We had their return tickets but needed to ensure that their seats were confirmed right through to London, for there was no direct flight and changes of airlines were involved. Having been assured that everything was confirmed and in order, Merilyn was the first to fly back. She had to get to Asmara to catch the London flight, but on booking in we discovered that the only seat available from Sana'a to Asmara was in the first class, so she had to be upgraded, and then, thanks to Ethiopian Airlines, had to spend a night in Asmara. We were thankful when we received her telegram saying she had arrived safely in London. These were some of the hazards of indifferent attitudes, but that was not all. Worse was to follow for Simon and Christopher, who had their own story to tell.

They were taken to Heathrow by taxi from Reading Blue Coat School knowing the flight would be unsupervised; they were on their own without a BOAC aunty to look after them. Their ticket read, London to Sana'a via Jedda on Saudiair (Saudi Arabian Airline). There was another teenager on the flight and the three sat together. It turned out that this other lad's father worked at the British consulate in Jedda. The first stop was Dharan where everybody was ordered off the plane for a passport check. The passports were taken from them, but only Christopher's was returned. Simon complained bitterly and was taken through passport control to the duty manager where he complained even more and, to his horror, saw his passport on the floor being used to prop up a table leg. Having made some official excuse, they had not realized the two boys were twins, they duly handed Simon back his passport and the two boys climbed back on board. The flight to Jedda was uneventful and the plane was full of pilgrims making the hadj. It is the duty of every Muslim to visit Mecca, which is near Jedda, once in a lifetime and this particular year the season for this ritual coincided with the Christmas holidays. They arrived at Jedda in the middle of the night and, having cleared customs, they realized that the hotel booking shown on their ticket was invalid because no such hotel existed. Luckily, the other boy's father intervened and took our boys to the consulate for the night and put Simon and Christopher on the Sana'a plane the next morning. Trevor was furious, but we were at least thankful that no terrible harm had been done to them.

After this experience, Trevor went to a lot of trouble to confirm their flight back to school, but need not have bothered. One thing was certain; he would book a route that avoided Jedda. So, from Sana'a they flew to Assab on the Red Sea coast in an old Ethiopian DC6, which struggled at take off because of the thin air at 7000 feet above sea level. Then, after a long descent to sea level, they landed on a gravel runway, disembarked, identified their luggage and waited in a tin shack in unbearable heat for another DC6 for the connecting flight to Asmara. Having flown over spectacular scenery across the Red Sea and mountains to Asmara, they once again found that no hotel booking had been made for their overnight stay. However, they were wiser now and persuaded the hotel to put them up but spent a miserable night with little or no money worrying because they still had no confirmation of their seats on the next day's plane. They got up early, crept out of the hotel and, now down to their last pennies, got a taxi to the airport. The airport was heaving with near panic as stricken people tried to get out before the war got closer. However, being resourceful, realizing it was a case of first come first serve, and determined to get on the London-bound plane, they barged their way through to the check-in desk where they were informed that the flight was severely overbooked. But somehow they got on the plane and, after some haggling, there were no seat allocations in all the chaos, even managed to sit together. Not surprisingly, they left Asmara much later than scheduled and understood there was to be one stop in Rome. After an interesting flight over the Great Rift Valley fault line, they noticed they were descending earlier than anticipated and were flying through very bad weather in the Mediterranean. When they got below the cloud line, they saw the Acropolis and Athens and there had been no announcement about an unscheduled stop in Greece. It was snowing and extremely cold. They did not stay there long. A VIP from first class was seen leaving the plane and immediately afterwards the doors shut and they flew off to Rome. They landed at Heathrow four hours late and were very relieved to find the school taxi waiting to take them back to their familiar routine of school life. Despite the hazards of their flights to and from Sana'a, they still managed to get their BOAC Junior Jet Club logbooks filled in and signed by the captain on each leg of their journey.

* * *

I returned to England in February earlier than I had planned, for a cousin who was housesitting for me cabled that she could not cope any more and asked me to come back directly. This I did and then it was the Easter holidays, which we spent in our Torquay home into which we had moved in 1972. When it came to the summer holidays, Simon and Christopher said 'do we really have to go out to the Yemen? It's so awful, there's nothing to do.' Since Merilyn was working in London by now, we decided not to go out but rather have Trevor join us for six weeks during the summer holidays.

Trevor was originally asked to go out to the Yemen for 18 months. That spread to four years, but in 1976 he managed to retire properly. He loved being retired and said it was the best thing he ever did. He had planned to retire at 55, but he was in fact 58, which was not too far off course. For the rest of his life he thoroughly enjoyed himself on his boat on the River Dart, fishing out at sea, gardening, building a greenhouse and growing exotic vegetables. With pride, he watched his children marry, graduate from university and become launched in their chosen careers. A contented man happy to reminisce for hours with his friends, he richly deserved his happy retirement after a very busy, full and eventful working life. Our lives were neither perfect nor conventional, but we made the most of wherever we were and, for the most part, we were happy. Trevor was awarded an MBE in the New Year's Honours' List of January 1977 and later that year we spent a very special day at Buckingham Palace when he received his honour. Merilyn and Christopher came with us (Simon was unable to attend). Trevor's oldest and greatest friend since childhood, Brigadier General Charles Sanders RAMC was serving as honorary physician to Her Majesty the Queen and was on duty on this auspicious occasion, so that added to the day.

* * *

Trevor sadly died of cancer in 1992. I miss him terribly but I know he would have been with me at the final winding up of the colonial era had he been alive. The occasion was a service of thanksgiving and commemoration to mark the end of Her Majesty's Overseas Civil Service in Westminster Abbey on 25 May 1999. I was allocated two tickets and Merilyn accompanied me. It was a moving and nostalgic, but not sentimental, service. The Dean of Westminster conducted the service, His Excellency the Rt

Hon. Sir Richard Luce, the Governor of Gibraltar, delivered the address. His father was Sir William Luce whom we had met and entertained in Ras al-Kaimah in 1969 when he came out of retirement to become the foreign secretary's special representative for Gulf affairs. His mother Margaret Luce has written a delightful book, *From Aden to the Gulf*, about Sir William's period as Governor of Aden and Political Resident in the Gulf from 1956 to 1966. Her Majesty the Queen and Prince Philip attended this very special service in a congregation of 1855 colonials. In the order of service the Queen paid tribute to the men and women who, for the last 160 years and in over 40 countries, had sacrificed so much in their distinguished service to the Crown in the dependent territories both before and after independence.

Her Majesty's Overseas Civil Service came to an end in 1997 when Hong Kong returned to China. This service was a fitting finale to the end of a proud and historical era.

Index

293

Index

Index

Index

Index

Index

St Helena, 1, 220–1
St James's Palace, 3
St Joseph's Hospital, 20
St Paul's Theological College, 151
St Peter's, 276
St Sophia, 275
Salima, 108, 112, 131–2, 159, 174, 189–90, 194
Salisbury, 84–5, 91, 106, 148, 151, 153–4, 158, 167–9, 171–2, 184, 190, 194, 196, 198, 219; *see also* Harare
Sally (nurse), 96
Samoa Islands, 100
Sana'a, 278–89
Sanders, Brigadier General Charles, 290
Sanders, Mr, 205
Saqr, Sheikh, 237, 240, 246, 269–70
Sarah (Ghani's wife), 97
Sarah (Mbabzi nanny), 176
Save the Children Fund (SCF), 128, 285
Saxon, 6
Scholtz, Dr, 10, 13, 16, 20, 42, 71–2
Schreiner, Olive, 60–1
Schreiner, W. P., 60
Schwarzkopf, Elizabeth, 91
Science Museum, 222
Scot, Frank, 134
Scotland, 65, 68, 145–6, 179
Scotland Yard, 96
Scott, R. F., 145
Sea of Marmara, 274
Second World War, 90
Selsey, 208–9, 211, 222–3
Senga Bay Hotel, 190
Seventh Day Adventists, 173
Severn Road Bridge, 223

Shackleton, Sir Ernest Henry, 145
Shares, Professor, 95
Sharjah, 233, 235, 242, 249, 258
Sharpe, Mary, 155, 173
Sharpe, Mike, 155, 169, 173, 197
Sheba, Queen of, 231, 243, 278
Sheffield, 7, 9, 12, 37, 116, 147, 167
Sheikha (little girl), 265
Shi-hu tribe, 242–3, 258–9
Shimmel Sheba, 257
Shiraz, 271–2
Shire Highlands Hotel, 118, 212, 216
Shire River, 107, 214
Shoesmith, May, 38
Shoesmith, Mr, 28
Shoesmith, Old Shoe, 28, 37, 38, 55, 59
Sieberhagen, Mrs Johnnie, 44
Simon (RAF dentist), 235
Simpson, Professor Keith, 96
Singapore, 2, 88, 91, 93, 95–9, 101–3, 106, 108, 113, 122, 124, 140, 146, 181–2, 247
Singh, Nagindar, 103
Sinoia, 168, 173, 184
Sir George Monnoux Grammar School, 84
Sir Lowry's Pass, 219
Sistine Chapel, 276
Slater, Deb (née White), 88–9
Smuts, Jan, 61, 71, 90
Smythe, Pat, 147
Snow, Peter, 258
Solomon, King, 278
Somaliland, xii, xiii, 83, 85, 140, 162, 204
Somerset West, 183
Sonning Common, 224, 226, 238
Sonning on Thames, 227

Index

Index